D1326920

Wine Snobbery

WINE SNOBBERY

An Insider's Guide to the Booze Business

Andrew Barr

faber and faber

LONDON · BOSTON

First published in 1988
by Faber and Faber Limited
3 Queen Square London WC1N 3AU
Reprinted 1989

Printed in Great Britain by
Richard Clay Bungay Suffolk
All rights reserved

© Andrew Barr, 1988

British Library Cataloguing in Publication Data

Barr, Andrew
Wine snobbery: an insider's guide to the
booze business
1. Wines industries & trades
I. Title
338.4′76632
ISBN 0–571–15212–0

CONTENTS

[v]

ACKNOWLEDGEMENTS

Had I not been given a first opportunity to express myself by John Diamond, then the consumer editor of *Time Out*, but now sensibly moved on to greater things, and offered a more prestigious stage by Georgina Boosey, Managing Editor of *Vogue*, this book would never have been written. I am also grateful to Georgina Boosey for giving me permission to expand and develop articles I wrote for *Vogue* into chapters seven and sixteen of this book.

Many wine-makers and members of the trade have shied away from any connection with a book such as this, and others who have been helpful have been unaware that they were being so or have preferred to assist me anonymously. On the principle that a journalist should not reveal his sources, I shall name none of them here. I would, however, like to thank Lance Foyster for all his years of constructive criticism.

This book is dedicated to my parents, because they do not drink.

INTRODUCTION: THE WINE SCANDALS

This book germinated from the Austrian 'anti-freeze' scandal, the consequence of biochemist Otto Nadrasky Senior's discovery that he could make dry wines sweeter and thin wines fuller-bodied by adding di-ethylene glycol. Di-ethylene glycol is a chemical which is commonly used in anti-freeze solutions for car radiators, and it is potentially fatal to humans, as it can cause liver and kidney failure.

The 'anti-freeze' story broke in Britain in the summer of 1985. One might have expected positive action to be taken to protect our health by the government body responsible, the Ministry of Agriculture, Food and Fisheries. After all, the revenue derived by the government from excise duty and VAT on wine sales amounts to £1,000 million a year. Unfortunately no one at the Ministry actually knew anything about wine. They did begin by issuing a recommendation that Austrian wines should be withdrawn from sale. This was not, however, an order. They then stated that they had the affair under control. This was far from the case. They set up a scheme with importers for testing suspect wines, yet it would have been in the interest of a dishonest importer to conceal such wines. The Ministry ended up depending on the help of journalists to determine which wines might be suspect. They might have made use of local authority environmental health and trading standards officers, except that these officials had been told by the Department of Health that 'no action is necessary'. Some trading standards officers did become involved, but only at the request of members of the public who brought them wines they feared were contaminated. Yet it was trading standards officers in South Yorkshire who had first discovered that contaminated wines were on sale in Britain. At first the Ministry failed to issue a list of contaminated wines; then, when they did so, the list lacked the most vital details – the producers' names.

A number of retailers continued to offer for sale wines which had been shown to be contaminated. As late as September 1986 Mojo Ltd were fined £500 for selling in April 1986 two wines contaminated with di-ethylene glycol in their wine warehouse in Leamington Spa, despite having being ordered by a trading standards officer some months earlier to remove the wine from sale. Mojo Ltd is a subsidiary of the Argyll Group, which showed pre-tax profits in 1986–7 of £368 million.

We are told that the Japanese authorities reacted far more stringently to the scandal, so stringently that for a while they even banned the sale of Australian wines, because they confused them with Austrian. But might they not have used the di-ethylene glycol scandal as an excuse for attacking the growing exports of Australian wines? Certainly they treated Japanese wine producers much less harshly. In 1985 di-ethylene glycol was found in wine produced by Manns Wine Company who made 'domestic' wines by blending imported and domestic wines. As a result of this scandal, imported wines were required to carry stickers saying that they had been tested for di-ethylene glycol, but this requirement did not apply to Japanese wine producers such as Manns. All that happened was that Manns closed down for a few months and were then allowed to reopen after a few directors had resigned and the company had formally apologized.[1]

In Germany, a number of wines were found to be contaminated with di-ethylene glycol, but in much lower concentrations. The authorities claimed that 'the wines were not deliberately falsified, but that unclean equipment in importing and bottling companies was at fault'.[2] Nonsense. German wines were found to be contaminated because German wine-makers were in the practice of adding illegally 10 to 15 per cent of Austrian wine to their own produce. The German Wine Institute, whose job is to inform the public about German wines, sent out press releases with such titles as 'German Wines "Harmless", says Minister for Viticulture,' and, five days later, ' "No Deliberate Contamination of German Wines," says German Wine Institute.' For his delay in publishing the dangers of drinking wine containing di-ethylene glycol, the Secretary of the Rhineland-Palatinate Ministry for Agriculture, Wine and Forestry was forced to resign.

Yet I would have thought that many wine producers and

merchants would have been delighted for the maximum publicity to have been given to the implication of the Pieroth group in selling contaminated wines. Here in Britain, where Pieroth's overpriced wines are sold by door-to-door salesmen, members of the wine trade have on several occasions accused them of misleading the public. In 1961 the House of Hallgarten, respected importers of German wines, took out an action against them, claiming misrepresentation. At that time the House of Hallgarten was owned by the Hallgarten family. In 1971, however, it was taken over by Pieroth. Fifteen years later, in the aftermath of the anti-freeze affair, Fritz Hallgarten, long since retired from the company, published *Wine Scandal*, an account of many of the major scandals of the last thirty years, from which he omitted the names of some participants. He had in fact written the book in 1976 but shelved it on the advice of 'an influential friend' in the wine trade, who told him that its revelations, even though they had appeared in various newspapers and magazines, could damage established wine merchants and even do harm to the wine trade as a whole.[3]

When I responded to the di-ethylene glycol scandal by contributing an article to *Vogue* on additives and organic wines, and wrote to the importer of one of these wines, asking how it was made, he said in his reply that he hoped that by the time the article would have appeared five months later, 'the whole glycol saga will be forgotten. The very mention of additives, whether natural or artificial, always raises question marks in the consumer's mind and it seems to me that any reference to additives seems to add another black mark to the image of wine.'

Members of the wine trade believe that if you ignore a scandal it goes away quicker; indeed, it may never become public at all. Certainly this approach has served politicians well. In the same way as sex scandals expose the fundamental dishonesty and arrogance of many politicians, wine scandals briefly expose what is rotten, but generally hidden, in the wine trade. It is the purpose of this book to illuminate those dubious practices which are normally exposed only by occasional wine scandals. Only by appreciating why wine-makers find it necessary to break the law is it possible to understand why wine tastes as it does, and why we buy the wines we do.

Perhaps, however, it *is* in the interests of the wine trade as a whole to encourage people to think that wine scandals are wholly unrepresentative. Wine merchants are scared that, if the truth were to come out, consumers would be content with cheap wines and could no longer be persuaded to spend extra money to achieve the image that producers have so carefully created. It is the purpose of this book to explain why we pay for that image. We may think that wine snobbery has disappeared: we no longer shrink from admitting that we drink Sainsbury's or Tesco's wines at home; we are no longer embarrassed by wine waiters in smart restaurants; we no longer try to get one over on 'friends' at dinner parties. But to suggest that wine snobbery is dead is merely to fall victim to the skills of the marketing and advertising men. Wine snobbery today is more subtle and insidious than ever before.

[1] *Wine and Spirit*, May 1987, pp. 48–9.
[2] Press release from German Wine Institute, 31 July 1985.
[3] Hallgarten, p. 8. (Full references are not given in the footnotes to books listed in the bibliography on pp. 265–6.)

PART ONE

THE FALL OF THE WINE SNOB?

It is sometimes said that wine has become popular because it has been demystified. Yet the boom began, not with demystification, but with a growth in wine snobbery. Certainly it was a reduction in prices which stimulated growth in wine consumption in the 1950s, following a halving of the duty on light wines in 1949, in an attempt to assist trade with France, which needed help to recover from the war. But the lower prices did not encourage the working classes to take up drinking wine. All that happened was that the middle classes began to return to it. The new generation of consumers had been brought up in the knowledge that claret and burgundy were good wines, but they had no idea how much they should cost. Wine merchants exploited their ignorance and snobbery by selling plonk under such names as Nuits-Saint-Georges and Châteauneuf-du-Pape. This practice was generally known and accepted in the trade, but not publicly exposed until 1966, when Nicholas Tomalin revealed in the *Sunday Times* that a company called Société des Vins de France, who supplied branded table wine to French families, had set up a bottling and labelling depot in Ipswich, where they blended two different table wines in varying proportions to produce a 'Beaujolais', a 'Nuits-Saint-Georges' and a 'Châteauneuf-du-Pape'.[1] The cat was finally out of the bag. Charles Kinloch, part of the group owned by the brewers Courage, relabelled their 'Beaujolais' Les Courtiers, and their 'Bordeaux' Auberge. The official wine-trade reaction to Nicholas Tomalin's revelations was defensive. The Secretary of the Wine and Spirit Association tried to argue that 'to the trade there are very clear advantages in having a standard product. And the general public would be appallingly confused if they had to cope with a myriad of tiny commune names.'[2] The vineyard-owning MP Ernest Marples wrote in the *Sunday Mirror*: 'a colossal confidence trick is being played on the British public. Far too many members of the wine trade are cheats and chisellers. The attitude of the Wine and Spirit Association – I call them the Wine and Fiddle Association – encourages dishonesty. They say they can put what they like on a label – although one word they never use is "Rubbish".[3]

In content, if not in context, what the Secretary of the Wine and Spirit Association had to say was right. If new consumers were not to be put off from drinking wine, then they needed to be offered some simple, standard names. That is what the sherry producers did. In an article in the *Economist* in 1960, it was stated that 'the British are at last becoming wine-drinkers', for two principal reasons: the fact that pubs and restaurants had at last started selling wine by the glass, attracting middle-class women, who had hitherto drunk gin and orange; and the substantial growth in the consumption of sherry in the 1950s, which the author of the article attributed to the advantage of sherry over other wines in being a standard product which could therefore be heavily advertised.[4]

From 1962 on unfortified table wines began to be turned into standard products which could be heavily advertised. If this had taken a long time coming, it was because of a Catch-22 situation in which the mass of the population would not take up wine-drinking until cheap, branded table wines were produced, and their existence made known to them by advertising; but it was not worth a company's investing in creating brands until it knew that the market existed. Someone had to take a chance. In fact the first branded table wines, the 'Club' range produced by Harveys of Bristol, proved a failure because they were too expensive. In order to offset the cost of promotion, including a television campaign, Harveys charged 16s a bottle: given a seven-fold increase in the Retail Price Index since then, this is the equivalent of £5–6 today. What was needed was a brand that could be retailed at 10s a bottle, that would appeal to the increasingly wealthy working classes. The problem experienced by 'Club' in balancing the price of the wine and the cost of advertising dissuaded other companies who started to sell branded wine from spending a lot of money on promoting them.

Most off-licence shops were owned by brewers, who were therefore in the best position to market branded wines. By 1967 50 per cent more table wine was being drunk than had been in 1963. Some of the brewers were marking time while their industry was investigated by the Monopolies Commission, whose report, it was predicted, would propose that the brewers divested themselves of their wine and spirits businesses;[5] but Grants of St James's, a subsidiary of Allied Breweries, (Tetley, Taylor-Walker, Ind Coope et al.), were worried that the Monopolies Commission would recommend the abolition of the brewery tie, and thus destroy the brewers' captive market in pubs, forcing them to rely entirely on the mass marketing of branded products. In 1967 they spent the then gigantic sum of £250,000 – perhaps equivalent to £2 million today – on a television campaign to promote the Nicolas range of branded table wines at 8s 3d a bottle. They sold a million bottles of these wines a week, accounting – incredibly – for half of all the table wines sold in Britain. In 1968 they launched their own Don Cortez brand with a promotional expenditure of £450,000. Derrick Holden-Brown, deputy chairman of Grants, stated that these campaigns were part of a long-term plan designed to encourage people to identify and pick up from the shelves 'a cheap, no frills, table wine as readily as they now buy a bottle of ketchup'.[6]

Demonstrably, the new class of wine-drinkers were not interested in famous names or fine wines. They were quite willing to buy wines by national brand in the same way as they were now buying beer. Indeed, consumer research showed that a major brake on the growth of wine consumption was that people were afraid of making fools of themselves by mispronouncing names, and too shy to betray their ignorance by asking for advice. It was said that 'meaningless descriptions like *appellation contrôlée* with which the French like to adorn their bottles are becoming even more meaningless and will perhaps soon finally disappear altogether as the mass-market grows'.[7] In 1970 Derek Cooper predicted that 'in future, for most people, wine will come, not with frightening names like Château Pichon-Longueville or Schloss Eltz Rauenthaler Siebenmorgen, but just red, white or rosé'.[8]

We should not be misled by the dominance of supermarkets in the wine trade today into thinking that it was competition from supermarkets which forced the big brewery groups finally to develop and market branded wines. In 1967 Roger Holloway, marketing director of Bass-Charrington Vintners, expressed a belief that 'supermarkets will never really present any great competition; a supermarket could never offer the range carried by an off-licence. The wine habit is growing so fast that there is room for everybody.'⁹ What the supermarkets did, however, was to force prices down. They only moved into the drinks business after the 1961 Licensing Act made it permissible to sell alcoholic products during normal shopping hours, rather than, as hitherto, only during pub opening hours; and only started doing so in a big way after 1965, when resale price maintenance on spirits was abolished. No longer did spirits have to be sold at a fixed price, as books are today. The supermarkets indulged in a price-cutting war which destroyed many well-established smaller off-licence stores.

The price-cutting war, though it started with spirits, ended up making wine very much cheaper. The Augustus Barnett off-licences, as well as Del Monico in Soho, branches of Tesco and various other stores, had long experience of selling cheap spirits, even before resale price maintenance was abolished. Augustus Barnett, set up in 1963, at first sold mostly spirits, but after a few years Brian Barnett started taking a lorry over to France and buying wine direct. He thus avoided one of the most inflationary elements in the cost of a bottle of wine, the cut taken by the middleman. At a time when the general structure of the trade was that an importer sold to a wholesaler who sold to a retailer – the system with which, as a legacy of prohibition, the USA is still stuck today – he was able, by 1967, to cut the price of table wine down to 3s 9d a bottle, less than half as much as the heavily advertised brands. By 1969 Augustus Barnett were selling 35 million bottles a year, 14 per cent of total UK wine sales.

Brands, as it transpired, were merely a temporary stage, the means of introducing new people to wine. *Appellation contrôlée* did not become a meaningless term, largely because, after Britain joined the EEC in 1973, we had to start obeying its conditions. It became illegal to sell wine from the south of France as Nuits-Saint-Georges or Châteauneuf-du-Pape. This was the point at which Sainsbury's started taking wines seriously. They went over to France and brought back 'country' wines, which still came from the south of France, but now were not ashamed to admit their origin. Today, Sainsbury's and Tesco between them sell as much wine, mostly under their own labels (Sainsbury's Corbières, Tesco's Anjou Rouge, etc.), as all the 'traditional' branded wines put together – about 15 per cent of all the wine sold in Britain.

The rise to prominence of supermarkets has helped to make wine more popular in two ways. Firstly, own-label wine in supermarkets is cheaper than branded wine in off-licences, for exactly the same reason as own-label coffee and washing powder are cheaper than their branded equivalents. The supermarkets do not need to support their brands with expensive advertising and public relations exercises. Sainsbury's and Tesco do advertise their wines, that is true, but they do so in order to enhance their corporate image, rather than to improve the sales of individual wines. More importantly, supermarkets have made it possible for women to buy wine without having to suffer a feeling of alienation in off-licences, whose atmosphere all too often resembles that of a betting shop. Market research conducted in the area round Nottingham found that, over the busy Christmas and New Year period in 1985, more wine was bought by women than men. Thirty-eight per cent of wine-buying was undertaken by women alone; 21 per cent by men alone; the rest by men and women together.[10] Another survey in the same year found that, nationally, 62 per cent of women who bought wines did so in a supermarket.[11] Certainly, 80 per cent of Sainsbury's customers are women.

The last step in the demystification and popularization of wine, after the mystique of wine names had been removed by the brands, and that of wine merchants by the supermarkets, was the wine bottle itself, inaccessible to anyone who lacked a corkscrew. The wine boom in Australia had occurred as a result of the introduction of wine boxes, which took off in 1971, and by 1986 accounted for 60–65 per cent of all wine sold. On the basis of their success in Australia, various companies attempted to launch boxes in the UK in the 1970s, but the boxes were too large (five litres) and therefore too expensive. The breakthrough came when Stowells of Chelsea launched a three-litre box in 1981. Within two years, boxes accounted for 10 per cent of all wine sales.

There is no evidence, however, that boxes brought any new people to wine-drinking. Between 1981 and 1983 the number of wine consumers increased by 7 per cent, little more than the average annual increase of 4.5 per cent between 1970 and 1985. The growth in sales of boxed wine would not have been so rapid if it had appealed to new wine-drinkers. No one who was not a confirmed wine-drinker was going to spend £7 on wine. This was a product which people who had already started drinking wine had been looking for.

Wine boxes did not appeal to people because they took away the mystique of corked bottles and reduced wine to the status of any other packaged beverage. Wine boxes, which were more expensive than comparable corked bottles, appealed to people because they thought, mistakenly, that they were convenient. Though packaging technology has now improved considerably, with early boxes there was no chance of the wine's surviving the four months it was supposed to after opening, even if the consumer did ensure that the tap was kept flooded, something no one had told him was necessary. Admittedly at one time wine boxes were something of an asset at parties: they dispensed with the need for the host to wear himself out opening bottles with a corkscrew every ten minutes; and you could drink more without feeling guilty about it; whereas emptying a wine bottle may seem excessive, four glasses out of a box do not. But the idea that there was something convenient about wine boxes derives from popular misapprehensions about wine bottles. It is thought that a wine bottle, once opened, should be emptied the same day: a half-empty bottle, with the cork shoved back in, may certainly go off after a day, even in a refrigerator, but it is more likely to survive for a week or more. Popular fear about 'wasting' wine by allowing it to go off in the refrigerator has been exploited by the launch in 1987 of two appliances new to the UK. The 'Vacuvin' enables you to pump out most of the air from a half-consumed bottle but I am not convinced of its effectiveness. If a wine is insufficiently stable to remain in good condition after air is allowed into the bottle, it is unlikely to make much difference if, with the aid of a 'Vacuvin', two-thirds of the air is removed. On the other hand if a wine is stable enough to survive for a few days after opening, then why bother with a 'Vacuvin' at all? The expensive 'Vintage Keeper' system, which replaces the air with a mixture of nitrogen and carbon dioxide, does work, but is it worth it? If you do not want a wine to spoil from contact with air, fill up a clean half-bottle with it, and insert a cork. If you recork it with a new cork, it may keep, depending on the wine, for *years*.

Wine boxes have not caused the mystique of the cork to disappear. Most wine-drinkers seem to prefer a corked wine over one which has been sealed with a screw-cap. But corks offer many disadvantages. For a start, they are not always removable. On several occasions I have had to give up trying to open bottles of ordinary

Italian wine, sometimes before, sometimes after breaking my cork-screw. It is possible that, as well as the cork's being too tight, the glue which has been used to stick scraps of cork together to produce a cheap 'conglomerate' cork has caused the cork to stick to the neck of the bottle. Certainly, the glue sometimes reacts with the wine to produce an unpleasant taste. Moreover, conglomerate corks do not seal the wine as effectively as a screw-cap, and as a result not only is the wine more likely to oxidize, it will also have been necessary to have added more sulphur dioxide before bottling. The answer, of course, is to use a better cork, made from a single piece of bark, but this costs the bottler about 10p, compared with 5p for a cheap cork.

In any case, between 2 and 5 per cent of all corks impart a 'corky' aroma and taste to the wine. This, it has recently been suggested, may be the smell of 2,4,6-trichloroanisol, which does not occur naturally in cork but is produced as a result of the process of sterilizing it with a chlorine solution, producing TCP, which is then converted by penicillin moulds into 2,4,6-trichloroanisol. In the past, most wine books taught us that corked wines were very rare, and that, if you tried sending a wine back in a restaurant, it would almost certainly not be genuinely corked. Admittedly, before the war a popular restaurant ploy was for a diner-out to order a bottle of white wine to go with his fish course, drink half of it, then complain that it was 'corked'. As he had by now finished his fish, it was too late to replace it with another bottle of the same wine, so he was given, to go with his meat course, a bottle of red wine for free. Today, however, the problem is that too many people will drink a corked wine rather than sending it back; being unconvinced of their ability to discern corkiness, they may wish to avoid embarrassment, and may even believe that the wine was meant to taste like that. Certainly, I have identified wines as corked which were not in fact spoiled – just very woody, a taste which one would hope to wear off after a few more years in bottle. Instead of using a cork, it would be more sensible to seal a bottle with a screw-cap; this way the wine would be more stable, and cheaper. Why not, indeed, use a plastic instead of a glass bottle? But I cannot think of any restaurant in this country which subscribes sufficiently to the principles of radical chic to offer wine in a screw-top or plastic bottle. Perhaps wine has not been demystified, after all?

[9]

Certainly, Britain is now a nation of wine-drinkers. As many Britons drink wine as the national drink, beer. In 1985 in Britain there were 27.5 million wine-drinkers out of a total adult population of 44 million. In 1987 market researchers found that 50 per cent of the population perceive wine as an 'everyday' drink, even though only 35 per cent drink it as often as once a month.[12] Yet wine is still a relatively new fashion. Like almost all fashions, it began by conquering London and then the South of England. It has not yet overrun the North, nor rural areas generally: 80 per cent of adults in the South, but only 50 per cent in the North, drink wine.[13] Whereas 20 per cent of Londoners drink wine more than once a week, only 1 per cent of Scots do so.[14] Relatively few people aged over fifty-five drink wine, since they had already formed their drinks tastes before the wine boom of the 1960s. As time goes on, consumption amongst people in this age group will rise. Given that between 5 and 10 per cent of the population are teetotallers, it seems likely that the proportion of wine-drinkers will eventually reach between 85 and 90 per cent of the population.

The amount of wine people drink is also continuing to increase. Wine-drinkers do not, for the most part, drink wine in sufficiently large quantities to be concerned by the growing weight of medical evidence indicting even apparently moderate consumption of alcohol, nor by the increasingly enforced drink-and-drive laws. The average wine-drinker consumes only three glasses each week; a man can drink this much every day without endangering any aspect of his health in any respect. (Women are now being recommended to drink no more than two glasses a day.) Despite hiccoughs, the amount of wine consumed by each wine-drinker has doubled since the early 1970s, and I expect it to double again by the end of the century. It may increase still further if the European Commission carries out its plans to harmonize indirect taxation rates within the EEC; though, at the time of writing, the Paymaster General has given his assurance that Britain will use its veto to obstruct this proposal, and doubtless the discussions will drag on for years. But if the plans are ever carried out, the duty on a bottle of table wine will fall from 74p to 7p. Competition in the wine trade is today so great that there would certainly be an immediate response by retailers to these changes. At current prices, the cost of a decent bottle of wine in a supermarket would fall from £2 to £1 a bottle. It is hard to know how much this would increase wine consumption, since wine is no longer an expensive form of alcoholic drink. In terms of the number of pence you have to pay per degree of alcohol, it is the same price as spirits, and much cheaper than beer. Hitherto, however, the increase in wine consumption has been directly linked to a fall in the price of wine, both absolutely, and relative to purchasing power. The average amount spent on wine in Britain has increased by only 40 per cent relative to the cost of living between 1964 and 1984, though in that period per capita wine consumption has trebled.

But does the fact that wine is cheap and popular mean that it has been demystified? Has it become popular in the sense of 'classless' – or does its rise reflect the growth of the middle class? Wine has always been a middle- and upper-class drink: in fact one definition of the difference between the working and middle classes – if indeed such a difference still exists – is that the former drink beer and the latter wine. As the founder of the Victoria Wine chain said in the 1870s, many members of the newly prosperous artisan class had taken up drinking wine because 'they look upon it as a more genteel thing than drinking a glass of beer'.[15]

The enlargement of the middle class in the last two generations has produced an extended period of Conservative political dominance; in turn the Conservative Party has since 1979 succeeded in establishing itself as 'the natural party of government' by further widening the middle class, by creating a share-owning, property-owning populace who as a result no longer identify with Labour's nostalgic vision of investing in outdated, nationalized manufacturing industries. It is interesting to see that the argument that the growing popularity of food and wine was due to the growth of the middle class, rather than to the increased wealth of the working class, was advanced as early as 1960, in his memoirs, by the restaurateur Mario Gallati.[16]

Has wine truly become a classless drink? Or is classlessness an image as much as a reality? Certainly the sales pitch of wine warehouses is to sell to the middle classes by exploiting an image of classlessness. These warehouses are situated largely in spartan buildings on main arterial roads leading out of the centres of towns towards wealthy suburbs, and offer a similar feeling of adventure to that derived from buying run-down Victorian houses in derelict areas of inner cities. In theory wine warehouses are cheap, certainly cheaper than wine shops, because they do not have to indulge in the expense of running expensive city-centre premises as well as a warehouse out of town. But they are not as cheap as supermarkets. Majestic, who dominate the wine warehouse market, with twenty-two warehouses, made the mistake of trying to compete with the supermarkets; they have now realized that this is not for them. Instead, their role is to sell to wealthy people who like to feel that they are getting a bargain. Giles Clarke, director of Majestic, when questioned about the likely areas of his southern-based chain's expansion, admitted: 'I'm not interested in the North. There is a lack of concentrated rich people there.'[17] In business terms he is probably right. In 1987 Boddingtons' Breweries sold their chain of five Whynot Wine Warehouses to the Canadian-based multinational Seagrams, the owners of Oddbins, into branches of which they have been turned. According to Ted Englefield, finance director of Boddingtons, the wine warehouse concept is 'still not proven in the North of England'.[18]

The first wine warehouses did offer bargains of a sort. They were a product of the recession of the 1970s, selling the stock of bankrupted wine merchants and wine importers from the warehouse where that stock was held. Today, however, the name 'wine warehouse' is appropriated by wine shops who wish to appear trendy – Grape Ideas Wine Warehouse, in Swiss Cottage in London, for instance. This militates against what remains the basic theory of a wine warehouse, as expounded by Ahmed Pochee, who, in 1972, left Oddbins, which he had helped set up ten years earlier, and founded the first wine warehouse in Wapping on the River Thames. He recommends piling cases high to the ceiling in order to incite potential customers into wanting to possess them. For this theory to work, it is important that the warehouse should sell to customers in minimum quantities of one case. Some of them do have retail licences, which would permit them to sell by the single bottle, but they pretend they do not, because that is not what they want to do.

[1] *Sunday Times*, 27 November 1966.
[2] Quoted in *Decanter*, May 1985, p. 16.
[3] Quoted in Derek Cooper, *The Beverage Report*, Routledge & Kegan Paul, 1970, p. 144.
[4] *Economist*, 28 May 1960.

[5] *Economist*, 1 June 1968.
[6] Quoted in Asa Briggs, *Wine for Sale: Victoria Wine and the liquor trade 1860–1984*, B. T. Batsford, 1985, pp. 128–9.
[7] Douglas Sutherland, *Raise Your Glasses: a light-hearted history of drinking*, Macdonald, 1979, p. 197.
[8] Cooper, p. 157.
[9] *The Times*, 4 January 1968, p. 18.
[10] *Nottingham Evening Post* survey.
[11] NOP survey.
[12] NOP survey.
[13] Gallup Poll commissioned for Stowells of Chelsea's *Wine Report*, 1985.
[14] NOP survey, 1985.
[15] William Winch Hughes to 1879 Commons Select Committee on Wine Duties, quoted in Briggs, p. 49.
[16] Mario Gallati, *Mario of the Caprice*, Hutchinson, 1950, p. 121.
[17] Quoted in *Wine and Spirit*, November 1985, pp. 44–5.
[18] Quoted in *Wine and Spirit*, November 1987, p. 9.

THE NEW SNOBBERY

When people talk about the 'wine boom', what they are referring to is the increase in the sales of light table wine as opposed to fortified wines such as port, sherry or vermouth. They mean the fact that in 1960 we each drank one litre of light and sparkling wine, and in 1985 we each drank ten.

Not only has it been a boom in light wine, but a boom in white wine. I have no statistics for the 1960s, but most of the wine we drank then was certainly red. That was why, when International Distillers and Vintners (who produce Smirnoff among other brands) decided in 1968 to launch a branded table wine of their own, they introduced a medium-sweet Portuguese red wine called Doçura. Today, when about 70 per cent of the wine we drink is white and 25 per cent red,[1] a mass-market branded wine such as this would more likely be white. Why has this transformation in popular taste occurred?

White wine has come into favour because it is considered to be lighter and less alcoholic than red. Certainly it seems lighter to taste and more refreshing – not least because it is usually served cool, and red is not. In fact there is no reason why white wine should necessarily contain less alcohol, indeed there is some reason why it should contain more, since a red wine loses alcohol during fermentation in ways that a white one does not – up to one-twentieth of its total if it is fermented in open vats, as is traditional in the Côte d'Or in Burgundy; the same if the grape stems are included in the vat, as is the usual practice in Beaujolais; and up to one-sixth of its total alcohol content as a result of the regular recycling of the pomace of skins in the vat in order to extract colour and flavour from them. But still it is popularly believed that white wine is less alcoholic than red, and there are those who would not wish us to be disabused – like the wicked old Frenchman whom Cyril Ray described as recalling that he had found it profitable in his time that 'nice young English girls' were unaware of the truth in this matter.[2]

Moreover, it is generally attested by experience that white wine is less likely to give you a hangover than red, though it is not clear precisely why. It has been suggested that the reaction which a number of people experience after drinking red wine is an allergic one, possibly caused by histidine, which occurs in the skins and pips of black grapes. Red wines contain more histidine than white because they are fermented in contact with their skins, whereas for white wine the juice is separated from the skins before fermentation. If headaches are caused by the histidine in red wines, this would explain why cheap red wine produces a headache, and expensive red wine does not. In the manufacture of fine wines, the grapes are pressed very gently, whereas grapes for cheap wines are often pressed very hard, in order to get as much as possible out of them, and this extracts many more chemicals from the grape-skins and pips. Alternatively, people could be reacting to histamine (a derivative of histidine) and tyramine formed during the malolactic fermentation – a secondary fermentation which converts malic into lactic acids and which occurs much more commonly in red wines than in white ones. In 1983, however, two American scientists carried out allergic skin scratch tests and antihistamine treatments in order to determine whether the reaction to red wine really was an allergic one. They pointed out that histamine and tyramine levels in red wine are very low, and concluded that the reaction to red wine is not an allergic one and is probably psychologically induced.[3] There are, however, other causes of headaches which apply equally to both red and white wines, cheap and expensive, such as the enlargement of the cranial blood-vessels by alcohol.

Whatever the truth of the matter, white wine has gained ground over red because it is considered to be lighter. The success of wine, though ostensibly due to the disappearance of snobbery, really is the reflection of another sort of social snobbery. The snobbery of one generation has been replaced by that of another: the snobbery of lightness. The closer an alcoholic drinks product approaches fruit juice or water, the more we seem to prefer it.

The taste for alcohol is an acquired one: innately we dislike it. The most popular white wines, particularly among 'nice young English girls', are German ones, which account for 45 per cent of all the white wines we drink. Whereas many French white wines have a slightly sweet taste, even if they are dry, due to their alcohol content, most German wines have a sweet taste because they contain some unfermented sugar and so do not need to be as high in alcohol. The slightly sweet taste of pure alcohol, which first evidences itself at a concentration of about 10–11 per cent, can be experienced, for those who wish, by drinking neat vodka. Because German wines at 7–9 per cent do not taste of alcohol, they appeal to beginners, who have not yet become used to a wine that tastes of alcohol. French white wines contain between 11 and 13 per cent alcohol, at which level it can be tasted.

Alcohol needs to be present in a wine, even at a concentration lower than that which can be detected. De-alcoholized wines, in which the 8–12 per cent of alcohol which has been removed is replaced by water, tend to taste acidulous and unbalanced. They have been deprived not only of alcohol's slightly sweet taste, but also of the body given to wine by alcohol, which also balances the taste of acidity. Moreover, it is thought that alcohol makes a wine smell more fruity, by affecting the vapour pressure of other compounds.

Our innate taste, however, is for fruit and sweetness, not for alcohol. This preference is the relic of man's days as a hunter–gatherer 30,000 years ago, during which a liking for sweet things was programmed into our genes: if a fruit was sweet this was a sign that it was ripe and ready to eat: For this reason some people continue today to mix not only whisky with ginger ale, but bitter with blackcurrant, lager with lime, and vodka and white rum with anything in cocktails.[4]

It is only through the medium of such sweet, fruity drinks that the taste of alcohol has become acceptable to many people. For example, in the 1950s teenagers took up drinking Coca-Cola, not least because it was a symbol of a brash new American lifestyle and therefore unpopular with older people in the aftermath of the war. These teenagers were then introduced to alcohol by a blend of Coca-Cola with white rum (strictly a *cuba libre*, popularly a Bacardi and Coke); perhaps they wished deliberately to frustrate the intentions of the manufacturers of Coca-Cola (originally a patent medicine and temperance drink), who did not want their product to be mixed with alcohol. In the 1970s mixtures of drinks became more extravagant. It may seem strange now to think that ten years ago Peppermint Park in London's Covent Garden was the 'in' place and that Pina Coladas were socially acceptable drinks. People took to the consumption of this particular mixture of white rum, pineapple juice and coconut milk so readily that it rapidly became a mass-market product and therefore a criterion of 'naffness'. Its great appeal lay in its being so sickly-sweet that you did not notice that you were drinking a great deal of rum. You could enjoy the effect of alcohol without the taste.

Younger and younger people are learning to cope with the taste of alcohol through sweet, fruity drinks. In the early 1980s wine-coolers – mixtures of wine, fruit juice and carbonated water, which contain between 1.5 and 3.5 per cent alcohol, took the USA by storm. Between their introduction in 1980 and 1986 sales grew from 0 to 600 million litres, 20 per cent of all wine sales. The marketing of these products has in some cases been directed at very young consumers indeed. In Australia Lindeman's marketed their Tropi-cana cooler in a pack with a straw very similar to a fruit-juice box; they were persuaded in 1987 by the health ministry to withdraw this pack, as it was thought to be too appealing to children. Certainly, the taste would have appealed. Tesco's Summer Fruits Spritzer tastes just like fizzy Ribena. Nevertheless, coolers have not taken off in Britain. This may be partly because of our weather, or partly because consumers know when they are being ripped off: it costs more than twice as much to buy a cooler as it does to make a far superior mixture at home. At the end of 1987 Seagrams announced that they were scrapping their Spectrum range of canned coolers and replacing them with a new Spectrum range of bottled 'spritzers', with less fruit and 30 per cent more alcohol.

The failure of coolers to sell in this country does not negate the theory that we naturally prefer sweet, fruity, fizzy drinks. For example a much brighter future seems to lie ahead for Belgian cherry beer (*kriek lambic*) which, at least in the versions available in Britain, is a high-quality product, sold at a justifiable price – about £1–1.50 for a 37.5 centilitre bottle. I marginally prefer Liefman's to Timmer-man's, though they vary from one bottle to another. Cherry beer is made by macerating cherries in young beer, which causes the cherries to ferment. It is bottle-fermented in a similar way to champagne, except that the sediment is left in the bottle. It has a bitter-sweet character which causes some people to identify it blind as a vermouth-based cocktail. It is interesting to note that in 1972 Professor Hough of the British School of Malting at Birmingham University predicted that we would soon be drinking raspberry-, strawberry- and other fruit-flavoured beers.[5]

Because sweet, fruity drinks satisfy our natural tastes they are, *ipso facto*, unsophisticated. So how is it possible to satisfy the desire of many consumers to appear sophisticated while at the same time continuing to cater to their preference for a drink that is sweet? One method is simply to call a sweet drink 'dry'. A clever example of this is Dry Sack sherry. In his book on sherry, Julian Jeffs says that sack – as drunk in the England of the first Elizabeth – was a sweet wine. Dry Sack is a medium sherry; therefore it is a very dry sack, though not a dry sherry.[6] Other manufacturers have been more cunning still. In the 1960s the sherry firm Croft found through market research that people thought the lighter a sherry was in colour, the drier it was, and therefore the more sophisticated. Croft invented 'pale cream' sherry, which looks like and has the texture of a dry sherry, but fulfils popular demand for the taste of sweet, cream sherry. They now sell 7 million bottles of their invention, Croft Original, in Britain each year – as many as the most famous of 'traditional' cream sherries, Harveys Bristol Cream. Croft Original was followed in 1984 by Croft Particular, made drier and lighter coloured than Croft Original (though sweeter and blander than Fino sherry), in order to appeal, they say, to Yuppies, who have become too sophisticated to drink pale cream sherries. In 1987–8 Harveys spent £3.5 million on launching John Harvey, their equivalent of Croft Particular – so clearly this is intended to be the taste of the 1990s.

The example of sherries which look like white wine suggests that, if drinks have become lighter in the last thirty years, this is in terms not of flavour, but of appearance. Moreover, the popularity of vodka in the last generation suggests that lightness of appearance has proved a far more potent force than lightness in terms of alcohol. When Smirnoff was launched in 1953, vodka was so little known in Britain that many publicans thought it was a type of wine. It rose to prominence as the 'fun' drink of social revolutionaries in the 1960s. As a nation, we now drink much more vodka than gin, and twice as much as brandy.

It seems that we live today in a world obsessed with image, in which our idea of 'preserving' buildings involves pulling them down but keeping the façade. The importance of appearance is evident from the small attention we pay to the taste and smell of what we drink. As long as it is not objectionable, it does not matter if a drink is not particularly good. One might, for instance, imagine that the taste of wine is an important factor in its selection. If so, how come wine boxes were so popular in the early 1980s? It was more expensive to put wine in boxes than in bottles, so the only area of possible saving was the wine itself. In 1983 the company responsible for 50 per cent of the boxes produced sent out a letter to the wine firms whose wine it packed complaining of the 'filthy' and 'disgraceful' condition in which they had received many of the wines. Yet when, in 1982, market researchers asked people for their opinion of wine boxes, 90 per cent of the respondents said 'average' or 'better than average'.[7] And these responses were not from novice wine-drinkers. Only someone who already knew that he liked wine would buy three litres at a time.

Our interest in the absence of negative attributes of taste rather than in the presence of positive ones is evident from the popularity of 'cold-fermented' white wines. The introduction of stainless steel fermentation vats and heat-exchangers has revolutionized the production of white wines in warm climates. No longer do they oxidize and lose their fruit as a result of excessively high temperatures during fermentation. But no longer do they offer any interest, either. They all taste the same. Many white Riojas used to be oxidized and virtually undrinkable; now most of them are so dull that they have lost all identity. The exceptions are those wines – Marqués de Murrieta and Tondonia from Lopez de Heredia – which are still made by the old methods, and among oak-aged dry white wines offer outstanding value for money. But the general run of cold-fermented white Riojas, though perfectly sound to drink, do not offer value for money, because exactly the same taste, or lack of it, can be found in cheaper wines from less prestigious regions, such as north-east Italy, from where Sainsbury's sell a Pinot Bianco del Veneto in cartons for £2.29 a litre, the equivalent of £1.72 a bottle.

If few of us are interested in how a wine tastes, then we cannot particularly care how it smells, since most of what we think of as taste is in fact smell. If you smell a wine in the glass, you inhale only those substances which become volatile at the temperature of the wine, which ought to be between 13 and 18°C. If you take a wine in your mouth, and particularly if you hold it there for a second or two, it very rapidly warms up to approach the temperature of your tongue – 38°C – and many more substances become volatile and are inhaled up the back of your nose from the inside. In fact we are even less interested in how a wine smells than in how it tastes. One of my favourite wine snob stories is the apparently genuine incident recounted by a Canadian correspondent to *Decanter* magazine. At a dinner party he took a sip of wine, turned to the young lady next to him and said, 'I just love the smell of Chardonnay.' She replied with all sincerity that she was wearing Chanel No. 10.[8]

If we were interested in smelling wine, we would not use the glasses we do. It is one thing to employ standard 'Paris goblets', or even tumblers, for everyday wine, which is for glugging, not sniffing. But what about a wine for whose superior quality you have paid a more substantial sum? How can you swirl a wine around in the glass, in order to encourage its contents to become odoriferous and to enable you to smell the odour before it dissipates, if the glass is not a large one, with a big bowl and tapered at the top? Virtually all wine glasses on the market are far too small, except for the deliberately gross 'Burgundy goblets' which I cannot imagine anyone buying other than as a joke. By far the best glasses for all fine wines are Berry Bros' red wine glasses (which cost £3.20 each), and it is no coincidence that these are what the majority of the wine trade use at home.

Sight has become a much more important sense than smell ever since primeval apes rose from all fours and began walking on two legs. Our sense of smell has been deteriorating ever since. Unlike many other mammals, our major instrument of sexual selection is now sight rather than smell, perhaps because in humans vision acts at a distance, whereas smell does not. We have not lost our ability to secrete pheromones – hormones to which members of the opposite sex react – but we are gradually losing our ability to detect and respond to them.

How else, if not in terms of its appearance, can one explain the popularity of sparkling mineral water, the most fashionable drink of the 1980s? We certainly do not drink it for reasons of taste. In a tasting of mineral waters conducted by *What Wine*? (now *Wine*) magazine, London tap water, both in its 'natural' form and after being made sparkling by passing it through a sodastream, was rated more highly than many brands of mineral water.[9] The leading brand since the first beginnings of the mineral-water boom in the mid-1970s has been Perrier, who account, according to their own figures, for 60 per cent, and, according to independently researched figures, for 35 per cent, of all mineral-water sales in the UK. Perrier has been so successfully advertised – currently they spend £1½ million a year – that it has become synonymous with mineral water in the same way as the Hoover brand name came to be identified with vacuum-cleaners in general. But do drinkers of Perrier actually prefer its taste to that of tap water which has been passed through a sodastream? Certainly, among self-perceived trend-setters, it has fallen victim to its own success in the same way as kiwi fruit, and has been replaced in favour by Badoit. This may be better suited to food in so far as it has fewer bubbles than Perrier; but how many of those of us who insist on drinking it actually enjoy the taste of a product with 170 milligrams of bicarbonate salts per litre? Certainly some parts of the country, such as Oxford, are provided with unpleasant-tasting tap water; but this can perfectly well be rendered neutral-tasting by passing it through a carbon filter; taking into account the purchase of the equipment, water filtered in this way would cost 14p per litre for the first hundred litres, and only 3p per litre thereafter.

So why *do* we drink mineral water? Not, on the whole, for reasons of health. Under the Natural Mineral Waters Regulations 1985, no water offered for sale in Britain may make therapeutic claims. Whereas in other European countries the term 'mineral water', as distinct from 'spring water', is applied to waters containing a high concentration of minerals which are supposed to produce a medicinal effect, in Britain it simply means that certain conditions regarding purity have been satisfied. We drink mineral water not because it is good for us, or even because we like the taste, but because it has become a socially acceptable drink which can be ordered and served without embarrassment at a party or restaurant. When Perrier became fashionable in the USA in the late 1970s, one of the jokes which became current told about a man who went into a bar and, thinking he ought to order the latest 'in' drink, asked for 'a Perrier and soda'.[10]

Mineral water is particularly acceptable if it contains bubbles. Bubbles have created the mineral-water market. It is estimated that three times as much sparkling as still mineral water is sold in Britain. Fizzy alcoholic drinks are also becoming more and more popular. Consumption of sparkling wines increased by 70 per cent between 1982 and 1987; and they now account for about 6 per cent of all the wine we drink. The principal reason for their popularity is demonstrated by their being served in tall, thin 'flûte' glasses, which are very narrow and are usually filled to the brim, making them quite inappropriate for smelling the stuff, but ideal for showing off the bubbles. That is the great appeal of sparkling drinks – ostentation. It was, after all, expressly with the intention of displaying the bubbles that flûte glasses were developed in the first half of the seventeenth century. They were initially used to serve sparkling ale, which was invented before champagne, but were popularized at the court of Charles II in the 1660s by the Marquis de Saint-Evremond, who introduced champagne to England. If the popularity of sparkling drinks derives from their appearance, then why not serve lager and mineral water in flûtes, too?

Beers have become increasingly fizzy over the years, in order to satisfy the demands of each new group of consumers for a product which is more ostentatious than the one drunk by their parents. Admittedly, beer has been a fizzy drink ever since its invention several thousand years ago. It possibly used to be drunk while it was still fermenting, as it went off very quickly afterwards, and as a result people developed a preference for fizzy beer. Cask-conditioned beer ('real ale') has always sparkled slightly as the result of a secondary fermentation in cask. But, to produce a really fizzy beer, carbon dioxide gas must be added. This was first done with bottled beers in the 1890s, but they did not become popular until after the First World War. In the 1920s, as in the 1950s, sales of bottled beer grew enormously, as young people took it up as a smart, young, go-ahead, sparkling drink. By the mid-1950s, bottled mild and bitter between them accounted for 50 per cent of beer sales – much the same as lager today – and enjoyed very much the same status as modern lager. In fact lager is even fizzier than bottled bitter, because it is served at a lower temperature, and the lower the temperature, the higher the proportion of dissolved carbon dioxide a liquid is capable of holding. Lager beer contains roughly 2 per cent carbon dioxide by volume, compared with 1.4 per cent in the case of bottled bitter.

Today draught bitter too is expected to be fizzy. Since the 1960s most draught beer has been brewery-conditioned and artificially carbonated: 'keg' beer, effectively bottled beer on draught. Had it not been for the efforts of the Campaign for Real Ale (CAMRA) in the 1970s, cask-conditioned draught beer might have all but disappeared by now.

In Yorkshire a draught beer is, quite absurdly, judged on the size of its 'head', and Yorkshiremen quite often send back pints in London pubs because they are not frothy enough. To satisfy public demand, Yorkshire publicans have for many years employed a device known as an economizer. A sparkler causes turbulence in the beer as it flows through the pump and therefore forces some of the gas out of solution and into the head. In order to fill the glass a large amount of overspill occurs, often more than double the capacity of the glass. The overspill is collected in a drip tray which returns it to the top of the pump, ready for serving the next glass. In 1987 it was reported that the economizer had been banned, partly as a result of the AIDS scare. In fact, a substantial number of publicans still use the system, although they have been instructed by public health officials to ensure that a clean glass is used every time and that notices are displayed to this effect.

But far worse crimes than the use of the economizer are carried out in order to give a good head. Beer which is made entirely from malt and hops, without replacing the malt with other cereals such as flaked maize or rice, or indeed simply with sugar, will retain a stable foam. But malt is expensive, and gives a beer too much flavour for a 100 per cent malt beer to be suited to mass-market tastes. The average malt content of British beer has fallen from 86 per cent in 1900 to – officially – 76 per cent today. Some people suspect that the 76 per cent is an overestimate; certainly British brewers are permitted to use as little as 60 per cent. Keg beers and the majority of British-brewed lagers almost certainly do not contain as much as 76 per cent malt, and propylene glycol alginate (E 405) has to be added to create a foam. It is suspected that this may be harmful, but as yet not enough research has been conducted to come to a conclusion. In order to promote a strong head on their beers, in the early 1960s some brewers in America took to using cobalt sulphate, which can reduce the body's ability to metabolize certain substances which maintain the life of cells in the heart, and consequently caused the deaths of about fifty people.

In the rest of Britain, although people do not demand so much froth as they do in Yorkshire, beers are required to have a head. This is probably the effect of advertisements showing lovable Cockneys, streetwise bears and cynical Australians drinking beer which has foam on top. Certainly, one reason for the fall in the popularity of cask-conditioned bitter since the 1950s is that it is virtually flat. Unlike 'keg' bitter or lager, it is not kept under pressure when in cask. When pressurized, carbon dioxide will dissolve to high concentrations, and then reappear as bubbles when the pressure is released. Roughly speaking, cask-conditioned bitter contains 0.8 per cent carbon dioxide by volume compared with 1.4 per cent in the case of keg bitter.

Partly because of its association with beer, connoisseurs have, throughout its history, condemned the popular taste for sparkling wine. When the new invention, sparkling champagne, was all the rage 250 years ago, the Maréchal de Montesquiou d'Artagnan, until then a regular purchaser of still champagne, asked his wine merchant, Bertin de Rocheret, for sparkling champagne because 'it is a fashion which rules everywhere, but more particularly among the younger generation'. Bertin de Rocheret replied that sparkling champagne was an 'abominable drink', that the bubbles destroyed the flavour of the individual growths, and that 'effervescence, I believe, is a merit in an inferior wine, and the property of beer, chocolate and whipped cream'. Two hundred years later, Morton Shand wrote that 'the outstanding example of the menace to the survival of wine is the *champagnisation* of all kinds of wine, quite irrespective of their suitability for gaseous treatment. Our spendthrift generation is convinced that the sparkling variety of any given wine must needs be its highest, because its costliest, expression. It would seem that in the United States wine, in common parlance, always implies a sparkling wine of sorts. It is arguable whether sparkling wine is really wine at all.'[11]

In fact, from the point of view of the wine-maker, carbon dioxide gas has various useful features. It accentuates the acid taste in wines and therefore makes them seem fresher, which is very useful for white wines made in hot climates which tend to suffer from a lack of acidity. It also protects wine from decay, because the pressure of gas trying to escape prevents air from entering the bottle. When the 'champagne method' was developed last century, making it possible to produce sparkling wines at will, it was used to preserve wines while they were waiting for customers. When it became difficult to sell red burgundies at the end of the century, even the *grand cru* wines were made sparkling by the new 'champagne method'. This method is still used today as an alternative to chaptalizing – the modern form of fortifying with brandy – the produce of bad vintages in cool vine-growing regions. It is used by a number of producers in the Mosel, even for the most famous wine of all, Bernkasteler Doktor; and also in the Loire, at Vouvray and Montlouis.

From the point of view of the consumer, as well as enhancing a drink's appearance, carbon dioxide both diminishes the taste of alcohol, which many people dislike, and at the same time enables the alcohol to be absorbed much more rapidly by the gut, thereby producing a much more rapid effect. This has rendered sparkling drinks sexually useful. As Denzil Batchelor once wrote, 'In the old days before World War I, [sparkling red burgundy] was a particular favourite of ladies of easy virtue and also of young girls who were inclined to wish that their virtue was not quite so difficult.'[12]

---

[1] The figures do not add up to 100 per cent because they ignore the consumption of pink wine.
[2] Cyril Ray, *Ray on Wine*, J. M. Dent & Sons, 1979, p. 24.
[3] Robert Masyczeck and C. S. Ough, 'The "Red Wine Reaction" Syndrome', *American Journal of Enology and Viticulture*, vol. 34, 1983, pp. 260–64. Six English doctors have recently suggested in the *Lancet* that migraines which occur after drinking red wine might well be caused by the tannins in the skins and pips of black grapes, rather than by histidine. They believe that tannins may inhibit the bodily enzyme PST, whose job it is to detoxify certain chemicals in the intestine. See Julia T. Littlewood *et al.*, 'Red Wine as a Cause of Migraine', *Lancet*, 12 March 1988, pp. 558–9.
[4] Embury, pp. 24–8, defines a cocktail as a combination of spirit and modifying agent (such as vermouth) in which the spirit must always comprise at least 50 per cent of the volume of the cocktail. Many of what we call cocktails are, strictly speaking, long, or (in American) tall, drinks.
[5] Cited in Christopher Hutt, *The Death of the English Pub*, Arrow Books, 1973, pp. 157–60.
[6] Julian Jeffs, *Sherry*, Faber & Faber, 3rd ed., 1982, pp. 51–2.
[7] Stowells of Chelsea research.

8 *Decanter*, May 1983, p. 11.
9 *What Wine?*, November 1985.
10 Maureen and Timothy Green, *The Good Water Guide*, Rosendale Press, 1985, p. 130.
11 P. Morton Shand, *Bacchus, or Wine Today and Tomorrow*, Kegan Paul, 1927, pp. 47–8.
12 Quoted in *Decanter*, April 1983, p. 20.

3

DRINKING OUT

Apart from our preference for apparently lighter drinks, there is another reason why we drink so much more white wine than red, which, along with our instinctive liking for sweetness, goes back to our berry-gathering days. We have an innate dislike of bitterness, since a bitter taste in a plant indicates that it contains poisonous alkaloids, a necessary means of chemical warfare resorted to by plants, which cannot defend themselves from predators by running away. In fact liking for sweetness and dislike of bitterness are the only two innate tastes we have: all others are acquired. Whereas liking for sweetness accounts for the preference of novice wine-drinkers for sweet white wines, dislike of bitterness explains why novice wine-drinkers are not attracted to most red wines, because these contain tannins. It is the purpose of tannins to interfere with the digestive process: they taste astringent because they react with the mucoproteins contained in saliva, thereby preventing it from performing its lubricating effect. The more we drink, the more astringent the wine appears, as we simply run out of mucoproteins.

In fact we drink three times as much red wine in Britain as we did twenty years ago, but it is not what it used to be: it is no longer so tannic. Piat d'Or, which accounts for 4 per cent of all red wine sold in this country, contains practically no tannin at all. After Doçura failed, largely – though this was not realized at the time – because it was Portuguese and not French, International Distillers and Vintners spent the mid-1970s testing out experimental blends on consumers to see if they could do better. In all the tastings they held, the preferred wine was a Liebfraumilch to which red dye had been added. This made them realize that it was the tannin in red wines which offended people and what they needed to do was to remove it, to make a red wine for white wine-drinkers.

Our innate liking for sweetness and dislike of bitterness dominate the consumption patterns of new or irregular wine-drinkers. To make the transition from novice to sophisticated wine-drinker, it is necessary literally to 'sophisticate' – to pervert – one's natural tastes. The ways in which we lose our preference for sweetness and overcome our hostility to bitterness are different. In the first case it is a question of satiety: until our taste for sweetness returns in our old age, as we grow older our tooth becomes progressively less sweet: that is why children have a sweeter tooth than adults. We lose our dislike of bitterness by taking pleasure in experiencing the sensation of danger. Drinking tannic red wine, or coffee, is unnatural and dangerous – and therefore pleasurable – in much the same way as riding in a roller-coaster. In both cases, however, our reason for doing so is to show ourselves to be sophisticated (in the sense of worldly-wise) by adopting tastes which can only be acquired with practice, by coming actually to prefer dry wine and red wine.

More and more people seem to be undergoing this transformation. Already – if only slightly – the consumption of sweet German wines is falling and that of dry French white wines is increasing. Already – if, again, only slightly – the general consumption of white wines is falling and that of red wines is increasing. I believe that, despite the prevailing fashion for lighter products, these will be the dominant trends over the next generation. After all, the wine boom is a boom in *table* wines; and dry white, and particularly red, wines go much better with food than sweet white ones. Certainly in the wine-producing and wine-drinking countries of Europe, more red wine has historically been drunk than white, for this reason. In the 1950s it was said of the Italians that they believed that wine *was* a food. Every meal had to include wine, but wine could only be drunk at a meal. If Italians drank little in the way of spirits, it was because they were not recognized as a food. [1]

In Britain today wine is most commonly taken with food: an opinion poll in 1982 found that 61 per cent of consumers normally drank table wine during a meal, compared with 7 per cent who habitually drank wine when they went out to a pub, disco or wine bar, and 13 per cent who usually drank table wine at a party. [2] It follows that if dry red wine goes better with food than sweet white, one would expect it to become more popular – especially as the growing importance of own-label wines from the supermarkets makes the transition from sweet white to dry red wines easier. Unlike the branded wines devised in the late 1960s to appeal to novice wine-drinkers, supermarket own-labels appeal to regular wine-drinkers. Whereas a 'traditional' brand – Hirondelle or whatever – will usually consist of only two or three wines, a supermarket might sell 100 or more wines under its own label. This eases the progression of the Liebfraumilch-drinker from sweet to dry wine: his confidence is boosted by sticking with the same brand while he crosses his own personal Rubicon. The traverse is made easier by supermarkets who offer a transitional style of wine which bridges the gap. Tesco in particular have succeeded in finding a range of white wines which are true to type but off-dry, and red wines which retain their regional character but have a great deal of soft, ripe fruit. Good examples are their own-label white Saumur, the red Quinta de Santo Amaro, made by the innovative Australian Peter Bright for the pan-Portuguese João Pires company, and their Finest Amontillado sherry, which stands half-way between the general run of commercial 'Amontillados', which contain little, if any, genuine Amontillado (that is, aged Fino) sherry, and old, unblended, unsweetened Amontillados which even hardened wine-drinkers often find too austere for their tastes.

Quinta de Santo Amaro, like many 'modern' red wines which are low in tannin and have been made for quick drinking rather than keeping, is best drunk cool, at 14°C. A major obstacle to any growth in red wine consumption is that it is drunk too warm. It is popularly imagined that red wine should be drunk at room temperature. This was certainly the practice in the nineteenth century. Since then, however, wine-making techniques have changed to produce less tannic wines. It is only the presence of tannin which requires that red wine is not served as cool as white: we are far more sensitive to bitterness and astringency at low temperatures. Moreover, the concept of what room temperature is has changed too since last century. Fuel is now (relatively) cheap, and people have central heating. Except in high summer, room temperature meant at most 16–18° last century, not the 20–22°C we enjoy today. Fine wine is best enjoyed at historic room temperature, which should *never* exceed 18–19°C; above that level too much alcohol evaporates and the smell of alcohol overwhelms the bouquet of the wine.

It is not difficult rapidly to alter the temperature of a wine as long as you remember that it changes very quickly when immersed in water in a kitchen sink or an ice-bucket, but very slowly when left to change temperature in the surrounding air. To bring a red wine up to room temperature of 18°C from a cellar temperature of 11°C in a room heated to 21°C takes two and three-quarter hours. To do so in a bucket of water at 21°C takes fourteen minutes. To cool a white wine down to 13°C from a room temperature of 21°C in a fridge at 5°C takes 1 hour 40 minutes. To do so in a bucket of iced water at 5°C takes eight minutes. If you want to calculate precisely how long a wine takes to warm up or cool down either at air temperature or when placed in a bucket of water, look up the tables reproduced in Emile Peynaud's *Le Goût du vin*.[3]

Until we have rid ourselves of the misconception that *chambré* means warm, red wine will never reassert its old dominance over white. This is because as a nation we do not have the habit of taking more than one drink with our meals. As we require what we drink with food to be refreshing, if we are taking only wine, then we will demand white wine, because white wine is perceived to be refreshing. This is exactly the same problem as besets producers of bitter beer in their struggle to resist the flood-tide of lager. Lager is perceived to be refreshing because it is usually served cool, whereas it is often held that bitter beer is served warm in this country. This misconception derives from the fact that it is served *relatively* warm compared with Continental beer, practically all of which is lager. Bitter is – theoretically – stored at a cellar temperature of 11°C, and served at the same temperature as 'modern' red wines, about 13–14°C. Both lager and white wine are, in fact, usually served far too cold – partly to satisfy the public taste for a refreshing drink; partly, in the case of lager and sparkling wines, to make them more bubbly; and partly to conceal their lack of taste. Those white wines and lagers which do have something to offer the taste buds are best served *at the same temperature* as bitter and 'modern' red wines.

The catalyst of change in taste in food and drink – and thus of the movement from sweet white to dry red wine – is the restaurant. The wine boom began with wine being drunk with food in restaurants on special occasions (and expense accounts) before it became a regular purchase for home drinking. People go out for the occasion more than for the food – this was even more true in the 1950s, when restaurant food was far worse than it is today. It cannot just be for the food, since any decent home cook can produce better food than 95 per cent of restaurants. Part of that occasion is the drinking of wine, even if this is not something people normally do: in fact more than half of all wine-drinkers today take wine only on such special occasions. In one opinion poll more members of the lower-middle and upper-working classes – or, if you prefer, socio-economic groups C1 and C2 – cited restaurants as the place where they usually drank wine than did members of the middle and upper classes. Might it not be expected that, as eating out becomes increasingly popular, the consumption of red wine will increase?

The general attitude that wine-drinking is an essential part of the experience of restaurant-going is reinforced by the efforts of restaurateurs to compel their customers to drink wine. This is because they make little money on food. That may seem odd, given a 250 per cent mark-up on the cost of raw ingredients and the high prices of restaurant food in Britain compared with France, but in neither country are consumers willing to pay the sort of prices for their food which would cover not only food costs (and wastage), but also labour costs (both cooking and serving), the expense of equipment, electricity, rent, rates, etc., and the restaurateur's profit margin. Therefore the profit margin is transferred to wine. A restaurant's food prices may be relatively low, but its wine prices will be high – so high, in fact, that many restaurants, while obeying the law which requires a menu with prices to be displayed outside the entrance, flout the requirement that an abstract of the wine-list, showing the price of at least six wines, also be displayed. A customer might be put off from entering the restaurant if he saw how much the wines cost, but once he is seated, he is unlikely to leave on this account.

The standard restaurant mark-up on wines in 100 per cent. This might be justified if restaurants had to tie up capital in long-term storage of expensive stock. But in fact most restaurateurs sell their wines before they have to pay for them. This is because wine merchants are so desperate for their custom that they extend one or two months' credit, and so polite and unbusinesslike that they don't make a fuss if payment is delayed. The service of wine involves restaurants in little expense – some breakages and pilfering by the staff, some bottles rejected as 'corked', and minimal staff time actually in serving the stuff. On top of this, they make a huge net profit.

Restaurateurs' dependence on the profits they make by selling wine is shown by their attitude to water. Using as an excuse the British habit of not taking more than one drink with a meal, restaurateurs do not offer free tap water to their customers. If it is asked for, usually a single glass is brought – often some time later. Happily for restaurateurs, people who go out to dinner do not do so in order to drink tap water. If they want water, not wine, they order mineral water, because this is socially acceptable in a way that tap water is not. For a bottle of mineral water, which costs about 50p in the shops, they can expect to pay up to £3 (or more). By charging this extortionate price the restaurateur protects himself against the losses incurred by customers not drinking wine. As a result, the consumer, who wishes whatever he drinks to be refreshing, and is neither given nor asks for water, chooses white not red wine, Beaujolais being the exception. Restaurants know that they should serve Beaujolais cool: that is why it is so popular. Beaujolais Nouveau popularizes Beaujolais for only a few weeks a year; the fact that it is served cool in restaurants does so for the rest of the time.

Restaurateurs' dependence on their drinks profits is also shown by the way they try to force their customers to drink as much alcohol as possible. There are still many restaurateurs who shunt customers into the bar on the pretence that their table is 'not ready', though this practice used to be more prevalent before the wine boom; now money can be made out of people drinking wine at the table. Restaurateurs rarely offer half-bottles, because they want each couple to drink two whole bottles. That is why a well-trained waiter always irritates customers by filling up glasses to the brim. According to a recent survey, 30 per cent of a typical restaurant bill is for wine and spirits.

The high price of wine in restaurants delayed the take-off of wine-drinking after the last war. Arguably, at the time of the first, partially abortive, wine boom in the 1860s, the prices charged by restaurants had prevented wine-drinking from taking off at all. A halving of duty on French wines in 1860–1 merely enabled restaurateurs to increase their profit margins. Claret in a restaurant cost 9s a bottle when it could be bought retail for 1s. As a result, in restaurants, people stuck to sherry and port, and did not acquire the habit of taking light wine with food.[4] Before the duty on French wines was halved once again in 1949, a bottle of ordinary claret in a restaurant cost 18s – equivalent to more than £10 today – and it was believed that 'the people of this country have almost given up the habit of drinking table wine with their meals'.[5] When the duty was reduced, restaurateurs once again chose the path of short-term profit – not passing on reductions in duty to their customers – rather than that of long-term profit resulting from increased wine consumption. In 1951 a bottle of claret in a restaurant normally cost about twice the price of a set meal at the same place; today it is the other way round. Restaurateurs were able to get away with mark-ups on wine of 200 per cent or more in the 1950s largely because, at the beginning of a wine boom, people were not regular wine-drinkers but were being introduced to it in restaurants, hence were not aware of the comparative retail price of the wine.[6] Moreover, wine was still considered a luxury, so people were prepared to pay through the nose for it. When he opened his restaurant at Thornbury Castle in Gloucestershire in 1966, Kenneth Bell tried charging less for the wine and more for the food, but soon had to give up on this idea. His customers did not understand what he was trying to do, and considered his prices for food to be excessive. In the USA today, the wine boom has been held up by restaurateurs taking profit margins as high as they ever were in Britain. According to one survey, two-thirds of American diners-out usually order wine by the glass rather than by the bottle,[7] and consumption of table wine is falling.

In Britain, restaurants account for 26 per cent of all wine consumed today. Is one to anticipate a substantial increase in eating out and consequently in the consumption of wine? The key here lies in restaurant prices. The question is often asked, why eating out is so expensive in Britain when it can be so cheap in France. The answer lies partly in economic factors – the use of family labour in France, lower property and rates costs – and partly in social factors – the French go out to eat as a way of life, whereas the majority of the British do so on special occasions only. Certainly, it should not be thought that restaurateurs are *necessarily* ripping consumers off. Between 1980 and 1983 63,500 new restaurants were opened and 60,500 closed.[8] The closures occurred not because the proprietors made enough in three years to retire to the Cayman Islands but because most of them went bust. But many of them go bust because they fail to offer their customers the service that is desired.

If the British go out to eat only on special occasions, might it not be because food is so expensive, and not the other way round? Food is expensive, according to restaurateur Peter Ilic, simply because most of his colleagues and competitors are interested in making as much money with as little effort as possible. In other words, they charge a few customers excessive prices rather than fill their restaurants and charge reasonable prices. Peter Ilic opened his first restaurant, The Lantern, in a run-down area of inner west London, in 1982. Six predecessors in the same site had failed. He was soon turning away 200 customers a night, and was forced to open two more restaurants simply to satisfy demand. The food is just as good as in the general run of neighbourhood 'French' restaurants, yet a three-course meal costs only about £8 a head. Peter Ilic has continued to try to find what he describes as even better means of offering value. In 1985 he received considerable publicity when he opened a restaurant called Just Around The Corner in north London where no prices are quoted on the menu but you pay as much as you think the food is worth, or as you can afford to pay. Some couples consume three courses and a bottle of wine yet leave only £5. He does not mind. Regulars who eat also in his other restaurants pay more here than they do there. This is not just out of embarrassment, but because people expect to pay higher prices in restaurants than he charges.

An alternative method might be to charge an entrance fee to cover the cost of the restaurateur's overheads and to allow him a profit margin, and then to charge for food and wine at cost. I suspect, however, that this would discourage people from ever entering restaurants at all, as it involves paying something for nothing. It would also mean that small eaters subsidized big eaters – though that is no more unfair than the present system in which wine-drinkers subsidize non-drinkers. There is, I fear, no answer to the price problem of West European-style restaurants in Britain. The gap in the market for such places is largely filled by Greek Cypriot restaurants, where people drink retsina; Indian restaurants, where they drink lager; and Chinese restaurants, where they drink tea. Here lies an insoluble brake on the growth of wine consumption of any kind, let alone the movement from sweet white to dry red.

[1] Giorgio Lolli *et al.*, *Alcohol in Italian Culture*, 1958.
[2] NOP poll.

3 They are absent from the English translation.
4 *The Times* leader, 8 September 1865.
5 *The Times*, 22 January 1949, p. 3.
6 Christopher Driver, *The British at Table 1940–80*, Chatto & Windus/The Hogarth Press, 1983, pp. 113–14.
7 National Restaurant Survey, 1987.
8 This figure is exaggerated as it includes wine bars, pubs, snack bars and hotels.

4

SMALL IS BOUNTIFUL

We may not all turn from white to red, but we seem to be graduating from cheaper to more expensive wine, for a number of reasons. To begin with, we are starting to drink less alcohol than we used to, and can therefore afford to take that alcohol in a more costly form. Although members of the anti-alcohol lobby believe they have proved conclusively that we are drinking *more* alcohol than we used to, it can be demonstrated no less irrefutably, and by equally creative use of statistics, that we are drinking *less*. Our annual consumption of alcohol in all its forms (expressed in litres of pure alcohol) fell from over eleven litres a head at the turn of the century to a little over four after the last war, then almost doubled in the next thirty years. During these thirty years alcohol consumption increased precisely in line with average earnings, which went up twice as fast as prices. The proportion of our incomes that we spent on drink remained at approximately 7 per cent.

Between 1975 and 1985 the amount of alcohol we drank *de*creased by 12 per cent – and a similar fall is to be expected to occur during the next ten years, not least because the anti-alcohol lobby is only just getting into its stride. In 1986 the Royal College of Physicians recommended a halving of the maximum safe daily levels of alcohol consumption. They pointed out that previous figures had been based on the point at which we were more likely to contract cirrhosis of the liver, but that research had now shown that our likelihood of contracting certain cancers was increased by a much lower level of alcohol consumption.[1] In response to the changing climate of opinion, drinks manufacturers have begun to produce and heavily to promote low-alcohol and de-alcoholized[2] products. Are they perhaps shooting themselves in the foot, giving in to the anti-alcohol lobby without a fight? Certainly the promotion of low-alcohol drinks encourages consumers further to reduce their alcohol consumption.

At the same time as we are beginning to drink less for reasons of health, more and more of us are becoming established wine-drinkers, and want to dissociate ourselves from new wine-drinkers – the sort of people that we ourselves once were. We do so by moving up-market. This process is encouraged by the various scandals, particularly the Italian methanol scandal, which affected only cheap wines. If we spend more money on the wines we buy, we feel that we will be more likely to be buying a safe and reliable product. This said, no one knows how many wine-drinkers are actually interested in progressing beyond Liebfraumilch. After all, not all fans of one-day cricket will ever come to take pleasure in attending five-day Test Matches.

The way in which consumers grow accustomed to a standard product and therefore seek a premium one can be seen in developments in the lager market. Here there is a problem of terminology, since for the marketers 'premium' lager does not mean better, but merely stronger, lager. Since few lager-drinkers are interested in the taste of the product, it would not be possible to make that a criterion. Nevertheless, whatever the meaning of the word, lager began in Britain in the 1950s and early 1960s as a premium product. It was sold in bottle, and it was expensive. The pseudo-Germanic lagers – about as genuinely German as actresses in pornographic films are genuinely Swedish – which were launched in Britain, with a huge advertising budget, in the early 1960s, failed to sell. Consumers were being offered a premium product without the chance to taste a standard one first. Lager took off in Britain when Harp was put on draught in 1966, and became an everyday drink. The lager-drinkers of today are returning to the expensive, frequently bottled, lagers which their parents rejected twenty years ago. In 1986 79 per cent of the lager we drank was standard lager (below OG 1040 – see table on p. 264), and 21 per cent was premium and Diät Pils lager (over OG 1040). Between 1985 and 1986 consumption of standard lager had grown by 3.5 per cent and that of premium lager by 19 per cent.[3]

People who become regular wine-drinkers, and wish to sophisti-cate themselves, 'trade across' from sweet to dry wines. The reason why the market in fine German wines is dead is that the sort of sweet wines with which many people begin their wine-drinking careers are perceived to be unsophisticated. If, at the turn of the century, Auslese wines from the top German estates fetched higher prices than any other wines, it was because they were mostly dry; today they are mostly sweet, and can be bought for £10 a bottle or less. It is even possible to buy 1975s and 1976s, many of which are ready to drink, at that price. English wines suffer from similar problems of image. Such cheap English wines as do exist have been sweetened with grape-juice concentrate imported from Germany, and bear no resemblance to more expensive English wines, the best of which are fragrant, delicate and austerely dry.

I have already suggested that the catalyst of the movement from sweet to dry is the restaurant. But do restaurants encourage the purchase of better wines? In fact their pricing structure serves as a discouragement. They mark up wines by a fixed percentage, say 100 per cent, which means that they make far more profit on expensive than on cheap wines. If good wine in restaurants were not so obviously a rip-off, more people might be encouraged to drink it. But, given the extra expense and effort involved in holding stocks of fine wine, there is no economic reason for restaurants to encourage consumers to drink it cheaply. It is easier to make the same profit on plonk. Then a restaurateur does not have to worry about the ignorance of his staff in wine service.

Historically, the chief exceptions to this rule have been found in the City of London, where there has always been a market for good wine, since long before the wine boom. If a number of City wine bars, such as The Pavilion in Finsbury Circus or branches of Balls Bros, take relatively small margins on fine wines, it is partly because they are owned by wine shippers, so there are no extra overheads, but principally because consumers in the City have always known what wine really costs. This is now changing. The new generation of enormously rich but very young bankers and brokers seems to be interested only in champagne. The wine shippers Corney and Barrow, who run the smartest wine bars in the City, charge 100 per cent more than their already high retail prices, and find no shortage of customers willing to pay.

Elsewhere in London escalating labour costs, and perhaps a feeling that, in London at least, the days of the restaurateur acting as a missionary for fine wine are now over, have forced many restaurateurs and wine-bar owners to increase their prices. As recently as 1984, the Davy's chain of pseudo-Victorian wine bars offered, for consumption at the Boot and Flogger by London Bridge, wines such as Château Latour 1962 for £30 and Taylor's 1945 for £45, in both cases less than half what they would have cost retail. The Tate Gallery restaurant which, it was alleged, Egon Ronay used deliberately to leave out of his guide so that not too many people would find out about its wine-list, still charges relatively little for fine wines, but no longer little enough to justify putting up with its food. Outside London, however, a number of good restaurants are still run by wine-lovers with a mission. They include Kenwards in Lewes in Sussex, Bowlish House in Shepton Mallet and the White Horse Hotel in Williton in Somerset, the Croque-en-Bouche in Malvern Wells in Worcestershire, Hope End Country House Hotel near Ledbury in Herefordshire, and Brooklands in Barnsley in Yorkshire, and, in Scotland, the Ubiquitous Chip in Glasgow, La Potinière in Gullane in Lothian, and the Peat Inn near St Andrews in Fife.

In most restaurants, regardless of their cost, fine wines are not treated properly. They are served in the wrong way by staff who mostly know no better. Even the smartest restaurants nowadays have great trouble finding *sommeliers* who have the slightest knowledge of wine. Unlike the position on the Continent, the status of a *sommelier* in Britain is a lowly one – so lowly that we do not even have a word to describe his job – and someone with enthusiasm for wine is more likely to choose to work in a wine shop. What is the point in spending a lot of money on a good bottle of red burgundy if it is going to be served too warm, and if the staff insist on filling the glass up to the brim every time you have drunk enough to get a chance of swirling it round to enjoy its bouquet? Not that this would be very effective, anyway, given the shape of glasses that most restaurants use, and the fact that many of them stink either of detergent or of varnish – the latter the result of mistakenly storing them upside-down on a shelf.

Fine wine is for drinking at home, in which case it will have to be bought from a specialist wine shop, that is, a shop which specializes in wine (as opposed to beer, spirits and cigarettes). Why not from a supermarket or corner off-licence? The image and ambiance are not right; fine wines are expensive items which most people buy deliberately, after consideration.

Specialist wine merchants can sell luxury items only by

establishing consumer confidence. Merchants, particularly those who are rarely visited by their customers and depend upon mail-order sales, rely substantially on their wine-lists in order to achieve this. If a wine merchant has intelligent things to say about the wines he sells, then naturally the consumer will suppose that he knows what he is talking about. The first wine merchant to realize the importance of a wine-list was Simon Loftus, the controversial, ex-hippy director of the wine side of the brewers Adnams of Southwold. He had their list re-designed eight years ago, since when it has been copied by a number of other merchants; indeed, one imitated it so closely that Adnams successfully sued them for breach of copyright. Despite his refusal to send lists to people who do not buy any of the wines he has selected, Simon Loftus has described the list as his company's 'major source of publicity', intended 'not just to sell wine', but to be 'browsed through in the loo. I see [it] on show in a lot of people's drawing rooms.'⁴ Other wine-lists which are long on opinion are produced by Corney and Barrow, Morris and Verdin and Windrush Wines. As a whole they are a better, more authoritative and not necessarily more biased source of information than many wine magazines, for which you have to pay.

Merchants whose customers lie close at hand, such as those in London, or who can persuade their customers to travel to visit them, supplement the authority of their wine-lists by holding regular tastings for their customers. Certainly tastings are a very effective means of selling wines, particularly from obscure regions, or from 'off-vintages' in Burgundy or Bordeaux. But that is not usually the purpose of tastings. Every few months, Bibendum in north London hold large tastings for their customers of wines which, at least in the case of their burgundies and Rhône wines, could perfectly well be sold over the telephone in a morning without being shown to anyone. Tastings, like wine-lists, are intended to establish consumer confidence – which is fortunate, since many of those people who attend tastings go for the experience, not in order to stock up their cellars, though even we non-buying tasters have been led astray on occasions. It is always possible to get invited to a wine merchant's autumn tasting – once. Practised liggers can, by posing as the wine correspondents of obscure free magazines no one has heard of, get themselves invited to trade- and press- as well as consumer-oriented tastings.

In both these respects, specialist wine merchants score over supermarkets and off-licence chains. But is there any valid reason for buying wine from them? After all, glossy wine-lists and 'free' tastings have to be paid for by someone. The Côtes du Buzet which Sainsbury's sell for £2.65 costs about £3.30 at specialists; the Vin de Pays des Côtes de Gascogne which Waitrose sell for £2.09 costs about £2.80 elsewhere. (These are Spring 1988 prices.) Specialist wine merchants seek to justify these differences by the service and advice they offer. Apart from such well-known services as free local delivery, many of them are now open on Sundays. Although the opening hours of retail wine merchants are restricted by the licensing laws on Sundays to 12–3 and 7–10 pm, these laws do not apply to the purchase of a case or more of wine. Retail wine merchants do not usually stay open outside licensing hours on Sundays, but 'wine warehouses' and other wholesalers do. Of wine merchants open throughout the day on Sundays, I would particularly recommend Winecellars in south London and Bibendum.

Supermarkets are, however, restyling themselves in order to compete, and I have little doubt that, in time, they will be open on Sundays too. Waitrose, who enjoy the most up-market customers of all the major supermarket chains, have found that their philosophy has come back into fashion. Unlike Sainsbury's, say, they have never been interested in marketing their products but offer them to their customers on a take-it-or-leave-it basis. Their wines are thus selected purely according to considerations of quality rather than those of turnover or fashion – or so their wine buyer, Julian Brind, assures me. They have recently increased the range of services they offer: in 1987 they introduced a discount of 5 per cent on purchases of wine over £100 and started lending out glasses for parties in return for a deposit (but no hire fee). Julian Brind thinks it possible that they will one day start selling immature fine wine to lay down, as the specialists do.

What specialist wine merchants offer that supermarkets and off-licence chains will never be able to replicate is exclusivity. Part and parcel of the sophistication of taste is the desire to buy something different from other people. Why else should a woman spend thousands of pounds on a one-off designer dress, if not in order to ensure that no one else will be wearing the same dress at the same function? In the case of wine, it is no longer naff to display a

Sainsbury's label on your table, but it shows you to be one of the masses: as wine becomes an item of mass consumption those people who like to entertain feelings of superiority want to go where the mass of the population does not. A wine becomes exclusive by virtue of where it is bought.

Shops which cater for people who desire exclusivity deliberately alienate those people with whom they feel the majority of their customers would not wish to identify themselves. I have for some years been testing this theory by walking into Berry Bros' eighteenth-century wood-panelled shop in St James's – which all tourists to London ought to take the trouble to visit – on some occasions wearing a suit and tie, on others in street clothes. In the former guise I am treated with deference; in the latter I am usually ignored – at least for a while, presumably in order to make me feel uneasy, so that I will not want to shop there again.

Specialist merchants can maintain their exclusivity only if they sell wines which are different from those available in supermarkets and off-licence chains. In general, because of their limited availability, and their desire to establish and maintain an exclusive image, the best wines from small growers and the most prestigious estates are available only from specialist merchants and not from supermarkets. When they can be bought in the latter they are, unlike everyday wines, no cheaper than in the specialists, because their limited availability means that the supermarkets cannot negotiate a discount for buying in bulk. Supermarkets do not work on substantially lower profit margins than specialist wine merchants; they merely buy, on the whole, at a lower price. That is why the Sainsbury's are multi-millionaires as a result of the grocery business, whereas wine merchants have to be wealthy to start in business, but rarely remain so afterwards. Waitrose stock a few good vintage and single-*quinta* ports, but a far smaller range and at higher prices than Berry Bros charge. Sainsbury's have for some years sold Les Forts de Latour, the second wine of Château Latour, at prices higher than one would pay at specialist merchants.

The wines from small estates which enjoy the greatest prestige are burgundies. Only the two most up-market of supermarkets, Waitrose and Marks & Spencer, sell burgundies from growers, and only half a dozen between them. Otherwise, supermarkets sell burgundies from merchants, who buy in and blend together the produce of different growers in order to be able to provide wines in quantities large enough to satisfy the demands of those customers who sell a lot of wine. Growers' burgundies at present enjoy a far higher reputation than merchants' versions. This is partly a matter of history. The proto-*appellation contrôlée* law of 1919 required, for the first time, that if a bottle of wine bore a name of origin on the label, then the wine had to come from the place in question. This in fact encouraged abuse. Pommard, for instance, had previously, except in cases of outright fraud, been applied only to fine wines, whether they came from the village of Pommard or that of Chass-agne-Montrachet. But now any wine from Pommard enjoyed the right to use that name, even if it was produced, not from the noble Pinot Noir, but from the ignoble Gamay grape, and overcropped to 150 hectolitres per hectare (see conversion table on p. 264). The law did not specify the permitted grape varieties, nor place a limit on the yield. But it did enable court cases to be brought to establish precisely how far the land entitled to claim a famous name extended. Certain vine growers, including the Marquis d'Angerville from Volnay and Henri Gouges from Nuits-Saint-Georges, took local merchants to court for selling wine which they did not believe was of a quality to be entitled to the *appellation* it boasted.[5] As a result, no local merchants would purchase their wines, so they had to start bottling themselves. At the same time, Raymond Badoin, the owner of the wine magazine *Revue du Vin de France*, persuaded such celebrated estates as those of Armand Rousseau in Gevrey-Cham-bertin and Leflaive in Puligny-Montrachet to bottle barrels of their wine for him, which he then sold to top restaurants and private clients in Paris. It was not, however, until the 1950s that the domaine-bottling of burgundies took off. Today the proportion of the vintage in Burgundy which is bottled at and commercialized by the estate ranges from 25 to 50 per cent, depending upon the state of the market. Unlike some merchants' wines, one can be fairly sure that these have not been adulterated.

It is not, however, the possibility of adulteration which makes burgundy from good growers superior to that produced by merchants. Whereas in most quality-oriented regions of France, such as Champagne and Alsace, merchants buy in grapes and vinify them themselves, in Burgundy merchants buy in wine. Yet the quality of red burgundy, more than that of any other wine in the world, depends on the skill of the wine-maker. How many Burgundian farmers are going to take the necessary care over the vinification of their Pinot Noir grapes when they know that the result is destined for a merchant's blending vat? The white Chardonnay grape is much less difficult to vinify, which explains why the white burgundies from leading Burgundy merchants, such as Louis Latour and Louis Jadot, are as a rule vastly superior to their reds. In his book on the region, Anthony Hanson says he does not expect the present situation to improve, because both grower and merchant see vinification as the grower's traditional responsibility.[6] Since the publication of his book in 1982, however, the quality of the red burgundy produced by such hitherto disregarded merchants as Moillard has improved enormously; and some of the better merchants, such as Bouchard Père et Fils, have begun to buy in grapes instead of wine. On the other hand there are many more good retail sources of growers' red burgundy than there used to be, thanks partly to a resurgence of interest, and partly to judicious use of the services of brokers. Perhaps the best of these sources are Domaine Direct, Haynes Hanson and Clark, Ballantynes, Morris and Verdin and Bibendum.

Outside Burgundy, and where merchants do buy in grapes and vinify them themselves, wines from the best growers are still superior to the produce of merchants. Growers who rely on the product of their own vineyard holdings make less wine than merchants who buy in from several sources, and are less likely to be able to offer wine in the sort of 'commercial' quantities required by chains of restaurants, supermarkets or off-licences. Therefore they are inclined to aim for the segment of the market where quality takes precedence over price. In any case, someone is far more likely to take care over the grapes he grows to be made into wine which he will sell under his own name than over grapes he knows he is going to sell to a merchant, or give to a cooperative, who will then sell on to a merchant. On the principle that, to do something properly, you have to do it yourself, a farmer is restricted, if he wishes to make the best possible wine, to the amount of land that he and his family can cultivate without having to employ hired help – depending on the terrain, anything between 2 and 20 hectares. It may well be that a merchant who buys in grapes makes better wine than a grower with so large a *domaine* that he cannot possibly keep an eye on all of it all of the time. Certainly Mastroberardino, the outstanding wine producers of Campania in central Italy, chose for many years to buy in grapes rather than own vineyards on the grounds that people take more pride in working their own land than in working on someone else's. They have only been forced to change their policy by a general exodus from the land.

However good a merchant's blend may be, a grower's wine will usually offer more individuality; clearly a blend of the produce of different growers dampens down the characteristics of each. It might be argued that the lack of interest we have shown in the wines of Alsace, which wine merchants have for years been ordering in restaurants, and telling their customers that they offer better value than any other dry white wines in France, can be attributed to the fact that, even today, the vast majority of Alsatian wines to be found in this country are the well-made but essentially unexciting produce of merchants' and cooperatives' blending vats. In the last few years, however, the number of growers who bottle their own wines has been increasing in Alsace, as it has in Champagne and Beaujolais. In part, the domaine-bottling movement has been a creation of the merchants as surely as an aspiration to drink fine wines which they cannot supply has been a creation of the supermarkets. The most celebrated and perhaps the best of the Beaujolais merchants, Georges Duboeuf, often puts the name of the producer alongside his own on his labels. It is almost as though he has gone out of his way to enable growers to set themselves up in business on their own. One grower recently to have taken advantage of the reputation Georges Duboeuf established for him and gone it alone is Jean de Saint-Charles, who makes Brouilly and Beaujolais-Villages at the Domaine du Conroy. Much the same is true of Champagne, where all the advertising to create the image necessary for it to sell as a prestige product has been carried out by the big merchant houses: the growers simply reap the benefits.

Moreover, in Britain there has been an enormous growth in the number of small specialist importers since the requirement to obtain a wholesale licence was withdrawn six years ago, and this has fuelled the domaine-bottling movement in France. After all, what has prevented many growers from commercializing their own wine in the past has been not knowing where to find customers. They can be persuaded to bottle their wine by customers who come to them.

In Champagne, for example, Jean-Paul Arvois, a part-time fireman, part-time vine grower in the village of Chavot was persuaded by Tony Westbrook, a builder who owns Champagne de Villages, specialists in growers' champagnes, to commercialize his wine. Previously he had sold his grapes to Moët et Chandon for obliteration in their blending vats. Admittedly these specialists are usually small fry. Their origins frequently lie in personal interest, and perhaps the desire to supply a few friends, rather than the dictates of commerce, and they are often run as hobbies. Some such firms have, however, outgrown their origins. Yapp, the grand-daddy of them all, started up in 1969 by Robin Yapp, then a full-time dentist, recently went public.

Precisely because they are run as hobbies rather than particularly profitable businesses, these specialist importers are a source of interesting and unusual wines which would probably not, in more commercial circumstances, have been imported into this country. After all, in those instances in which they do stock individual and interesting wines, even the most up-market of supermarkets find that these fail to sell. Because the wines offer unexpected tastes, customers complain that there is something wrong with them. No supermarket would risk selling the obscure wines from South-West France, rejoicing in such unmemorable names as Pacherenc du Vic-Bilh and Vin d'Entraygues et du Fel, which are imported by Sookias and Bertaut, two couples whose interest in the region stemmed from the Bertauts' purchase of a house there in 1973. Some of the wines sold by Sookias and Bertaut may taste a bit weird, but they are stimulating and reasonably inexpensive. For example the red Côtes du Frontonnais from Château Flotis is, at £3.50 a bottle, cheap enough for regular consumption, but quite individual, being made 50 per cent from the Negrette grape, which is found almost nowhere else in the world, not least because, the owner Philippe Küntz has assured me, it is just as difficult to cultivate as Pinot Noir in Burgundy, and produces similarly low yields.

We should, however, be careful of preferring growers' to merchants' wines because of our subscription to the maxim that 'small is beautiful'. This leads us to delude ourselves. How small does a grower have to be to be beautiful? The châteaux of Bordeaux produce what are, strictly speaking, growers' wines from single estates, but no one could describe the *cru bourgeois*

Larose-Trintaudon, which produces nearly a million bottles a year, as 'small'. I often suspect that the Campaign for Real Ale (CAMRA) are deluding themselves in their adherence to the view that the beer produced by 'small' regional brewers is *ipso facto* superior to that produced by national brewers. Certainly a lot of good beer is produced by regional brewers, and a lot of very dull beer is produced by national ones. But beer is a large-scale industrial product in a way that wine is not. Youngs, the London brewers, are small and therefore beautiful in the eyes of CAMRA, yet they own 145 pubs of which the Alexandra in Wimbledon alone sells 2,500 pints a day. Even in a pub owned by one of the big groups it is possible to buy good beer, though it does usually come as a surprise rather than as fulfilment of an anticipated pleasure. I have on occasions enjoyed excellent draught Bass, Burton Ale (in Allied Breweries' pubs[7]) Courage Directors' and Flowers Original (Whitbread's version). Bass-Charrington's bottled Worthington White Shield is the only genuine India Pale Ale still made and, arguably, the finest beer in Britain.

More seriously, our blind preference for pygmy producers leads others to deceive us. If a domaine name always helps sell a wine, and at a higher price, then, regardless of whether it is the produce of a single domaine or not, it is better to give a wine that dignity. In their advertisements Sainsbury's have done their best to suggest that they sell wines which are small and therefore perfectly formed. At the end of 1984 they advertised their pink champagne as made by 'a small family concern'. This company was later revealed to be Charbaut, who sell 2 million bottles a year. Subsequently they advertised that their white champagne was made by a grower called Roger Duval – actually it came from the house of Duval-Leroy, who also sell 2 million bottles a year.

In Germany, Liebfraumilch produced by cooperatives announces that it is 'estate-bottled'. In France, cooperatives in Chablis and Cahors vinify the grapes sold to them by their members in communal vats and then commercialize the produce under the names of various members of the cooperative. One should beware of confusing the Chablis produced by the growers Gérard Tremblay and René Dauvissat with those bearing the names of Suzanne Tremblay and Jean-Claude Dauvissat, which are cooperative blends. They are perfectly good wines, but that is not the point. You can discover if you are being done by looking on the corner of the label for the bottling number 'emb 8906', which the cooperative use. In Champagne, growers sell their grapes to a cooperative, and then buy back the cooperative's wine, which they then sell from their farm door, bearing a domaine name, as though they had made it themselves. In theory, RM (*récoltant-manipulant*) on the label indicates a grower's champagne, and CM (*coopérative-manipulant*), that produced by a cooperative. But, depending on whose estimate you accept, anything between 15 and 50 per cent of 'growers' ' champagnes are the product of a cooperative's blending vat. This patently contravenes *appellation contrôlée* laws for champagne, which state that, if a grower uses the terms *propriétaire* or *viticulteur* on the label, then the wine must come from grapes grown in his own vineyards. A similar exercise, with different consequences, is carried out by smallholders who also work the vineyards of the classed-growth châteaux of Bordeaux. They bring in their own grapes to be vinified together with the produce of the château, and then take away an equivalent proportion of the finished wine to commercialize under their own label. The abuse of estate names by port producers will be discussed in a later chapter (see Chapter 10).

In some instances the misuse of estate names is misleading only because confusion is encouraged by ridiculous labelling regulations. It should not be necessary to point out *ad nauseam*, in every article and book which deals with English wine, that this bears no relation to British wine, which is made in this country from imported grape-juice concentrate. It is quite absurd that wine produced from grapes grown in Wales should have to be described as English wine in order to distinguish it from factory-made British wine. If the term 'British' wine were not permitted, then we would not be misled by the abuse of the image of British country houses by its producers. For example, Vine Products and Whiteways, a subsidiary of Allied Breweries, produce British wines under both the Concorde and Rougemont Castle labels. The former name is not misleading; the latter is. The abolition of the term 'British' would not, however, have stopped the German company Ferdinand Pieroth from selling British wine as 'Barnsgate', a name which might have caused some of their customers to have confused it with the English wine from Barns-gate Manor, a vineyard which they own in East Sussex, whose label declares that the wine has been 'estate produced and bottled at Barnsgate Manor'.

In the drinks trade in general, it would seem that the misuse of estate names is not as great as it used to be. In the late nineteenth century Ceylon tea was much in demand, being lighter than Indian and more reliable than China tea. Single-estate teas had a high-quality image, and fetched a premium price. In 1890 two White-chapel dealers were fined £10 for having sold a blend of China and Assam tea under the name of the well-known Ceylon estate Sogama, in contravention of the recently introduced Merchandise Marks Act; and the well-known firm of Kearley and Tongue were fined £10 for intention to deceive: they had invented an estate name – 'Blackmore Vale' – which they displayed on the label followed, in large letters, by the description 'Pure Ceylon Tea', followed in very small letters, partially obscured, by the phrase 'blended with India and China'.

In fact the misuse of estate names on blended products in order to make them appear more prestigious can be compared to the use of hand-pumps to serve 'keg' beer, a malpractice which is rife – and which demonstrates quite how genuinely many of the bigger brewers are committed to cask-conditioned 'real ale', which they have only started selling again in the last few years because the success of CAMRA persuaded them that it would be good for their image. Selling keg beer on hand-pumps contravenes either the Trades Descriptions Act 1968 or Food Act 1984 or both, because the presence of a hand-pump leads consumers to expect that this pump will be used to draw cask-conditioned beer from the cask, and not merely used to enhance the status of filtered, pasteurized keg beer. In 1986, however, the Hampshire Trading Standards Officer refused to proceed against Hunter's Wine Bar in Lyndhurst following complaints that they sold on hand-pump Eldridge Pope's keg Huntsman Best Bitter, on the grounds that neither Act was being broken. In the February 1987 issue of *What's Brewing*, the news-paper of the Campaign for Real Ale, pubs owned by Eldridge Pope, Camerons of Hartlepool and Greenall Whitley were cited as serving keg beer on hand-pumps. Greenall Whitley were quoted as having replied that 'careful market research shows that the majority of the public prefer their beer to be drawn through a hand-pump' – which is, of course, the whole point.

[1] Royal College of Physicians, *The Medical Consequences of Alcohol Abuse*, 1986.

[2] 'De-alcoholized' drinks contain less than 0.5 per cent alcohol; 'alcohol-free' drinks contain less than 0.05 per cent.

[3] Figures from a speech given by Derek Cook, UK Sales Director of Carlsberg, to the Brewers' and Distillers' Seminar held by Wood Mackenzie in November 1986.

[4] Quoted in *Decanter*, September 1983, p. 58.

[5] Theodore Zeldin, *France 1848–1945*, vol. 2, Oxford University Press, 1973, p. 758; Hanson, p. 43.

[6] Hanson, p. 138.

[7] Allsopp, Benskins, Friary Meux and Taylor-Walker.

THE GREY MEN

The next two chapters look at outside influences on our drinks purchases. Do we make up our minds for ourselves, or do others make them up for us?

Unlike, say, cars, which travel at different speeds, handle in different ways, and offer different standards of comfort, there are no objective criteria for differentiating between different wines. All wines are a solution of ethanol in water. Some Germans have tried to 'prove' that their frequently maligned dry wines are better than dry French white wines because chemical analysis shows them to contain more sugar-free extract – which in theory means more body and flavour – but the practice of judging a wine by its chemical analysis has not caught on in Britain.

Moreover, the wine market is quite different from that for other drinks. There are specialist retailers in other drinks markets; there are pubs selling real ale, and CAMRA guides to them. But there is not the same daily turnover of advice and information, because there is not the same range of products. There is a range of branded products from which the consumer chooses. Only in our choice of wine do we rely on the opinions of 'experts'.

This expertise has become increasingly in demand in the last few years. More and more newspapers and magazines have taken to including wine columns. Obviously, to a certain degree this reflects a general increase of interest in wine and in particular the extension of the habit of wine-drinking to new classes of society. I cannot believe, however, that articles in any number of glossy, especially free, magazines and in local newspapers on subjects such as the declaration of the 1985 port vintage really have much impact on consumer expenditure – or even are necessarily of interest to readers. To a substantial extent, the purpose of wine columns is to attract drinks advertising. Certainly that was why Cyril Ray was asked to begin his wine column in the *Observer* in 1958.

Newspapers and magazines are economically dependent on advertising. On average, daily papers and consumer magazines derive 40 per cent of their revenue from advertising; Sunday papers derive 55 per cent. The *Sunday Times* magazine was started in 1962 by its then new owner, Roy Thomson, principally in order to attract advertisements. Advertisers are not amused by articles which are critical of their product, and few newspapers or magazines are strong enough to be able to afford to alienate advertisers. In 1961 the *Observer* was shown to be weaker than those who advertised in it. Members of the Society of West End Theatre Managers, upset by some theatre reviews by Mr Puff in the *Observer*'s Quick Theatre Guide, withdrew almost all advertisements. The *Observer* fought for several weeks but in the end had to compromise by curbing Mr Puff's activities.[1] Today the large number of new, up-market magazines competing against each other puts the advertisers in an even stronger position. On occasions a tacit understanding is reached between editor and advertiser, and a product is mentioned in an article in expectation of an advertisement being paid for. This relationship is sometimes made explicit, in the form of what are called 'advertisement features' or 'advertorials'. More often, it is not. As a result, many articles in magazines end up, in effect, as puffs, as advertorials posing as editorials.

Free speech among wine writers is more likely to be found in newspapers and general interest magazines – who derive only an average 5 per cent of their advertising revenue from drinks advertisements – than among specialist magazines, whose advertising revenue is derived almost exclusively from drinks advertisements. In theory, for impartial, expert comment on wine one would read a wine magazine. The economic facts dictate that this is in fact the last place you are likely to find such comment. *Decanter* considers itself to be a consumer magazine, offering consumer advice; indeed, it boasts on its letterhead that it is 'the world's best wine magazine'; but how can these claims be justified when its contributors are not allowed to criticize advertisers, actual or potential – and, indeed, are often pressed by the magazine's advertising department to mention a particular company, who will then be prepared to buy space? An uncritical attitude on the part of wine writers is often defended on the grounds that critics should mention what they like, and simply ignore what they do not. But how, by definition, can a critic be uncritical? As well as recommending good wines to buy, particularly in supermarkets and off-licence chains where there is otherwise no source of advice as to what one should choose from up to 200 different wines, giving consumer advice entails, for example, examining the latest hype – be it Beaujolais Nouveau, *en primeur* claret, wine-coolers or whatever – and trying to determine whether it is a rip-off or not. The idea that one should write only about those wines which are worth drinking is a dereliction of the first duties of a journalist. It is also highly misleading. Is one to assume that a product which is not written up is condemned by omission? If so, this will only increase the pressure from advertisers for favourable editorial mentions to be a condition of their paying for advertisements. It is the job of wine writers to expose scandals, not to sweep them under the carpet – which is the habit, rightly or wrongly, of members of the wine trade. Yet Nicholas Tomalin, who eventually exposed the long-established malpractice of applying famous names to blended table wines, was not a wine writer but an investigative journalist, who was killed seven years later while covering the Arab–Israeli Yom Kippur War. Although, fifteen years earlier, Raymond Postgate had published his *Plain Man's Guide to Wine* partly out of a desire to prevent the wine trade from passing off wine under assumed names, not all of the recent boom in wine writing has been consumer-led.

If it is not the job of the wine writer to give impartial and sometimes critical consumer advice, then what is his job? Does it perhaps lie in perfecting means of describing sensual pleasure? If so, one would presumably have to accept that it is the job of the art critic to try to describe the aesthetic appeal of paintings, and of the music critic to put aural sensations into words. If so, we must presumably commend such descriptions as those given by Charles Metcalfe, Associate Editor of *Wine* Magazine, in one of his articles in the wine trade magazine *Wine and Spirit*, a report on some tastings of German wines. After associating the Hattenheimer Wisselbrunnen 1981 from Schloss Rheinhartshausen with strawberry ice cream, the Johannisberger Erntebringer Spätlese 1982 from Deinhard with browned rice pudding, and the Erbacher Rheinhell Spätlese 1983 from Schloss Rheinhartshausen with baked bananas, he went on to describe the Forster Jesuitengarten Eiswein from Reichsgraf von Bühl as having 'the pungent fragrance of old-fashioned sweet peas, but a softness as well, as if they had been stewed in butter but retained their perfume'.[2] Tasting terms are useful as a mnemonic to oneself, but to publish them is nothing but wine snobbery. Matters have been made worse by a generation of aroma scientists who insist that each aromatic compound that appears on the print-out of a gas-chromatograph corresponds to a particular description of flavour. For linalool you must say 'lavender', for ethylmaltol 'strawberry', for β-ionon 'violets', and so on. I suppose, however, that it is better to say that a wine smells of peanuts than to describe its bouquet as being one of 5-(3-hydroxylethyl)-4-methylthrinxol.

One alternative to such descriptions is marks. The American wine writer Robert Parker has come in for a great deal of criticism for his 'intellectual self-indulgence'[3] in believing that he can detect sufficiently fine distinctions between wines to validate his marking those he tastes on a 100-point scale. He has now extended this practice by including his wife's assessments of the restaurants they visit during their wine-tasting trips. Are we meant to conclude that Troisgros (91.75) are better than Alain Chapel (91.15)? Many of those people who criticize Parker use a 20-point system: I don't see that there is any difference. Whatever form they take, marks permit wine writers to indulge themselves, and consumers to ignore any comments that have been made, disregard any description of the style of a wine or its state of development, and simply buy those wines which have been awarded the highest marks. That, I suspect, is the practice of the majority of subscribers to Parker's bi-monthly newsletter, the *Wine Advocate*. Marks, like tasting terms, should be restricted to being *aides-mémoire* for the markers. When, at a tasting arranged by a newspaper or magazine, I am asked to mark out of 20, on the basis of 2 for appearance, 4 for aroma or bouquet, 6 for palate, etc., I ignore these criteria and simply give it more or less than 12, depending on whether I like it or not – which, to some extent, defeats the point of awarding marks in the first case.

At least marks involve a genuine attempt to offer consumer advice – which is something many wine writers fail to do. The reason is that they are not truly journalists. They are amateurs. This again is explained by economics. Many magazines are not particularly interested in the quality of the copy presented for their wine column, providing it is innocuous enough. What matters to them is that the right image is created for their magazine; for the middle-class, up-market status of wine-drinking has not yet been tarnished by its growing popularity. They feel that wine writers write for love of wine only, and in their heart of hearts believe that the writers ought to pay the magazine, not the other way round. This belief is reciprocated by the many amateur wine-lovers who are perfectly prepared to write, as a hobby, for nothing. As a result, magazines on the whole pay very little for wine articles. If professional journalists are not prepared to work for these fees, amateur ones will.

Moreover, in some cases the argument that wine writers ought to pay the magazine for being published is justified. That is to say, many wine writers are in fact wine merchants wearing another hat. Few professional journalists can afford to visit wine regions and, since magazines will not pay, they are forced to rely on the liberality of public relations companies and national promotional organizations, who show journalists what they want to see rather than what is most important or interesting. This means that the person best suited to write an article in a specialist publication on a specialist topic is less likely to be a professional wine journalist than the very merchant who imports the wines in question. Yet he is the one person who ought to be barred from writing about a region which it is in his commercial interest to promote and about the overall quality of whose wines he cannot possibly write impartially. What is wrong with wine writers asking specialist wine merchants for information? This is, after all, what other journalists do. They go to the experts. It is ridiculous that wine writers should be expected to be experts themselves. Cyril Ray has always protested that he is no expert, but a journalist, interested in wine, who has known the right people to ask. 'A journalist's job is to know who the experts are, to consult the right expert at the right time, to get the facts right, and to make them readable.'[4]

If a merchant is to write about a wine, wine region or wine company with which he is professionally involved, he should at the very least declare his or her interest. To do otherwise would be downright dishonest. Many merchants are honourable about declaring their interests. Others, however, are more cynical. Serena Sutcliffe is a wine importer who also writes articles for *Decanter* and *A La Carte*, and has published a book on Burgundy. In her articles are to be found frequent recommendations for the wines of the Haut-Poitou Cooperative. In her book she is remarkably complimentary about the wines of the Burgundy merchants Delaunay and André Delorme, of Robert and Michel Ampeau in Meursault and of the Domaine des Varoilles in Gevrey-Chambertin. She imports these producers' wines – a fact which I have never seen mentioned in any of her books or articles. I would have thought it relevant.

But are the genuine wine critics any better? As it is difficult for professional wine journalists to make a living solely from writing, many involve themselves part-time in the wine trade. For example, Derek Cooper, presenter of the Food and Wine Programme on Radio Four, is president of the Vintner Wine Club, owned by Arthur Rackham. Hugh Johnson is president of the *Sunday Times* Wine Club and selects a substantial proportion of their wines. Moreover, wine writers would seem to enjoy quite enough in the way of perks to compensate them for being badly paid: all those press trips abroad where they are wined and dined at someone else's expense, not to mention the regular and continuous supply of free samples. One elderly wine writer, a notorious freeloader, has admitted to me that every year he asks Sainsbury's to send him one bottle of each of the wines on their list to 'taste', thereby supplying his vinous needs for the next twelve months. Press trips, however, are not free: a comeback is required, in the form of an article puffing the wines of the region or producer the journalists have just visited. As a result, these trips can prove very effective for the company hosting them. In a later chapter, for example, I will argue that the generally held belief that blended champagne is superior is a load of nonsense, put about by the big champagne houses to justify their high prices. If few members of the wine trade or wine writers are prepared to consider this possibility, it is because they have all at some time or other fallen prey to the public-relation skills of the big champagne houses. Many of them have spent a few days at a champagne establishment having stuffed down their throats, along with *nouvelle cuisine* food and of course champagne, the dogma that champagne is a blended product. Free trips are clearly detrimental to good journalism and are not even very useful. The only way to see a region properly, to ask the right questions of the right people, is to go on one's own. Yet many wine writers are not interested in doing this: they are quite satisfied with a life which depends on the enjoyment of free samples and free holidays. That is why a good wine merchant is much more likely to be informed about what is currently happening in a particular region than a wine writer. He can afford to pay for his trips.

The system of sending out samples is not much more satisfactory than that of press trips. Inevitably, the most interesting wines are often those which are in too short a supply for a sample to be sent. Thus *Decanter* achieved the wrong results on both recent occasions when it held a Meursault tasting because no one sent in sample bottles of wines from the best growers. (More will be said about this in the chapter on wine-tastings.) Robert Parker makes a point of buying most of the wines he tastes so that his integrity will not be affected and is reported to spend $100,000 a year on tasting-samples.

There would not be such scope for press venality if its influence were not so great. The power of the press as affects the drinks trade can be seen in the resurgence in the 1980s of adulteration fever. This is the work of journalists writing about 'E' numbers and carrying out their job of exposing the Austrian di-ethylene glycol scandal of 1985 and the Italian methanol scandal of 1986. In 1987 one piece of market research suggested that people were more worried about additives than about excess alcohol intake, because they believed they could simply moderate their drinking if required.[5] Another poll in 1986 found that more than 60 per cent of people are concerned about additives, preservatives and colouring; and 75 per cent of the above 60 per cent said that this concern applied to beer and lager.[6] Samuel Smith's Natural Lager, brewed in conformity with the subsequently outlawed German pure-beer laws, was produced in response to this report. Public additive-consciousness about wine has produced a vogue for so-called 'organic' wines. I must confess to a certain degree of involvement in starting this fad because of an article I published in *Vogue* in the spring of 1986.

Press cries of 'adulteration' may well produce long-term changes in what we drink, particularly if present-day fads are enshrined in legislation. For example, if it is ever enacted that wine-makers must state the sulphur dioxide content of their products on the label, methods of vinification would probably be changed in order to reduce the amount of sulphur dioxide used, necessitating the use of more chemical sprays in the vineyard, and the production of duller, safer wines.[7] A century ago, it has been argued,[8] adulteration-mania was a major cause of the fall of sherry from popular esteem. Sherry had hitherto been perhaps the most highly regarded of all the white wines imported into Britain, and, in the 1860s, good examples sold at the same price as Le Montrachet. In 1873 Johann Thudichum, in a series of lectures on wine in which he did not so much as mention white burgundies, declared that 'France produces no white wines which can be compared to those of Jerez'.[9] It was Thudichum, however, who launched an adulteration scare by attacking the practice of adding plaster of Paris to sherry must before fermentation. This is in fact a harmless means of increasing the tartaric acid content of the eventual wine – but the public were in no position to judge. In his book, *Facts About Sherry*, Henry Vizetelly wrote that 'the public grew alarmed, and for a time the subject formed a common topic of conversation at all dinner-tables, where by the lady at your side you found sherry generally declined with thanks'. He added that 'the alarm soon subsided and people returned to their old ways'.[10] But did they? In 1901 King Edward VII sold off 5,000 cases of sherry, and it was commented that 'now nobody thinks of sherry, excepting perhaps a few old fogies'.[11]

Naturally some writers wield more power than others. This depends principally on whether they write readable prose. As Cyril Ray has put it, 'the reader doesn't give a bugger if you know anything about wine – he wants to read an interesting article.' That, certainly, is why Auberon Waugh's writings on wine have proved so popular, when no one would describe him as a wine expert. On the other hand, some writers who are not great prose stylists exert considerable influence because they give straightforward consumer advice in the right place at the right time. If Jane McQuitty exerts more direct influence on wine sales than any other wine writer, that has far less to do with her abilities as a taster than with the fact that she writes for *The Times*, which has not yet been deserted by its readers in droves, and on a Saturday, which is when most people think of doing their wine-shopping.

In the USA, the influence of wine writers is much greater, and not just because Americans admire the written word more than the British. As a consumer you are not allowed to taste before you buy; therefore you have to take advice, which few American wine merchants are equipped to give. The power of Robert Parker through the *Wine Advocate* has acquired semi-legendary status. Parker himself belittles his reputation for single-handedly making or breaking a vintage in Bordeaux, which he says derives from the fact that he strongly favoured the 1982 vintage at a time when the dollar was strong and Americans were just starting to become interested in fine wine. He says that he owes his success substantially to the fact that consumers had received a lot of bad advice before he started the *Wine Advocate* in 1978, not least because most American wine writers are general journalists who devote themselves to wine only part-time. (For example, until he retired in 1987, the principal job of the doyen of American wine writers, Frank Prial of the *New York Times*, was that of foreign correspondent.) Yet, despite his influence and integrity, not all the advice that Parker gives is sound. Like many English wine writers, his only foreign language is French. He knows a great deal about Bordeaux, Burgundy and the Rhône valley, but about such countries as Portugal he is, to judge from the comments in his *Wine Buyer's Guide 1988*, much less well informed. To suggest, for example, that 'vintages in Portugal seem to have relevance only to the port trade' is absurd. For his fuller section on Germany, he may well have taken the advice of a specialist wine merchant. If so, he has made a few mistakes in the transcription. I was particularly interested to see, from the Mosel-Saar-Ruwer, Geltz-Zilliken recommended among the 'Outstanding' producers, and Forstmeister-Geltz-Erben among the 'Excellent' producers, since they are in fact the same estate.[12]

Some British wine merchants make sure they have made their annual buying trip to Bordeaux before Parker publishes his tasting notes on the previous year's vintage at the beginning of May, otherwise all the good wines will have been bought by American importers on Parker's recommendation. Parker's influence is, if anything, greater among wine merchants than among the American wine-buying public. There is not the same tradition of knowledge-able wine merchants in the USA as in Britain, not least because for Americans to visit France is not as easy as it is for us. But even in Britain, in some cases, wine writers are very influential even among wine merchants. D. Byrne and Co. is one of two good merchants in Clitheroe. Philip Byrne, who buys their wine, does not go to France much. Instead he reads what wine writers have to say, and tries those wines which they have recommended. He says that 'a wine writer can break a vineyard'.[13]

Thus, if the wine trade is happy to let wine writers live parasitically on its flesh, it is because the relationship works two ways. Writers tell members of the trade what is going on, as well as vice versa. Moreover, being nice to wine writers is both more effective and cheaper than advertising. Certainly a couple of years ago Majestic Wine Warehouses were spending £15–20,000 a year on wooing the press, including £5,000 on sending out samples; certainly national promotional organizations think nothing of spending £1,000 a head on journalists going abroad on a press trip – but the latter figure is less than the cost of a single full-page advertisement in a wine magazine. If there were no wine writers, there would be many fewer of the small specialist merchants, who cannot afford to spend much money on advertising and therefore rely on write-ups by wine writers as much as on word of mouth to spread the news of their existence. Their dependence on wine writers is comparable to that of smaller regional breweries on CAMRA, which was founded in 1971. This organization may presently boast only 20,000 members, yet a number of breweries have admitted to me that, had CAMRA not existed, they would have been swallowed up by one of Watney's, Whitbread's and the like. A wine merchant is happy to send writers samples of his wines to taste, even if no one actually buys the wines as the result of favourable write-ups, because the merchant can quote what the writer has said in his publicity. Of course, he quotes selectively – and often inaccurately. That is why the Consumers' Association, who publish *Which? Wine Monthly* and the *Which? Wine Guide*, alongside the *Good Food Guide* under the *Which?* umbrella, do not permit merchants to quote their comments, on pain of future exclusion. (These ethics do not, however, prevent the *Which? Wine Guide* from advertising itself by quoting the complimentary remarks of other journalists.)

Indeed, many merchants seem to imagine that the sole function of wine writers is to support the wine trade – presumably on the grounds that, if there were no wine trade, there would be no wine writers. When I wrote a letter to *Decanter* criticizing their practice of publishing articles by wine merchants, one of those I mentioned, Liz Berry, the owner of La Vigneronne in South Kensington, replied that she found it 'a great shame that there are so many "angry young people" [sic] in the wine trade'.[14] In other words, she believes that wine writers are part of the wine trade – which is, or at least ought to be, complete nonsense. I am afraid to say that some wine writers agree with this stance. One wine-writing friend, no longer an angry young man, has defended his acceptance of 'freebies' to me on the grounds that the purpose of wine writers is to promote wine and the wine trade as a whole. That excuses him if he doesn't give the PR people their pound of flesh in terms of column inches after each press trip abroad.

There are no entry qualifications to become a wine writer or wine merchant. To become the first you have to be pushy, to become the second, you need lots of money. All professional training is done on the job. There is, certainly, the wine trade's equivalent of a degree qualification, the title of Master of Wine. But to become a Master of Wine it was, until recently, necessary to have spent five years working in the trade; it was not a qualification which could be acquired before entry. Most wine writers cannot help but learn something about wine, if only by a form of osmosis as a result of all the tastings they attend and free samples they receive. Wine merchants, however, can perfectly well leave the job of tasting and choosing wine to a few importers. They don't have to be able to select the stuff themselves. All they need to be able to do is to sell it. In 1986 the buying policy of The Noble Grape wine warehouse in Wapping was described in the gossip column of the wine trade magazine *Wine and Spirit*. Their wine buyer was said to ask his suppliers to tell him what they thought he should sell and then to ring round to ask them how to describe their wines in his list – not having tasted them himself.[15]

Matters used to be worse. It was evident from the evidence given by wine merchants to the 1852 Commons Select Committee that most of them knew nothing about wines beyond the two or three in which they dealt.[16] In 1860 Gladstone extended licences to grocers, which made things worse still. Charles Tovey mentions one grocer's wine list which speaks of 'Sherry direct from Bordeaux' at the following prices:

Sherry, Chateau d'Yquem	40s. per doz.
Ditto, Finest Sauterne	34s. per doz.[17]

I said in the previous chapter that, for many wine merchants, particularly those situated outside London and substantially reliant on mail-order sales, their annual list is a major sales force. Many consumers sit and study a pile of wine-lists, comparing range and prices. To steal a march over his competitors a merchant likes to announce a new 'discovery' – a wine which is underpriced because no one else has heard of it but which will become rapidly more expensive once it becomes known – as a carrot to customers and a sop to wine writers. It may well be true that the wine in question is listed by none of his competitors – until the following year. But is it a discovery? and, if so, did the merchant discover it?

Certainly, there are real discoveries. Since 1969 – long before it became fashionable – Robin Yapp has been ambling down the Rhône valley, digging out the best growers. He says that a merchant does not need to be either intelligent or assiduous to discover the best grower in a particular *appellation* – he just has to get there first. Until recently he had supposed, with the rest of us, that no wine of any consequence was produced in the forty-mile gap between the vineyard areas usually described as the Northern and Southern Rhône. However, in 1985, he chanced upon the wine produced by Jean-Marie Lombard, one of two growers in the village of Brézème, in the middle of that gap, at the one restaurant in Lyons to list it. His friend Gérard Chave, the leading producer of Hermitage, who was with him at the time, in fact knew of this wine, and had been instrumental in persuading Jean-Marie Lombard to bottle his own production rather than to continue to take it to a distant cooperative. But Chave had thought it would be of no interest to Robin Yapp and had therefore forgotten to tell him about it. It is an absolutely classic, 100 per cent Syrah, Northern Rhône wine, and as yet underpriced. But even this wine was not previously unknown, just forgotten. One hundred and fifty years ago the English wine writer Cyrus Redding described Brézème as a wine which was 'scarcely known' but was 'beginning to be sought after'.[18]

Most 'discoveries' are less genuine than this. Some are simply poached off rivals who have made less of a fuss about the wines. Michel Ferraton makes what is, alongside 'Thalabert' from the merchants Paul Jaboulet Aîné, the outstanding wine of the Crozes-Hermitage *appellation*. I first encountered the 1983 vintage of this wine at a tasting given by Justerini and Brooks, and bought a few bottles. I was therefore a little surprised, some while later, to read in Adnams' opening offer of 1985 red wines from the Northern Rhône of Michel Ferraton, described by their buyer Simon Loftus as 'a major newcomer to our range of producers . . . it was only after several months' cogitation that he formally agreed to sell to us (and to allow me to choose his other customers in England).' In his autumn 1984 list, Mark Savage of Windrush Wines made a great song and dance about his discovery of Château Le Tertre Roteboeuf in Saint-Émilion, under the auspices of Pascal Delbeck, the wine-maker at Château Ausone, one of the two leading estates of the region. Even so, John Armit of Corney and Barrow had no compunction about announcing in their autumn 1986 list the introduction of Château Le Tertre Roteboeuf, 'the most exciting discovery we have made in Bordeaux for a long time'. The wine is remarkable – he is right about that – but so is the price Corney and Barrow are asking for it.

The majority of discoveries are not even poached; they are not made by wine merchants at all. They are made by brokers, or else specialist importers, whose job is to dig around their chosen regions of the world, to make discoveries. They act as middlemen between producer and vendor, working for a 10 per cent commission. Merchants need not worry lest they are found out for claiming brokers' discoveries as their own. Brokers play the game, and do not reveal themselves to the public. Brokers I have spoken to have expressed the concern that, were I to undeceive their customers, wine merchants might feel that they were being shown up as fools, give up making 'discoveries', and return to selling famous names which might not be so individual nor offer such good value but which are certainly easier to sell. So long as brokers remain, in the words of one of their number, 'grey men with briefcases', wine merchants will not fear to sell red burgundies from Gaston Barthod-Noëllat and Virgil Pothier(-Rieusset) instead of Jadot and Latour, Northern Rhône wines from Bernard Faurie and Marius Gentaz-Dervieux instead of Jaboulet and Chapoutier, and Alsatian wines from Louis Rolly-Gassman and André Ostertag instead of Hugel and Trimbach.

I do not wish to criticize the system of buying through brokers. If anything, it is cheaper than buying direct. Suppose a merchant wished to track down a new grower in a particular village in Burgundy. If he went to a broker, he would have to pay 10 per cent commission which on, say, 100 cases at £70 each, would amount to £700 – much less than the cost of travel, accommodation, entertainment expenses and loss of potential earnings if he actually went and did the job himself. Moreover brokers, because they are buying larger quantities, sometimes on behalf of several clients in various countries, ought, at least in theory, to be able to negotiate a better price than an individual wine merchant. There are wine merchants who insist on bypassing brokers and buying at source themselves. It does not work out any cheaper: certainly Nicholas Davies of the Hungerford Wine Company, who makes a point of buying direct from Bordeaux châteaux wherever he can, as he prefers to enjoy a direct relationship with his suppliers, does not save his customers any money as a result.

If they are not out digging for wines, what do wine merchants do with themselves? Some of them certainly have to make a living by selling the stuff – but not all. It is not, after all, much of a living. At the bottom, it is no sort of a living at all. Graduates, even in London, work as shop assistants for between £4,000 and £5,000 a year. They are paid so little, not because their employers are mean, but partly because of the laws of supply and demand – like publishing, the wine trade, though a business, carries the respectability of a profession – and partly because their employers cannot afford more. Thanks to the activities of brewery groups in the 1960s and of the supermarkets in the 1970s, the Good Old Days are gone for ever. Wine merchants operate on a 25–30 per cent mark-up – which most accountants would regard as economic suicide in a business in which such huge amounts of capital are tied up in stock. The accountant for Lay and Wheeler, one of the most successful of wine merchants, once told me that he had had to forget the basic principles of economics when he entered the wine trade. To operate successfully as a wine merchant, it does no harm to be able to tap some source of private income. As has been said of both wine-making and wine retailing, the way to make a small fortune in the wine business is by starting with a big one.

The wine trade is the repository of unintelligent and unsuccessful male Sloane Rangers. It has long replaced the Church as a means of getting rid of younger sons who are not suitable for the Army. What is true today was true a hundred years ago when, according to Charles Tovey, the job of a wine merchant was frequently adopted 'as a *dernier ressort* by those who, lacking education or ability for the learned professions, and who could not succeed in living upon their wits, have an idea that there is something respectable about a "Wine Merchant", and they embark in a business for which they are wholly unqualified'.[19] What the wine trade offers is respectability. Its status in Britain can be compared to the historic status of barbers in France. Before the Revolution, barbers were the only tradesmen accorded the privilege of wearing swords, whereas at the same time in Britain, wine merchants were the only tradesmen allowed an *entrée* into country society – for both trades required culture, taste, discrimination, and the absolute confidence of the patron in the tradesmen concerned.[20]

[1] Malcolm Southan, 'The Adman Cometh' in Richard Boston (ed.), *The Press We Deserve*, Routledge & Kegan Paul, 1970.
[2] *Wine and Spirit*, October 1985, pp. 33–5.
[3] David Peppercorn in *Decanter*, December 1986, p. 99.
[4] Cyril Ray, *Ray on Wine*, J. M. Dent & Sons, 1979, p. 12.
[5] Adsearch report.
[6] Gallup poll.
[7] See Chapter 16, pp. 239–43.
[8] Julian Jeffs, *Sherry*, 3rd ed., Faber & Faber, 1982, pp. 103–8.
[9] J. L. W. Thudichum, *Cantor Lectures on Wines*, 1873, p. 37.
[10] Henry Vizetelly, *Facts About Sherry*, 1876, p. 59.
[11] *Newcastle Weekly Chronicle*, 1901, quoted in H. Warner Allen, *Number Three Saint James's Street*, Chatto & Windus, 1950, p. 205.
[12] Robert Parker, *The Wine Buyer's Guide 1988*, Dorling Kindersley, 1987, pp. 394, 398–9.
[13] Quoted in *Wine and Spirit*, March 1987, p. 24.
[14] *Decanter*, September 1987, p. 15.
[15] *Wine and Spirit*, July 1986, p. 74.
[16] *Fraser's Magazine*, 1855, quoted in Asa Briggs, *Wine for Sale: Victoria Wine and the liquor trade 1860–1984*, B. T. Batsford, 1985, p. 30.
[17] Charles Tovey, *Wine and Wine Countries*, 2nd ed., 1877, p. 40.
[18] Cyrus Redding, *A History and Description of Modern Wines*, 1833, p. 116.
[19] Tovey, p. 19.
[20] Dennis Wheatley, *The Seven Ages of Justerini's*, 1949, pp. 30–31.

6

IT REFRESHES THE POCKETS OTHER BEERS
CANNOT REACH

Few wine-drinkers place absolute confidence in their wine merchant.

Certainly, the proportion of the population which shows a serious interest in wine, though small, is significant. An opinion poll in 1986 found that 25 per cent of all wine-drinkers had visited a vineyard, and 5 per cent of all wine-drinkers had attended a wine-tasting. About 25 per cent of wine-drinkers are 'regular' consumers; but this merely means people who drink wine at least once a week. Fifty-five per cent of those who drink wine, take wine only on special occasions, which in many cases means only on birthdays and/or at Christmas and at no other time. Thus the majority of wine-drinkers are not the sort of people who read wine writers or take advice from wine merchants. They have neither the desire nor the confidence nor the money to experiment in their wine purchasing, even on the basis of good advice. One survey found that only 9 per cent of customers in specialist off-licences asked for advice.[1] According to another survey 50 per cent of people always buy the same wine. Among the comments made to interviewers carrying out this survey were: 'You tend to stick to the names you know,' and 'I've bought a different bottle in the past and the wine was awful.'[2]

Thanks to its naval tradition, and, since the Industrial Revolution, to its dependence on food imports to feed its population, Britain has for many hundreds of years been the wine shop of the world. As was written by the Secretary of the Duke of Wurtemberg in 1592, 'there is no vine-growing in this kingdom; but, if you want wine you can purchase the best and most delicious sorts, of various nations, and that on account of the great facility which the sea affords them for barter with other countries.'[3] To the majority of consumers this is in fact a disadvantage. I cannot begin to guess how many millions of different wines are made in the world each year, nor how many thousands of these are imported into Britain. Given a choice so impossibly wide that no one, not even professionals who taste up to fifty wines every day, can ever get to try more than a small sample of what is available, it is no wonder that the majority of wine-drinkers rely on those names of which they have heard. That is why advertising is so important in the wine market. According to English wine producer David Carr-Taylor, 'This business is 80 per cent marketing of the wine and only 20 per cent actual growing and making.'[4]

The principal means of advertising a product lies in the promotion of a brand name. The use of advertising and the existence of brands are mutually dependent. Both the advertising industry and mass-market brands are products of the Industrial Revolution, which distinguished producer and consumer for the first time. This encouraged a degree of adulteration which had not been possible in agricultural societies where producer and consumer usually lived in the same village. The way in which consumers in an industrial society could best be sure of buying a product that was not adulterated was by relying on the reputation of a well-known brand. Traditionally, wines and spirits had been sold, usually in cask, to be bottled by and labelled with the name of the merchant who bought the cask. The expansion of the wine market as a result of the increased wealth of the working classes, the growth of the middle classes, and the reduction in duties on light wines effected by Gladstone in 1860–1, then brought unscrupulous dealers into the trade – and ignorant merchants, who could easily be duped. Therefore brand names on which consumers could rely became just as important for wines and spirits as for other products, and the advertising industry developed as a means of promoting them.

But given that the main role of advertising lies in the promotion of brands, how relevant is advertising in the table wine market as opposed to the other drinks markets? In 1985 £140 million was spent on drinks advertising, but only £10.9 million of this on table wines. Branded wines such as Piat d'Or and Hirondelle account for only 15 per cent of wine sales. But are these 'traditional' brands the only brands of wine there are? A brand is a name which distinguishes that product from any other. That name can only be relied upon if its exclusive use is protected by law. Certainly the development of trade marks legislation during the second half of the nineteenth century, which made the growth of brands possible, served largely to protect such branded, standard products as port and sherry, which are manufactured products in a way that table wine, made simply from freshly fermented grape juice, is not. But brands of table wine are protected by their own legislation. During the course of this century wine laws have been introduced to protect the reputations of famous wine-producing regions, beginning with *appellation contrôlée* in France in 1935. These laws ensure that, within the countries respecting them, claret, burgundy and champagne are not just types or styles of wine, but brands, whose reputation is no less jealously guarded than that of trade-marked brands.

Not until we joined the EEC in 1973 were we in Britain obliged to respect other member states' wine laws. Before that Beaujolais, for example, was only a 'type' of wine which could, and did, come from anywhere. In 1966 the *Sunday Times* showed fourteen bottles of 'Beaujolais' to a committee of ten French experts, who said that none of the wines were distinctly Beaujolais, though four *might* have been real. Four were doubtful and six definitely bogus.[5] It might well have been possible for the Burgundians to protect their brands' reputation in Britain by taking out civil actions for 'passing off' wines as something which they were not. This is what the Champenois did. They took out a civil action against the producers of Perelada Spanish champagne, and in 1960 were granted an injunction restraining the producers of Perelada from calling their product by any name that included the word 'champagne'.

But it was not *illegal*, that is to say, a crime, to sell wine from the South of France as 'Beaujolais', or Spanish sparkling wine as 'champagne'. Lengthy and unwieldy civil injunctions could only be brought out against individuals, not against the generality of those who took advantage of the reputation of famous names. In 1958 the champagne industry had tried to stop the producers of Perelada Spanish champagne by bringing a criminal prosecution against them under trade marks legislation, but they lost the case.

In the USA (which is not a member of the EEC!) chablis and champagne are still types of wine, which may well come from anywhere. The same, sad to say, is true of sherry in Britain. Though a product sold simply as 'sherry' must by law have been produced in the Jerez region of Spain, we still, until 1996 at least, have Cyprus sherry and British sherry. This iniquitous arrangement was imposed on Spain as a condition of its entry into the EEC, in order to protect the interests of the British sherry industry, which makes a vaguely sherry-like wine out of imported grape-juice concentrate. The uniquely unprotected position of sherry within the EEC is, one suspects, the result of the Spanish government's giving the British government a *quid pro quo* in return for some unspecified concession made by the latter. When, in 1967, the Jerezanos had tried to protect the good name of sherry on the same grounds as the Champenois had succeeded with champagne, they lost their case. They were told that they had left it too late, that South African sherry, for instance, had been sold as such in Britain for over a century and therefore enjoyed 'squatters' rights' to the name. But Spain's Treaty of Accession to the EEC does not mention South African sherry, which may now no longer be sold. It permits only the terms Cyprus, British and Irish sherry – a decision made at the last moment by the Council of Ministers, overturning the recommendation of the European Commission. If there was horse-trading, it was not unprecedented. The good names of port and madeira have been protected in Britain by Act of Parliament ever since the First World War, when we made this concession to the Portuguese in return for their selling us wolfram which we needed to make armaments.[6]

The ferocity of the Champenois in protecting the reputation of their brand is quite remarkable. In the spring of 1982 Sainsbury's ran a campaign of advertisements for their own-label sparkling Saumur, in which they suggested that many people would find great difficulty in telling Sainsbury's Sparkling Saumur from champagne. This is true enough. There are plenty of instances of experts in blind tastings believing that a sample of champagne was in fact sparkling Saumur. Nevertheless Moët et Chandon, on behalf of the champagne industry as a whole, took out an interim injunction in the High Court, forbidding Sainsbury's from repeating the advertisement on the grounds that it would be likely to lead to sparkling Saumur being passed off as champagne. Sainsbury's were not prepared to fight the case and caved in a couple of days before the hearing. So never again can Sainsbury's use in one of their advertisements the word champagne 'in connection with' a wine not produced in the Champagne region. Nor, after 1993, will producers in other regions of sparkling wine made by the *méthode champenoise* be allowed to use that term on the label. The Champenois, it seems, will stop at nothing in their determination to ensure that the name 'champagne' is their property alone. In 1975 they obtained an injunction forbidding the makers of Babycham from describing it as 'champagne perry', and even succeeded in having the use of the name 'Babycham' itself prohibited, though this latter ruling was reversed by the Court of Appeal on the grounds that the champagne industry had not been able to produce a single witness who had been confused by the Babycham label. The Champenois have not, however, taken the French government to court for marketing, through its state tobacco monopoly, a brand of cigarettes called 'Champagne'.

Champagne was deliberately created as a brand. The name had been used in the Middle Ages only to describe the open plain which was better suited to the cultivation of cereals than to that of vines. The wine of the region only came to be called champagne at the beginning of the seventeenth century, possibly at the instigation of Nicolas Brûlart, Chancellor of France and a major proprietor of vineyards in Champagne. Its image as the smart wine drunk by the smartest people in Paris was also a deliberate creation of that time.

The brand name 'champagne' is not congruent with the place name Champagne. Not all wines produced in a particular region are entitled to use the brand name of that region, perhaps because they have been made from grapes grown on unsuitable soil or from the 'wrong' grape varieties, or perhaps because of politics. In Champagne those soils which may be planted in grapes for champagne production were specified in 1927. Some suitable soil was missed, but it is too late now for it to be included. Claude Taittinger says that 'there would be a revolution if one peasant became a multi-millionaire because his land is classified, while his neighbour's land alongside is not'.[7] Brands have a reputation, which they must protect. Brands denote a particular style of wine, which may not necessarily come from the place in question. It may seem ridiculous, but only one of the twenty-three vineyards in the village of Nierstein is allowed to use the regional name Niersteiner Gutes Domtal, though this covers thirty vineyards in fourteen other villages.

Not only are regions brands, but so are whole countries. When you are not knowledgeable about wine, what you are most likely to remember about a wine is the name of the country it came from. One piece of market research found that, whereas two-thirds of those interviewed wanted to see a wine's country of origin stated on the label, only one-quarter were interested to know what region it came from – and only one-third wanted to know who made it.

Many people have quite fixed – if not necessarily correct – ideas of a country's products. Spanish wines have a bad image, being thought of largely as cheap, nasty, red party plonk, which is likely to give you a headache. This impression is substantially derived from experiences of cheap Spanish wines on holiday. It can be dispelled by advertising. Wine merchants had for a long time thought the wines of Rioja to offer particularly good value for money, but they could not sell them. In 1977 Rioja producers combined to promote their wines in Britain. Between 1976 and 1986 sales of Rioja in the UK increased by 1,400 per cent. When the campaign began, one of its basic strategies was that, wherever possible, all references to Spain would be avoided. This would no longer be necessary. Wine merchants have become so confident in the ability of Wines from Spain (part of the Spanish Government Trade Office) to sell wines for them – and so despairing of their ability to sell wines from regions which are not advertised – that they decide what wines to import on these criteria. In 1985 one company, Espavino, gave up trying to sell their Rueda because, they said, no one knew the name, but announced that they were going to add a wine from Penedès to their list in 1986 'because Penedès is being supported by Wines from Spain'.[8]

It is important for the governments of southern European countries – France, Italy, Spain, Portugal, Greece – to promote their wines, because wine plays a major part in their economies. It accounts, for example, for 9 per cent of the French Gross National Product. Whether or not a country promotes its wines successfully or not seems to make all the difference to whether it succeeds or fails in selling its wines in Britain. Though they have proved enormously successful in the USA, thanks largely to the size of the Italian immigrant population, here in Britain Italian wines enjoy a smaller share of the market than they did in the mid-1970s. Yet the Italian authorities have done little to reverse the decline. Have they grown fat in the knowledge that their wines enjoy guaranteed sales in thousands of *trattorie*? Certainly it is rumoured that they regard the UK market as a relatively easy one for their wines. The Italian Trade Centre possesses a magnificent shopfront in Piccadilly, where an *enoteca* – a wine library – sits behind smoked glass, open to the public for only ten hours a week, and even then giving an impression of being closed. Their budget was increased five-fold between 1986 and 1987, to £1 million per annum. But the key is not how much money you have so much as how you use it. The more money the Italians have, the more they will be able to spend on appallingly bad advertisements and aimless marketing exercises – such as tastings which are attended by no one but the converted, and receptions at which there are apparently no hosts, and where nothing seems to happen.

The German government does not advertise its country's wines in Britain. Advertising is carried out instead by the producers of branded Liebfraumilch – Blue Nun, Black Tower, *et al.* As a result, consumers acquire the wrong impression of German wines, thinking that they are all like Liebfraumilch, and consequently when they 'trade up' from the bland, semi-sweet wines with which they began their drinking careers, they ignore fine German wines. Perhaps the German government is right not to spend money on advertising, since wine is an unimportant element of the German economy compared to that of France or Italy. But the reason why they do not advertise is that the German 'economic miracle' since the last war has been founded upon a fundamental belief in a free trade economy unlike the protectionist economies of Mediterranean Europe.

The same can be said of Californian wines, which failed to take off in late 1970s, despite a large amount of free publicity from wine writers and substantial public interest, because this interest was not sustained by a promotional campaign. The Americans, like the Germans, believe in *laissez-faire*, not in paying taxes to fund promotions on behalf of their business competitors. Anyway, at the beginning of the 1980s Californian wine producers could sell all their wines on the American market; only since 1982 has the dollar become so strong against the franc that French imports have become cheap. Exports of Californian wines to Britain plateaued after 1981, then fell. In 1985 the Californian wine producers joined together to promote their wines, with assistance from the United States Department of Agriculture. It may be too late. In terms of both fashion and value for money, Californian wines cannot compete with those of Australia or New Zealand.

As a general rule wine producers do not advertise until they have to. Market-oriented producers, such as Torres in Penedès in eastern Spain, advertise their own brands; many others are peasant farmers with little understanding of foreign markets and a feeling that, if people want to buy their wines, they will come to them. They only club together to advertise their products as a last desperate attempt to shore up a declining market.

It was in such dire circumstances that sherry came to be advertised in the 1920s. It had gone out of fashion at the end of the nineteenth century, and was then all but killed off by the cocktail habit of the 1920s. A number of sherry shippers joined together and pooled their advertising money for a promotional campaign in which they put forward the argument that sherry was more versatile than cocktails, had a cleaner taste, offered better value for money, and was better for your health. The campaign succeeded. People began to give sherry parties instead of cocktail parties and at the majority of the latter it soon became customary to offer sherry as an alternative.

In the 1930s beer came to be advertised for the same reason, and with similar success. Consumption of beer increased by 45 per cent between the mid-1930s and the mid-1940s. In 1938 a majority of the licensees of forty pubs in London told market researchers that the generic advertising which was proving so successful for beer would not succeed for wines. However, after the war, the wine trade became desperate. A survey showed that, on the day before they were interviewed, 86 per cent of respondents had taken beer but only 1 per cent had taken wine; and members of the Wine and Spirit Association admitted that, if the trend continued, there would soon be no demand for wine at all. So a campaign to encourage people to drink more wine was launched in 1950. By 1960 we were drinking more wine in total, and three times as much unfortified table wine, as we had before the war.

Before the 1950s members of the wine trade had regarded advertising with horror. When Walter Sichel started advertising Blue Nun, it was considered scandalous. 'Advertising was beneath one's dignity. It was felt that if it was necessary to advertise a wine it couldn't be much good.'9 When Sandeman had decided in the 1920s to start selling their basic ports under their own name rather than that of the companies which imported them, and to support their decision with an advertising campaign featuring the famous Don with a black cape and hat, they were condemned by both importers and retailers, and accused of selling 'grocer's port' rather than a drink suitable for gentlemen.

But how much effect does advertising have on what we drink? A truism which applies to all luxury products is that people don't need them. Therefore we have to be persuaded to buy them. A survey in 1976 found that 59 per cent of the population thought advertising made people buy things they did not want.[10] One of the oldest chestnuts in the advertising industry is to say that 50 per cent of advertising is effective – but no one knows which 50 per cent it is. There are no means of measuring advertising's effectiveness other than consumer research; after all, the fact that a product's sales increase following an advertising campaign does not necessarily mean that the increase was due to the campaign. If statistical correlation implied a causal correlation, we would have to make a connection between the decline in the birth-rate and the fall in the stork population in Sweden after the last war. But market research is a very clumsy instrument. For example, in 1987 a New York survey found that only 4 per cent of consumers were influenced by advertising in deciding what liqueur or brandy they purchased at off-licence shops. Most consumers apparently relied on previous knowledge of a brand or on word of mouth. But, even in New York, people aren't going to admit that they buy a product just because it has been well – or heavily – advertised. They might feel that such an admission would make them look dumb.

The success of Sainsbury's advertisements for their own-label pink champagne, introduced in the autumn of 1984, shows how much more successful an advertising campaign can be than has been anticipated. Sainsbury's ordered around 3,000 cases of pink champagne, which they advertised as being produced by 'a small family concern' by the costly maceration method, which involves letting the skins of the black grapes macerate in the juice for the first few days of fermentation, in order to give a pink colour to the wine; the usual, cheaper method is simply to pour red wine into finished white champagne. The new product sold so well that Sainsbury's buyers had to dash over to Champagne and get hold of a further 5–7,000 cases of pink champagne, cobbled together from several sources, each case of which cost them £10–15 more than in the original consignment – but they had to sell all the champagnes at the advertised price of £6.45 a bottle. I doubt if they made much of a profit on those wines, and they got into trouble with the Advertising Standards Authority for their pains, because the various champagnes in the second consignment patently did not come from 'a small family concern', and were not made by the maceration method, as their advertisements continued to declare almost right up to Christmas. This said, it is possible that the success was due not so much to the advertisements as to the appearance on their shelves of an own-label pink champagne the year after a second successive election victory by a right-wing Conservative government had accelerated a boom in conspicuous consumption.

What can certainly be said is that advertising, though the great god of our time, is not all-powerful. It cannot succeed unless there are underlying reasons to buy the product. If we imagine the power of advertising in the drinks industry, substantial though it is, to be greater than is in fact the case, this is partly the result of widespread misconceptions concerning the reason for the present popularity of lager. Many members of CAMRA are so devoted to their avowed cause of saving 'traditional', cask-conditioned bitter beer that they find it hard to understand that people actually like drinking lager. Letters and articles in CAMRA's monthly newspaper *What's Brewing* frequently express the view that people buy lager only because it is heavily advertised. They point to the fact that lager accounts for 42 per cent of the beer drunk in Britain but 60 per cent of the advertising expenditure. This is not the point, however. If more money is spent on advertising lager, it is because it is a more heavily branded market than bitter, a substantial proportion of which is still produced by a number of small(ish), regionally based breweries. It is also because the lager market is growing, and the bitter market is not. Money is patently better spent on advertising in order to gain a larger market share of a growing market than to win a larger proportion of a declining one. People do not drink lager instead of bitter because it is more heavily advertised. They drink lager instead of bitter because they prefer it. Lager has been favoured by social changes over the last generation, by the desire of a growing number of people to consume a light-coloured, light-tasting, refreshing, fizzy drink. How can the lager boom have been created by advertising when the big brewers began advertising lager heavily in 1962 yet it did not take off until five years later, when it was put on draught and lost its image as an expensive bottled beer which male drinkers considered to be suitable only for women?

If one fundamental reason underlies the success of lager, it is the fact that it is perceived to be more refreshing than bitter. Oddly enough, advertisers did not realize this until 1973, when, after a decade of expensive advertising campaigns, lager accounted for only 15 per cent of all beer sales. Hitherto lager had been advertised as a smart drink for those in the know. In 1973 Heineken picked up the theme of refreshment, and used it in their famous campaign – still running – which shows Heineken refreshing the parts other beers cannot reach. Lager sales increased by 50 per cent when it was used for refreshment during the hot summers of 1975 and 1976. If we look upon lager as a whole as a brand, the fact of its being perceived to be refreshing is described, in marketing terms, as its unique selling point (usp): a marketing asset which is unique to that brand and is not possessed by its rivals – in this case, bitter.

To be successful commercially, a product must have a usp. If a product does not have a genuine, intrinsic usp, then the marketing men have to set about inventing one. The way this works can be seen from the marketing of champagne over the last three centuries.

Champagne's usp was originally the fact that it sparkled. In the first half of the eighteenth century, it was the only wine that did. It sparkled because the sugar from the grapes did not all convert to alcohol before the onset of winter, when the cold weather caused the wine to stop fermenting. If the wine was put in bottles in March, it would be rendered sparkling when fermentation started up again in the spring, and the carbon dioxide gas was unable to escape. This method was not applied to other wines because, until the means was developed in the nineteenth century of measuring the amount of unfermented sugar left in the wine at the time of bottling, it was unreliable and therefore expensive. In the second half of the nineteenth century wine-makers in Germany started to add sugar and yeast to a fully fermented wine, enabling it to referment reliably a second time in bottle. This method was not adopted by the Champenois until the very end of the century, not least because the Germans had got there first: a fact that did not prevent the Champenois from christening it the *méthode champenoise*. Since the 1960s German wine-makers have adopted a system of fermenting the wine entirely in vats, and bottling the sparkling wine under pressure at low temperature, to prevent the carbon dioxide gas from escaping. The Champenois now shout loudly that their method is superior.

Is it? Tank-fermented wines are not *ipso facto* inferior to bottle-fermented ones. If in practice they are not usually as good, it is because they lack the up-market image of wines made by the *méthode champenoise*: they cannot achieve the same prices and therefore their makers cannot afford to produce wine to such a high standard. Quality in a sparkling wine is determined by the quality of the raw product, and by the length of time the wine spends in contact with the yeast cells during the second fermentation. Whereas sparkling wine made by the tank method usually spends only a month in contact with the yeast cells, one made by the *méthode champenoise* spends two years or more. In fact, because there is greater surface contact between the wine and the yeast cells in a tank than in a bottle, it would not take as long to produce a sparkling wine of the same quality, if desired. Czech lagers, which are fermented in tank, not in bottle, take two to three months to develop a yeast-derived bouquet similar to that of champagne; the most outstanding example of this characteristic is probably Budweiser, which is now widely available in Britain, but should not be confused with the bland and heavily advertised American Budweiser, which was so named last century in 'homage' to the Czech beer.

In order to 'prove' that their wine was superior to other wines made by the 'champagne method', the Champenois also developed the argument that their soil was intrinsically superior. Certainly the chalk content of the soil helped it to sparkle before the *méthode champenoise* was developed. Certainly its lime content produces grapes with a relatively high acidity, which is important for sparkling wines, since the acid level falls by up to one-third during the second fermentation; but acidity can perfectly well be added. It is not the soil in Champagne which is so important, but the climate and the grapes. Until English sparkling wines take off, Champagne will remain unique in producing sparkling wines from Chardonnay and Pinot varieties of grapes, which particularly well suit the yeasty character of wines produced by a double fermentation, in a climate which is sufficiently cool to enable the grapes to enjoy a long growing season yet retain a sufficiently low sugar content and high acid levels.

The one successful usp to have been developed for champagne is the invention of the marketing men and the product of advertising. Champagne has successfully been turned into the *sine qua non* of celebration, sometimes by dubious methods. In 1902 George Kessler, Moët et Chandon's agent in the USA, somehow succeeded in substituting a bottle of Moët for one of German sparkling wine at the launch in a New York dockyard of the German Kaiser's yacht, and in having Moët served at lunch after the ceremony. The resulting publicity for champagne so infuriated the Kaiser that he recalled the German Ambassador from Washington.[11] Today, champagne is so closely associated with celebration that the phrase used to describe a James Bond fantasy-type of existence – fast cars, slow yachts and beautiful women – is 'champagne lifestyle'.

This image has enabled champagne as a whole to maintain its usp. But what of the individual brands of champagne? They all convey the image of a 'champagne lifestyle', so that cannot be used to differentiate them. So how is this done? How are brand identities created? The most obvious way would be to base them on differences in taste. That is, after all, how the various châteaux of Bordeaux create their brand identities. But champagne is different from claret. We buy claret – theoretically at least – for the taste. We buy champagne for the image; the taste is irrelevant. That is why it is of no real consequence that most of the champagnes from the big houses taste more or less the same. Champagne houses make much of the skill in blending so that the wines conform to a 'house-style', but how many people, in a blind tasting, could distinguish Moët from Mumm from Charles Heidsieck. . . ?

Bottles of ready-made champagne are purchased from the Centre Viticole de la Champagne at Chouilly and from Marne-et-Champagne in Épernay by well-known champagne houses when they do not have sufficiently large stocks of the champagnes they have so carefully made and blended themselves in order to meet demand. If the big champagne houses buy ready-made champagne and slap their own labels on it, how can they possibly each claim to have a 'house-style' of their own? This particular scandal is called the *sur lattes* scandal – *sur lattes* means 'on lathes' and applies to those bottles of champagne maturing in other people's cellars which the big houses buy.[12] There is nothing new about it. A hundred years ago, Charles Tovey wrote:

the more the public is enlightened with respect to the growth and manufacture of champagne, the sooner will the absurd delusion as to the superiority of certain brands be dispelled. It is no secret to the well-informed English wine merchant that most of the champagne houses, when their original stock of any year is exhausted, supply themselves from the stock of *speculateurs*, and that identically the same wine so purchased will, when advanced with the brand and the label of the big house, fetch from ten to twelve shillings per dozen more than when introduced into this country under the modest auspices of a smaller shipper. How long will such a system last? Surely the time will come when champagne drinkers will become wise. . . .[13]

How are the brands of champagne to be distinguished from one another, if not by taste? By image. Take Pommery and Lanson, for example. According to Lanson's assistant export director, Bernard Peillon, when the yogurt manufacturers BSN bought the two brands in 1983, they had similar prices and similar images. BSN therefore targeted Pommery 'at the 35-plus age-group – the man who drives a Mercedes', and Lanson 'at the 25–35 age-group, the BMW-driver. Lanson is the champagne for Yuppies.'[14] Both houses have conducted startling advertising campaigns in order to establish these brand-images for themselves.

Much the same is true of lager. Lager as a whole enjoys the usp of being perceived as refreshing. Individual lagers do not have usps. Nor do the majority of lagers taste noticeably different from each other. Admittedly, at the temperature they are usually served one's palate is so numbed that it would be difficult to detect any differences that might exist. But whether these differences exist or not is irrelevant. A lager-drinker chooses his preferred brand according to the image put forward in the advertisements. If he prefers Hofmeister to Fosters, it is because he is more readily able to identify himself with a Jack-the-lad bear than with a sarcastic Australian, not least because he believes that such an identification will impress his friends. If he chooses Carlsberg, it is because he wishes to be thought of as someone who has good taste – and, quite by accident, he is.

The Sales Director of Carlsberg, Derek Cook, freely admits that 'people don't drink always any more by taste. They drink with their eyes, they drink because of advertising promotions and so on, and because of what they want to be seen drinking.'[15] When bottle-conditioned Guinness was withdrawn from Scottish pubs and replaced by the patently inferior brewery-conditioned version, their Marketing Director Gary Luddington claimed that 'there is no perceptible difference in taste and appearance. Blind-taste tests were made by our brewers and they could not tell the difference.'[16] Guinness, admittedly, has always been regarded as the exception which proves the rule in the beer market – a drink which is very much an acquired taste achieving mass-market success. But the majority of Guinness-drinkers take it too for its image, not its taste. This is perhaps fortunate, since it is becoming increasingly difficult to find unpasteurized Guinness – look for the returnable bottles – in English off-licences, though it can still be found in many English pubs.

There is a very good reason why the majority of lagers and champagnes are not merely indistinguishable from each other, but lack any noticeable characteristics at all beyond being cold, fizzy and alcoholic. The successful mass marketing of any product depends, even more than the product's having a usp, on its not being objectionable. An excellent product with an appealing usp is unlikely to succeed if it has a definite flavour. This will only put off some consumers who would otherwise have bought the product because it suited their self-image, and will certainly not win any more consumers, as those who find it suits their self-image will buy it anyway. It is often said that if Guinness were to attempt to launch their stout on the market today, they would fail miserably.

A product is made non-objectionable by making it bland. When a *Sunday Times* journalist asked one of the brewers of Harp Lager in 1974 to explain its success, the brewer replied, 'It's not so much what you can say for it. It's just that there's not much you can say against it.'[17]

[1] John Gordon and Associates for Stowells of Chelsea, 1985. In this context 'specialist off-licence' includes both specialist wine merchants and branches of off-licence chains.
[2] Qualitative Research and Planning of Greenwich for Food and Wine from France, 1984. Admittedly only ninety-three people took part in the group discussions!

³ J. Rathgeb, quoted in Francesca M. Wilson (ed.), *Strange Island: Britain through foreign eyes 1395–1940*, Longmans, Green & Co., 1955, p. 26.
⁴ *Decanter*, November 1982, p. 12.
⁵ *Sunday Times*, 4 December 1966, p. 8.
⁶ David Sills, address to the Symposium on Historic Appellations of Origin, held in Jerez in 1987.
⁷ *Decanter*, July 1985, p. 25.
⁸ Alan Westray of Espavino, quoted in *Wine and Spirit*, August 1985, p. 49.
⁹ Quoted in *Wine and Spirit*, January 1986, p. 61.
¹⁰ Advertising Association, *Public Attitudes to Advertising*, 1976.
¹¹ Forbes, p. 157.
¹² See Tom Stevenson, *Champagne*, Sotheby's Publications, 1986, pp. 192–3.
¹³ Charles Tovey, *Wine Revelations*, c.1881, pp. 32–9.
¹⁴ Quoted in *Decanter*, July 1987, p. 37.
¹⁵ Quoted in *Brewers' Guardian*, July 1986, p. 7.
¹⁶ Quoted in *What's Brewing*, April 1986, p. 1.
¹⁷ Quoted in Roger Protz, *Pulling a Fast One: What the brewers have done to your beer*, The Pluto Press, 1976, pp. 61–7.

7

WINE-TASTINGS ARE BUNK

Comparative blind tastings are frequently held and published by newspapers and magazines, as an alternative to relying on the prejudiced and often ill-informed views of wine writers and merchants. 'Blind' means that the tasters do not know what the wines are until they have tasted them. This is essential to avoid prejudice, in precisely the same way as the criminal record of an accused person is not made known to the court until after judgment has been passed. Just as more serious crimes are judged by the consensus of a jury, so are panels of tasters convened in order to judge wines in a blind tasting. The difference is that, for tastings, experts are used. The results of a tasting appear more authoritative if they appear to be the consequence of the deliberations of a committee, especially if a number of eminent members of the trade bearing the letters MW (Master of Wine) after their names can be shown to have attended. In fact they can be depended upon with even less confidence than the decision of an untrained jury.

Many of the experts are prejudiced. They tend to be merchants or importers commercially involved in the wines of a particular region. The wines they are called upon to judge will almost always include some which they sell. One of the basic principles of what lawyers call 'natural justice'[1] is that no man should be a judge in his own case. Of course, the tasting being blind, they will probably not know which their own wines are; and there are many instances of experts marking their own wines down in tastings. They will, however, impose their own prejudices, based on a predilection for the wines in which they are commercially involved. When *Decanter* magazine held a blind tasting of 1980 and 1982 vintage ports, to try to establish which was the better vintage, those tasters whose houses had declared the 1980s preferred the 1980s, and those whose houses had declared the 1982s preferred the 1982s.

Tasting is entirely a matter of personal preference. Most tasters would give a higher mark to a champagne with a 'good yeasty nose' than to one without. But Moët's oenologist Edmond Maudière says that 'If a champagne does have a yeasty nose, it's a defect. It results from having too many generations of yeast cells develop in the bottle.'[2] Would he be wrong to mark a champagne down for having a yeasty nose? Of all wines, perhaps red burgundy is the one over which experts most consistently disagree. I wonder how a panel convened to compare 1983 red burgundies, and including in their number both the wine writer Clive Coates and the wine importer Joseph Berkmann, both acknowledged authorities on the region, would judge Alain Hudelot-Noëllat's Chambolle-Musigny. Having tasted the wine on the same occasion, just after it was bottled and shipped, Clive Coates described it as 'clean, stylish, concentrated and balanced', whereas Joseph Berkmann, who was meant to be trying to sell it, wrote that it was 'a weak little wine, governed by a taste of rot'. Tasting by committee seeks to perform the impossible by aggregrating personal preferences.

I would always prefer to read one man's views on a particular wine than those of a committee. One man may be biased – but he says what he thinks. Moreover, just as consumers learn to judge a film review according to the tastes of a reviewer, and may perfectly well go to a film because Dilys Powell did not like it, or avoid a film to which Derek Malcolm has given a good write-up, so, in the world of wine writing, it is possible to come to understand the prejudices of one taster. For example, Robert Parker's taste in red burgundies is for big, rich wines, such as those made by Jean-Marie Ponsot in Morey-Saint-Denis, and among ports he likes the soft, fleshy style of Fonseca. He freely admits that he is obsessed with young wine – with fruit – and for this reason he doesn't go to tastings of old wines. Knowing his predilections, one can judge his comments accordingly. For all their foibles, Robert Parker and Clive Coates deserve far more attention for what they have to say than do the views of one-off committees convened to hold comparative tastings.

Not only does judgement by consensus seek to sum up personal preferences, it groups together decisions which are made on wholly different criteria. Does one judge a wine according to its typicalness or its individuality? Should one expect the character of the vintage to dominate the style of the house, or vice versa? In a tasting of 1984 clarets, should one prefer those wines which taste more austere and more predominantly of Cabernet Sauvignon than usual because their Merlot crop failed, or those wines which have been produced to conform to a house-style, either by rejecting a significant proportion of Cabernet Sauvignon from the final blend or by including some Merlot from the previous vintage? In a tasting of 1983 white burgundies, does one rate more highly those wines which have overcome the unusually hot weather conditions of the vintage and emerged as characteristically lean and stylish, or those which have sought to express the particular character of that year and ended up resembling Californian Chardonnays rather more than the usual run of white burgundies? What usually happens is that some experts choose one criterion, and some another. But these are subjective questions, and how they can be determined by a committee within the context of comparative blind tastings beats me.

A committee will never choose a wine of individuality to come top. Just as many people will hate it as love it. The same applies to choosing the best film at the Cannes Film Festival or the winner of the Booker Prize. The same, indeed, applies to the now historic failure of England's cricket selectors to pick Phil Edmonds. A committee chooses well-made mediocrities, and elevates blandness to the status of a virtue. For example, in *Wine* magazine's 1985 International Challenge, Gold Awards were awarded only to 'the most superlative wines in each tasting . . . wines had to be of the highest quality *and* to represent value for money'. Among the Gold Award winners in the Rhône section were Tesco's Châteauneuf-du-Pape les Arnevels, a pleasant and inexpensive but mediocre wine from 1982, the worst vintage in the region this decade. Among the also-rans was Château de Beaucastel 1981, a great wine and cheap for its quality. Whereas Sainsbury's Côte-Rôtie 1982 received a Gold Award, Cornas 1983 from Guy de Barjac and Hermitage 1983 from Gérard Chave, two of France's finest wines and at the time very much underpriced, came nowhere.[3]

Of course the problem in the *Wine* magazine tasting was that Château de Beaucastel, Guy de Barjac's Cornas and Gérard Chave's Hermitage were nowhere near ready for drinking. They had to be judged on potential, not, as they undoubtedly were, on actuality. The problem is that judging on potential is very difficult, particularly in a blind tasting, where you are having to compare a wine that is attractive now with one that tastes pretty disgusting. As Robin Yapp has written in the context of a tasting of immature vintages of Gérard Chave's Hermitage, which he imports, 'A good rule of thumb for aspirant wine merchants searching for good Rhône red wines is to remember that the nastier the stuff tastes when young, the better it is likely to be ten years later.'⁴ I wish 'experts' would realize this fact when they try tasting young top-class German wines. A cross-section of wine writers and members of the wine trade who tasted a range of twenty-six German wines under £5.50 for the April 1987 issue of *Which? Wine Monthly* managed to give bottom place to the best wines in the tasting; I refer to such underpriced splendours as Schlossböckelheimer Kupfergrube Riesling Kabinett 1985 from the Nahe State Domain, Oberemmeler Hütte Riesling Kabinett 1985 from von Hövel, and Forster Pechstein Riesling Kabinett 1985 from Bassermann-Jordan. If nonentities received higher marks than these wines it was because they were more ready to drink; but eighteen-month-old fine German wines should not be marked down simply because they require to be aged as long as classed-growth clarets.

Some wines which taste thoroughly unpleasant when young – at least to the palates of tasters who expect immediate gratification – turn out to be quite something. When Penfold's Grange Hermitage was first shown to tasters in 1957, it was commented that 'it tastes of crushed ants', and that 'it would make a good anaesthetic for my girlfriend'.⁵ A similar reception greeted Sassicaia, the prototype of modern Tuscan Cabernet Sauvignons, when first tried in the late 1940s. Both these wines are now accorded international acclaim.

Because the criterion in comparative blind tastings is – usually – actuality and not potential, wines whose commercial future depends on doing well in a tasting have to be made to be as forward as possible. In Australia wines sell at good prices only if they have been awarded medals at one of the sixteen wine shows – basically public comparative tastings – held each year. These are serious affairs, unlike some of their European equivalents, such as the wine fair whose jury one Portuguese merchant declined an offer to join when he was told that it was the policy to give an award to everyone who entered. In Australia many producers make wines in order to win medals: the classic example of this is the German expatriate Wolf Blass whose Cabernet-Shiraz Black Label unprecedentedly won the revered Jimmy Watson Trophy at the Melbourne Show in three successive years in 1974–6. He makes his wine in such a way that it will be close to its best when first sold at between three and five years of age. Like many other Australian wine-makers, in order to ensure that his wines are perfectly balanced as soon as they are released and offered for tasting, Wolf Blass blends together the produce of different regions of the country, in order to overcome the vagaries of the weather. He says that 'blending products together' – a skill which he learnt at Avery's in Bristol – 'is the art of wine-making'.[6] For their outstanding Chardonnay, Petaluma combine grapes from the Clare Valley with those from Coonawarra, 200 miles away – tantamount, in terms of distance, to blending Châteauneuf-du-Pape with burgundy. In 1984 Mitchelton Winery in Victoria bought grapes in Mount Barker in Western Australia and trucked them 2,000 miles across the Nullarbor desert.

It is largely because they mature sooner that Australian and Californian wines tend to beat those from Bordeaux and Burgundy in a blind tasting. Indeed, it was a blind comparative tasting of Californian wines against French which put them on the map, both in Europe and in America. Steven Spurrier had organized this tasting, in American Bicentennial Year, 1976, in order to gain publicity for his Paris wine shop, Caves de la Madeleine, and had rigged it so that the French wines would win: against Californian Cabernet Sauvignons he pitted first-growth clarets, and all the tasters were French.[7] In fact the Californian wines won, transforming public perception of their quality overnight. But making a wine to win tastings is quite different from making a wine that people will actually want to drink. Wines with high levels of acidity – as clarets and burgundies are, or at least historically were – tend to taste quite unpleasant when young, particularly if they are not taken with food. Yet it is the acidity which makes them digestible, and enables them to keep. It is unfair to compare Californian and French wines in a blind tasting. The former tend to be more alcoholic, richer, sweeter and lower in acidity; therefore they show more impressively in tastings. But if one sits down to eat, the French wine is almost certain to be finished first. Wines from different regions are made in different styles which simply cannot be compared. When the Spaniard Miguel Torres' Gran Coronas Black Label 1970 'beat' Château Latour 1970, Château La Mission Haut-Brion 1961 et al. in the 1979 Gaut-Millau 'Wine Olympics', the manager of Latour is supposed to have commented that, while the Torres wine might do 'for a bawdy night out', it was hardly the wine to serve 'for an elegant luncheon'.

Even if wines from the same region are tasted against one another, they cannot be judged if they come from different vintages. If wines developed at an even pace, this would be possible, but they don't. A young vintage will always show more flatteringly than one which is in the process of ageing but has not yet evolved. For this reason it is never possible to compare two port vintages which have been declared 'back to back', like 1982 and 1983. When I tasted them together when the 1983s were released in 1985, the 1983s all showed better – because they were younger. A comparative tasting of wines from different vintages is only possible if all the wines from all the vintages are fully mature; and this is never practicable, because not only particular wines but also individual bottles mature at different rates. If one is to compare wines from different vintages, it is essential to taste, not blind, but seen; for in that case one can judge the wine according to one's experience of its likely state of development.

Whatever comparisons a taster is trying to make, whatever criterion he has decided to apply, his job is frequently made much harder than it should be by his being asked to taste too many wines at once. I believe that the maximum number of wines which can be covered satisfactorily in a single session is about fifteen to twenty. Otherwise tasters have to taste so fast that they will be able to judge only on superficiality and not on complexity. The need to taste rapidly helps explain why tasters tend to give higher marks to the more obvious flavours of Californian Chardonnays and Cabernet Sauvignons than to more subtle white burgundies and clarets. Moreover, when too many wines are tasted at once, tasters are swayed by the order of tasting. If, in a sequence of fifty wines, no. 14 is fair, no. 15 good, no. 16 poor and no. 17 good, then no. 17 will probably receive a higher mark than no. 15 because it stands out so much from no. 16 and the taster does not have the time to return to no. 15 to compare it directly with no. 17. And fifty wines is not an unusual number to taste in one go. *Wine* magazine regularly includes between thirty and sixty wines, usually from the same region in various vintages, in a single tasting session.

The tasting of too many products at once may help explain the extraordinary results achieved by a tasting of olive oils held by the

Independent in the summer of 1987. A group of cookery experts, not professional olive-oil tasters, compared twenty-two oils, when in fact professional tasters say that they cannot manage more than five in a session. Top of the virgin and extra-virgin oils tasted came Safeway's own-label, which I personally find good and cheap but rather coarse; bottom came Badia a Coltibuono, which is not as good as it was and certainly not worth six times as much as the Safeway oil but nevertheless a far superior product.

Perhaps it does not matter how many wines are tasted in a session, since the same wine tastes differently on different occasions, partly because wine does vary from one bottle to another, particularly if it has not been filtered or pasteurized, partly because tasters vary from one day to another, and partly because of various other factors, such as the temperature of the room. There are a number of instances of the same group of tasters rating the same wines quite differently on separate occasions. Before Christmas 1984 both *Wine* (then *What Wine?*) and *Which? Wine Monthly* published results of comparative tastings of everyday ports. Two people took part in both tastings. Fonseca Bin 27, which was placed top of the *Which? Wine Monthly* tasting, came fifty-second out of seventy-nine ports tasted by *What Wine?* Churchill's Vintage Character, which was awarded two stars by the *What Wine?* panel, came third from bottom in the *Which? Wine Monthly* tasting. In the autumn of 1983 both *The Times* and *Which? Wine Monthly* published results of comparative tastings of non-vintage branded champagnes. Three people took part in both tastings. In *The Times* tasting, the Peter Dominic brand Lambert came bottom, and Piper-Heidsieck second bottom. In the *Which? Wine Monthly* tasting, Lambert came top and Piper-Heidsieck second from top.

But then there is another reason for the enormous variation in the results of tastings of non-vintage champagnes – so great that almost every house is able to boast of its success in one tasting or another. It all depends on who provides the samples. The question of bottle age is crucial in any tasting of non-vintage champagnes. Mediocre wines which have spent a year longer in bottle will tend to be rated more highly than better wines which are still a bit green. This is fair enough, since most people buy champagne for immediate consumption, not for laying down. However, it does mean that the results of tastings of champagnes which depend on samples sent in by importers can easily be manipulated. A canny importer will keep a special case of well-aged non-vintage champagne specifically for the purpose of sending out for tastings. Bollinger is an excellent champagne, but it needs longer ageing than most. In 1985 Liz and Mike Berry, owners of La Vigneronne, gave up selling it on the grounds that it was being sold too young. A sales representative from Bollinger's importers visited the shop, noticed the absence of his company's product, and insisted that the Berrys came round to the office for a tasting. On the way, they stopped at an off-licence and bought a bottle of Bollinger. In the ensuing blind tasting, everyone liked the sales representative's nicely matured sample, and disliked the very green wine the Berrys had bought in the off-licence.

Dependence on samples sent in by importers prejudices the results of many a comparative tasting. In June 1985 *Decanter* magazine published the results of a tasting they had held of white burgundies from Meursault and red burgundies from Gevrey-Chambertin. The intention behind the tastings had not been to taste as many wines as possible and select the best of each village, but to get an idea of the overall standard. Fifteen wines were tasted. The tasters were neither excited nor disappointed. But then – among the Meursaults at least – they did not taste the best wines of the *appellation*: no Domaine des Comtes Lafon, no François Jobard, no Jean-François Coche (Dury). A good but scarcely outstanding merchant's blend, Sélection Jean Germain 1981, came top. Two years later *Decanter* held another Meursault tasting, this time with the intention of '[looking] for the best that Meursault has to offer'. Well, someone did not look very hard. Certainly they tasted more wines, forty-two this time; and they chose not one top wine, but thirteen. But, once again, no Domaine des Comtes Lafon, no François Jobard, no Jean-François Coche(-Dury). How can *Decanter* defend its reliance on free samples being sent? As a result, its attempt to look for 'the best that Meursault has to offer' included as many merchants' blends as wines from single estates. The former are commercial wines, which the producers want to sell; whereas the best estates have to fight off buyers, and therefore do not need to send samples. But *Decanter* could have included wines from the missing growers if they had spent £40. Their wines are all available in Britain.

This said, comparative blind tastings can be very useful. They can demonstrate, for example, that expert tasters cannot tell malt whisky from cognac. In 1977 *Decanter* staged a blind tasting of malt whiskies and cognacs, with seventeen tasters representing whisky distillers and cognac shippers. Only five of the tasters succeeded in identifying in every case which were the malt whiskies and which the cognacs. On another occasion it was found that tasters – admittedly not experts – could not tell malt from blended whisky. In 1983 two surgeons at St Mary's Hospital, Paddington, asked eight members of their unit to try to distinguish, blindfold, between six whiskies, of which three were malts and three were blends. Four of the tasters were regular, experienced whisky drinkers; the other four were not. However, they all came out with much the same results. Despite – or perhaps because of – trying each sample several times, they were about 50–60 per cent successful in distinguishing malt from blended whisky.[8]

As in the case of malt whisky, so in the case of champagne, blind tastings have served to demonstrate that higher prices mean a more exclusive image, not a better product. In November 1985 Channel 4's *The Wine Programme* set up a tasting of most of the champagnes widely available in this country, and placed Sainsbury's own-label (then £6.45) second, ahead of all the well-known *grandes marques* at twice the price, with the exception of Krug, which cost four times as much. In their July 1987 issue *Decanter* published the results of a tasting of forty-two *blanc de blancs* champagnes; that is, champagnes made 100 per cent from the white Chardonnay grape rather than, as usual, from a blend of Chardonnay with the black grapes Pinot Noir and Pinot Meunier. The panel recommended sixteen wines, ranging in price from £9–19. They tasted the champagnes blind, with regard solely to quality, and without regard to price. Neither Krug's Clos du Mesnil (£60 a bottle) nor Taittinger's Comtes de Champagne (£35) was thought good enough to recommend. Top of the tasting came Waitrose's own-label, 1982 vintage, at one-seventh the price of Clos du Mesnil.

Blind tastings have often demonstrated champagne to be a rip-off, though we are not allowed to say so. After all, the champagne industry took Sainsbury's to court for stating, in the advertisement for their own-label sparkling Saumur, that 'at a recent [sic] *Sunday Times* wine-tasting even an expert was fooled'. Robin Young, who organized the tasting, was invited by the Champenois to give evidence in the court case. His evidence would not have favoured them. He had sorted out some other tastings in which other experts had identified various champagnes as 'cheap German sparkler', 'essence of boiled sweets with fizz', and 'inferior *vin mousseux*'. In fact Sainsbury's caved in and the case never came to court. As Allan Cheesman, the head of Sainsbury's wine department, was heard to remark on this occasion, 'All publicity is good publicity, as far as sales volumes are concerned.'[9]

Whisky and champagne are perhaps exceptions: tastings are the right context in which to judge them, because they are intended to be drunk on their own. Most wine, however, is supposed to be taken with food. Tasted with food, it cannot be spat out: it must be swallowed. In such circumstances it is not really possible to taste more than five or six wines at any one time. Thus, if this principle were carried into practice, those members of the wine trade who regularly taste between thirty and fifty wines a day ought, in theory, to eat eight dinners a day. Most of them are fat enough as it is, not to mention the state of their livers. However, this is an argument which appears to be favoured by M. Delmas, the manager of the Bordeaux first growth Château Haut-Brion. When told by someone who had drunk Château Haut-Brion with Château Lafite that he had found the Lafite rather better, M. Delmas simply replied that he had made the Haut-Brion to be drunk with meals, not with Château Lafite.[10]

---

[1] A technical term, which does not mean what we imagine natural justice to mean.
[2] Quoted in *Decanter*, July 1985, p. 31.
[3] *Wine*, January 1986, pp. 15–27.
[4] *Decanter*, September 1983, p. 35.
[5] Quoted in Jancis Robinson, *The Great Wine Book*, Sidgwick & Jackson, 1982, p. 231.
[6] *Wine and Spirit*, August 1987, p. 49.
[7] Loftus, p. 120.
[8] Stephen Chadwick and Hugh Dudley, 'Can Malt Be Discriminated from Blended Whisky?' in *British Medical Journal*, 24–31 December 1983.
[9] *Wine and Spirit*, May 1984, p. 78.
[10] I am indebted for this story to the wine merchant Joseph Berkmann.

PART TWO

INTRODUCTION:
ART AND AGRICULTURE

The second part of this book is concerned with the response of producers to those consumer demands which have been described in the first part. This is not the usual way of looking at wine production. Marketing – finding out what the consumer wants, and then giving it to him – is a dirty word in the wine trade, whose members tend to regard wine as a production- rather than a market-led commodity, as something whose intrinsic character cannot be altered to suit the demands of the market. Consumers are offered wine on a take-it-or-leave-it basis. They are not given the option of asking for what they want.

Certainly, such an enormous variety of wine is made that there is quite likely to be something for every taste. Certainly, wine appears, and is said, to be an agricultural product, dependent on the vagaries of the climate, and to differ in this respect from such manufactured drinks products as beer or whisky or gin. Even the supermarkets and big retailers, however great their buying power, are by and large unwilling to instruct wine-makers what to produce – though there have been exceptions. Five years ago, on an occasion now legendary in the wine trade, Angela Muir, wine buyer for Grant's of St James's, marched down to La Mancha in central Spain and told Protasio Rodriguez, the supplier of their Don Cortez brand, that, 'with very little effort, you could turn this product from a thoroughly bad to a pleasant one'. Very little effort – but a lot of money. She persuaded him to spend £500,000 on installing equipment to permit temperature-controlled fermentation, which has revolutionized the white Don Cortez.

But *is* wine an agricultural product? The agricultural product is grapes, not wine, which is a processed food product, like bread. Fermentation, in which yeasts excrete alcohol as a by-product of their growth, and accidentally cause grape-juice to be converted into wine, is a process of controlled decay, and the character of the wine is determined by the way in which control over the decay is exercised. The most important person, the wine-maker, did not, in many cases, grow the grapes himself.

Wine production has always been market-led. In the late Middle Ages, the greatest of French wines was red burgundy, which growers in other regions tried to copy by planting the Burgundy grape, Pinot Noir. Champagne, however, enjoys a colder climate than Burgundy, so the Pinot Noir grapes planted there did not ripen fully: the resulting wine was pink, not red. The young aristocrats who owned vineyards in Champagne succeeded in persuading the French court that pink wine was the thing to drink. By the early eighteenth century the tables had been turned, and growers in Burgundy were trying to copy champagne, devising various means of obtaining less colour in their wines. They interplanted white grape vines among the black grape vineyards, and placed alternate layers of straw and grapes on the press, in order to prevent too much red colour from being taken up from the skins during the pressing process.[1]

This transformation was repeated recently by Californian wine-makers, using the Zinfandel grape. A large number of Zinfandel vines were planted in California during the early 1970s, in anticipation of a boom in red wine drinking to coincide with an increased interest in food. However, by the time these vines came into production three years later, fashion had swung round, and what people wanted was white, not red, wine. To turn a vine from the production of red to the production of white grapes of similar quality and in equal quantity by field-grafting would have taken five years. Californian wine-makers refused to be fazed by this surfeit of black grapes. They simply vinified the black grapes as though they were white ones, separating the must as soon as possible from the skins of the grapes. Unfortunately the resultant wines were just as much a failure as eighteenth-century Champenois copies of red burgundy: they were pink, not white – and pink wines were even more unfashionable than red. The wine-makers remained unfazed. They rechristened these pink wines 'Blush Wines' and, despite the generally disappointing taste of the end product, a new boom was born. Still, it shows that, even today, the forces of nature cannot entirely be overcome. The following chapters look at how far producers are able to succeed in overcoming nature's desire to ensure that wine is a predominantly agricultural product.

[1] Claude Arnoux, *Dissertation sur la situation de Bourgogne*, 1728.

A KIND OF MAKE-UP

Our fundamental taste is a liking for sweetness. With wine, this has not always been easy to supply.

Much is made of the phenomenon of noble rot, to which are attributed the world's most celebrated sweet wines, those of Sauternes and the Auslesen, Beerenauslesen and Trockenbeeren-auslesen of Germany. Noble rot is well publicized, because it makes a good story. The grapes look decidedly unpleasant: when, in 1967, American federal inspectors found Louis Martini processing Semillon grapes affected by noble rot at his winery in California, they ordered them to be destroyed as unfit to be made into wine – American law stipulates that any wine that is offered for sale must be made fom 'clean' and 'healthy' grapes.[1] Noble rot is produced by the action of the same fungus, *botrytis cinerea*, which causes grey rot, destroying the aromatic substances contained in the grape-skins, imparting an unpleasant taste of its own, and causing the wine made from the affected grapes to oxidize. But, given suitable climatic conditions at the end of the growing season, with mists in the morning and sunshine in the afternoon, as is common in the autumn in the Sauternes region because of the interaction of the cold, spring-fed River Ciron with the warmer River Garonne, botrytis proves beneficial, and contributes a unique taste to a wine, by degrading tartaric acid into glycerine and gluconic acid and secreting a number of other substances which have not yet been identified.

The 'discovery' of noble rot is a romantic and frequently retold story. Schloss Johannisberg was owned in the eighteenth century by the Bishop of Fulda, whose permission was needed before the harvest could begin. In 1775, as the grapes were reaching ripeness, a messenger was sent from the estate to Fulda, 100 miles away, but for some reason his return was delayed by a matter of weeks. In the meantime the grapes had become affected with noble rot. This story may or may not be true, but it is hardly unique. The use of nobly rotten grapes in the production of Tokay is supposed to have been 'discovered' a century earlier, when Prince Rákóczi, the ruler of Transylvania, delayed the harvest on his estate at Oremui until late November, because a war was going on. Doubtless the miracle of nobly rotten grapes was known earlier still. Knowledge of their properties was allegedly not brought to Sauternes from Germany until the 1830s. If so, then what were the *vins pourris* (rotten wines) for which Sauternes was already esteemed in the seventeenth century?

Until recently, nobly rotten wines could not be produced to demand. Producers in Sauternes and the Rhine valley simply waited and hoped for suitable climatic conditions. But in California in the 1950s, Alice and Myron Nightingale, who now make wine for Beringer, believing that Californian conditions were not suitable for the natural development of noble rot, devised a method of inducing it artificially indoors, after the grapes had been picked. Their method today is to lay bunches of grapes in trays, spray on the botrytis spores, wrap the bunches in plastic, and blow alternate blasts of warm and cool air over them for two weeks, in order to replicate the alternate conditions of mist and sun in the vineyard.[2] Admittedly, scientists do not as yet understand the biochemical effects of botrytis sufficiently well to be able to outperform nature. But, even if they did, would conservative European wine-makers ever embrace a practice which runs counter to their insistence that the superiority of their produce derives from the particular autumn weather they enjoy?

It is often said that one of the advantages of botrytis is that it contains an antibiotic called botrycine which causes the wine to stop fermenting when it has reached between 13 and 14 per cent alcohol, leaving some unfermented sugar in the wine. But naturally occurring German wine yeasts are in any case incapable of fermenting a wine beyond 13.5 per cent alcohol. If the must is very sweet, yeasts find great difficulty in working, which is why German Beerenauslesen and Trockenbeerenauslesen usually contain only about 8.5 per cent alcohol. So much for botrycine, whose antibiotic properties would scarcely appear to be esteemed very highly by the Sauternais, judging from the amount of sulphur many of them add to their wines to prevent them from re-fermenting in bottle. Apart from contributing a special taste which not everyone likes, noble rot is simply a means of concentrating the sugar content of the grapes by causing the water in them to evaporate, an effect which could equally well be achieved by letting the grapes overripen on the vines, or by drying or freezing them.

Sauternes, Auslesen, Beerenauslesen and Trockenbeerenauslesen are not necessarily made from nobly rotten grapes. Usually only a certain proportion of the grapes is affected with botrytis, and sometimes none at all. The new German wine law of 1971 introduced a provision that Beerenauslesen and Trockenbeerenauslesen could be made from grapes which were merely overripe, and not nobly rotten, in order to cover the produce of very warm autumns, such as 1959, in which the requisite conditions for the development of noble rot did not occur. 1983 was a similar year. I cannot recall having tasted any 1983 Auslesen which tasted of botrytis other than the great Fritz Haag's Brauneberger Juffer-Sonnenhur Gold Capsule, from the Middle Mosel. Those 1983 Auslesen which do not taste of noble rot are no worse for its absence. Largely because they can be made in years in which noble rot does not occur, Eisweine have recently become very fashionable among German vine growers. They are produced by allowing the grapes to dry on the vines, and then picking them as soon as they freeze. The grower picks the grapes at 4 o'clock on the first winter morning on which the temperature has dropped to –7°C or below. In the Mosel in 1986, that happened to be Christmas morning. One cannot help wondering why growers do not harvest the grapes in more clement conditions and then freeze them in their cellars, as Sauternes producers are beginning to do with grapes which have been diluted by rain. Indeed, why freeze the grapes at all? In Jurançon in south-west France, grapes are allowed to dry on the vines but are picked at the end of the autumn, in November, not in the depths of winter. The absence of frost does not prevent some outstanding wines from being produced under this *appellation*, not least by Jean Chige at Cru Lamouroux. Eisweine are produced because they are thought to be prestigious, rather than as an economic proposition – or even because they taste particularly good. I have tasted some very concentrated young Eisweine, but no one has any idea how they will turn out when mature. In his book on dessert wines, *Liquid Gold*, Stephen Brook says that 'many Eisweine strike me as overaggressive and one-dimensional.'³ We shall have to wait until well into next century to find out how they develop.

Though they owe nothing to modern technology (other than alarm clocks), the deliberate production of Eisweine is a recent innovation. Rather than resort to such an elaborate procedure, for many centuries vine growers have found drying the grapes after picking to be the most effective means of concentrating their sugar content in order to produce sweet wine from them. This method was certainly used by both the Greeks and Romans, but it predates them. It is still very widely employed in Italy, where the wines thus made are described as *passiti*, except in Valpolicella and Soave, where the term *recioto* is used. Muscat (*Moscato* in Italian) is one of the varieties treated in this way, and the wonderful Moscato *passito* made in Strevi in Piedmont by Domenico Ivaldi is a lamentable reminder of how the best French Muscat wines used to taste when they were made by this method. *Passiti* wines, however, are made from all sorts of grape varieties: I have even tasted a really good *passito* Pinot Noir from Umbria. They are also made dry as well as sweet. In the case of *recioti* Valpolicella, the dry version is probably superior; in the case of the little-known but not inferior Sagrantino di Montefalco *passito*, both are equally good. The best examples I have tried are those made by Fratelli Adanti in Perugia, which they sell under the name Sagrantino d'Arquata.

All these *passiti* wines are expensive. From a commercial point of view, the drawback of drying grapes lies in a 50 per cent loss in bulk as a result of evaporation. That is why Domenico Ivaldi's Moscato *passito* costs twice as much as the best Muscat de Beaumes-de-Venise, that of Domaine des Bernardins. It was by drying grapes on straw mats that Muscat de Beaumes-de-Venise used to be made last century. But when the wine was granted its *appellation contrôlée* in 1945, one of the conditions was that it must achieve a minimum of 21.5 per cent 'total' alcohol (the result of adding together the fermented and unfermented sugar contents). To be sure of achieving this level, the wines had to be fortified like port – and that is how they are made today. Fermentation is usually stopped when the wine has reached an alcohol content of 15 per cent, leaving about 110 grams per litre of residual sugar.

Stopping fermentation with alcohol is suited, however, only to such substantial wines as port and the various Muscat wines of the

South of France. The most effective and economical means of sweetening more delicate wines is to add sugar. Surprisingly, this method does not enjoy a very long history. Until the sugar-beet industry took off in the 1840s, sugar was neither readily available nor inexpensive on the Continent of Europe. In England it was a different matter – we had our West Indian colonies – and in the seventeenth century travellers noticed that English gentlemen added sugar to their wine, something which they had not seen being done anywhere else. So well established was the taste for sugared wine that in taverns wines were mixed with sugar in the cask.[4] If sugar was unavailable 'sugar of lead' was sometimes used instead. This was lead oxide (litharge), which produces lead acetate, a fungicide, in the wine; it kills cells and is therefore poisonous. In Nancy, in 1696, wine sweetened with litharge caused the death by convulsion of more than fifty people. The merchants concerned were prosecuted, but only one was fined.

Following the introduction of beet-sugar, liquid sugar – a solution of sugar in water – began to be used in Germany in order to improve Mosel wines from poor vintages in the 1840s and 1850s. This practice was disapproved of by Rhine growers, who did not have the same problems. In 1886 the legality of liquid sugar was tested in the courts when a vine grower in the Mosel was charged with adulteration. He defended himself by claiming that he had done no more than any other grower in the Mosel. As a result of this case it was accepted that Mosel growers might reasonably add sugared water up to a quarter of the volume of the wine; this permission was eventually overturned by the new German wine laws of 1971. By then producers had adopted another method of sweetening; the addition of unfermented, or partly fermented, grape-juice (Süssreserve) to a finished wine.

Sweetening a wine with Süssreserve is not a new method, though some authorities have reacted to it as though it is. In their book on the Mosel, published in 1972, Otto Loeb and Terence Prittie describe the method of sweetening wine with Süssreserve as 'highly suspect. Unlike the discriminating addition of sugar, [Süssreserve] can change the intrinsic nature of the wine and reduce [its] alcoholic strength. The growers who made use of [Süssreserve] in the early years after the Second World War were well aware of the dangers. They kept quiet, even though they were not breaking any wine-laws.'[5] In the eighteenth century the pioneers of stopping the fermentation of port by adding brandy had kept quiet too, for at the time this was considered to be highly suspect. In a famous exchange of letters in 1754, English wine merchants resident in Oporto wrote to their agents up the Douro valley to complain of the growers' 'diabolical' practice of adding brandy to the wine before it had finished fermenting; they had no objection to the addition of brandy *after* fermentation. Their agents replied that they only fortified the ports they sent them because 'the English merchants wished the wine to exceed the limits which Nature had assigned to it, and that when drunk, it . . . should be like the sugar of Brazil in sweetness. . .'.[6]

Both stopping fermentation with brandy and sweetening a wine with Süssreserve in fact enjoy a long history. When ports were first being fortified during fermentation – a practice which did not become general until the nineteenth century – this method had already been common in France for the production of sweet white wines, *Vins des Liqueurs*, for more than fifty years.[7] The term *Vin des Liqueurs* was also in the seventeenth century applied to unfermented grape-must, that is to say Süssreserve, which was then drunk straight. Under the name of Rhenish in the Must, it was very popular with English women and children[8] – but it did not necessarily come from Germany. Most of the wine sold in England as Rhenish in the Must was in fact cheap table wine from the Cognac region, to which sugar or honey had been added, and sometimes essence of clary seeds, in order 'to give this mixture a delicate flavour'.[9] The real thing was difficult to make. Unfermented grape-must was prevented from fermenting by being put in a cask which was pitched on the inside, or in which sulphur matches had been burned, or which had, we are told, been rubbed on the inside with cheese. The cask was then sealed and the must chilled by placing the vessel in a well or river for a month; the must then kept fresh for a year or more. Increasingly it was not drunk on its own but added by wine merchants to tired wines or to the acidic produce of poor vintages, sometimes causing the wine thus treated to re-ferment.[10] In the mid-nineteenth century a large business developed in the South of France involving the production of unfermented grape-must for export to the Rheingau, where merchants 'used it to great advantage in the manufacture of their wine'.[11] No wonder they did not express the same need for beet-sugar as producers in the Mosel.

So why did Süssreserve hit the market with such a shock after the Second World War? In part, it was a matter of technology. The then-celebrated Seitz factory at Bad Kreuznach developed filters which were fine enough to remove yeasts, thus ensuring that the addition of Süssreserve to a wine before bottling did not cause it to re-ferment. But the revolution in its use was impelled by demand from a new generation of wine-drinkers, first from American soldiers occupying Germany after the war, then from all those people who took up wine-drinking for the first time, and wanted an inexpensive sweet wine that was low in alcohol. It is easy to deride wines such as Liebfraumilch, but they have contributed substantially to the wine boom in Britain. Today 30 per cent of the wines we drink are German, two-thirds of them Liebfraumilch.

Süssreserve was necessary because, naturally and traditionally, the majority of German wines were dry. This fact surprises the majority of wine-drinkers. I must admit that, when I visited the Mosel in 1985 I did not at that time believe those producers who assured me that, before the war, German wines were dry. To a certain degree, they *are* trying to mislead us. They have invented a tradition, in order to justify their recent conversion to the production of dry wines in order to satisfy the demands of the home market. They also want to overturn the down-market image of German wines in Britain as inexpensive sweet wines for novice drinkers. The American wine merchant Peter M. F. Sichel, who remembers tasting German wines before the war, says that they were no drier than they are today. He says that the idea that German wines used to be dry has been propounded in order to give a historical underpinning to the creation of dry German wines intended to accompany food.[12] Some wine-makers agree with him. According to Manfred Voepel, the chief wine-maker for Deinhard, in reference to the group of leading Rheingau producers who have formed the Association of Charta Estates in order to promote the consumption of dry German wines with food, 'Charta is not an old style; it is a new invention.' Though these new dry wines have proved very successful in Germany, they have not taken off in Britain, where they are frequently condemned as 'doughnut' wines – ones with no body in the middle. It was rash of the most forceful exponent of this style, Erwin Graf Matuschka-Griffenclau of Schloss Vollrads in the Rheingau, to have forecast in 1981 that by 1986 almost all the wine produced in Germany would be dry.[13]

Historically, however, German wines *were* dry. If consumers wanted to drink them sweet, they had to add sugar. In his *London Journal* Boswell describes a supper in July 1763 at which 'every man drank his bottle of Rhenish with sugar'.[14] Early last century the pioneers of modern wine writing, Cyrus Redding and Alexander Henderson, stated that German wines were dry. Redding said that they averaged 12 per cent alcohol, much the same as dry Auslesen today.[15] Henderson said that 'in general [the wines of the Rhine] are drier than the French white wines'.[16] The same could be said of dry (*trocken*) German wines made today – they appear to be drier than French wines, in part because they contain less glycerine, which is a by-product of the malolactic fermentation which white burgundies usually undergo but German wines do not. Not only were German wines dry in the 1820s, but most of them remained so until the 1960s. As late as 1964, the English wine merchant Allan Sichel wrote that 'The majority of German wines are dry or medium dry and can be drunk throughout the whole meal with pleasure.'[17] In that sense, Charta and similar wines are not a new invention but a return to tradition after the fad of a generation. If sweet wines have held sway for a while, it is partly because the development of the modern form of Süssreserve brought what had once been rare and expensive wines within the reach of ordinary consumers for the first time, and partly because the new German wine law of 1971, by laying down the minimum potential alcohol content for Spätlesen and Auslesen, has encouraged producers to make sweet wines bearing these names from *any* grapes which attain the requisite potential alcohol content. In the past they might well have allowed these grapes to ferment out naturally, and restricted their use of the term Spätlese to the produce of genuinely late-picked grapes, and of Auslese to wine made from the ripest bunches.

There is no reason why Auslesen should necessarily be sweet. The only legal criteria for their manufacture are that all the grapes used must be fully ripe and that they must contain at least enough sugar to produce a wine of between 10.4 per cent (for Riesling in the Mosel) and 12.5 per cent (for grapes other than Riesling in the Rheingau). The upper figure is a normal strength for French dry wines. The purpose behind the introduction of the selective picking of grapes in order to produce Auslesen in the second half of last century was not to produce wines with a residual sugar content, but to produce wines which were low in acidity. Writing at that time, Johann Thudichum and August Dupré described the growth of selective picking of grapes in order to produce Auslese wines as a recent advance which had made it possible to produce wines for drinking younger than thitherto.[18] A similar explanation lay behind the development of sweet wines using Süssreserve in the 1950s and 1960s. People wanted wines which could be drunk young. Allan Sichel said that, if the wines of the Rheingau were not as good as in the past, it was because they were being made 'less austere and less dry than they used to be, in the attempt to meet the heavy demand from the public for younger and fresher wines'.[19]

In the past, Auslesen were not necessarily intended to be sweet, but they often turned out that way. When they did, they were looked upon as something abnormal. Ernst Loosen, wine-maker at Weingut St Johannishof in Bernkastel in the Middle Mosel, says that his grandfather would have thought it a fault deliberately to make sweet wines. Thudichum and Dupré wrote that an Auslese 'easily loses the character of Rhine wine, and becomes a sweet, liquorous product, resembling Muscat or Sauternes'.[20]

There are a number of reasons why an Auslese should have turned out sweet. According to Bernhard Breuer, who makes some excellent dry wines at his estate (Weingut Georg Breuer) in Rüdesheim in the Rheingau, the term Auslese historically applied to wines which were sweet because they had stopped fermenting by accident. Fermentation was brought to a halt by the failure of yeasts to work properly, by the onset of an exceptionally cold winter, or by a barrel catching cold from being placed too close to the cellar door. Auslesen were thus, he says, the produce of selected barrels rather than of selected, fully ripe grapes.[21]

It is true that before the war individual barrels of the best German wines were bottled separately, rather than being 'equalized' by blending them together, as has always been the practice in, say, Bordeaux. The barrels often differed significantly from each other, and doubtless some Auslesen were sweeter than others. Certainly there is a difference in sweetness today between the barrels of Auslesen which are still bottled separately by some of the best producers in the Mosel-Saar-Ruwer, such as Forstmeister Geltz in Saarburg – but then the wine-maker here, Hans-Joachim Zilliken, stops fermentation in individual barrels at different stages. Bernhard Breuer is wrong, however, to deny that, before the war, the term Auslese applied to the selection of bunches of fully ripe grapes.

Auslesen sometimes ended up sweet because, depending on the temperature of the cellar, German wines stop fermenting at anything between 10 and 13.5 per cent alcohol. If some unfermented sugar remains in the must, then the wine is sweet. It is possible to ferment a German wine beyond 13.5 per cent alcohol, but only by using yeasts imported from France. Weingut Carl Finkenauer in the Nahe have succeeded in producing a dry Beerenauslese, but apparently it had too much alcohol – it must have been over 15 per cent – to be in balance. I am intrigued to know how the Wehlener Sonnenhur Trockenbeerenauslese 1959 which Michael Broadbent recorded in his *Great Vintage Wine Book* he had tasted in 1965 could possibly have reached the 20 per cent alcohol he mentions. Unfortunately he failed to note either the name of the grower or how the wine tasted.[22]

Whereas Auslesen are made from selectively picked bunches of grapes, Beerenauslesen and Trockenbeerenauslesen are produced from selectively picked, individual grapes (*Beere* means 'berry'). The musts are so high in sugar that yeasts find it very hard to work, and exhaust themselves easily. Beerenauslesen and Trockenbeerenauslesen have on occasions refused stubbornly to ferment at all, and often ferment very slowly. Most wines usually take about a week to ferment, but in 1959 the celebrated estate of J. J. Prüm at Wehlen on the Middle Mosel made a Trockenbeerenauslese which went on fermenting for two years. Normally a Beerenauslese will contain between 100 and 150 grams per litre of residual sugar, and about 8.5 per cent alcohol. This phenomenon of a naturally sweet, low-alcohol wine continued to amaze wine connoisseurs even as late as the 1950s when the popular explanation of why they had stopped fermenting was the vague assertion that 'the sugar and alcohol have "balanced" each other'.[23]

Such a 'balancing' act, however, only occurs in the produce of exceptionally warm vintages. Today, below the heights of Beerenauslesen and Trockenbeerenauslesen, it is the wine-maker who 'balances' the wine, in one of two ways. Either he allows the wine to ferment out naturally, and then adds Süssreserve – as is the most general practice in the Rhine valley – or he stops fermentation. The latter is the most common method of producing sweet wines in the Mosel, where there is a demand for delicate wines low in alcohol. Fermentation can be halted in one of a number of ways. Some less sophisticated producers simply add large amounts of sulphur, which causes the wine to stink in its youth and forces the purchaser to keep it for many years before drinking it, while waiting for the sulphur to wear off. This method, though 'old-fashioned' in conception, is quite a recent development: in his book on German wines, published in 1951, Alfred Langenbach discusses the preservative action of sulphur in detail but makes no mention of its use to stop fermentation.[24] More advanced wine-makers stop fermentation by centrifuging or filtering out the yeasts: it is sometimes suggested that these procedures diminish a wine's potential quality. When, in the course of researching *Liquid Gold*, Stephen Brook asked Pierre Dubourdieu, the owner of Château Doisy-Daëne in Sauternes, and possibly the only producer in the region to use a centrifuge, what he thought of the observation of some oenologists that this method was over-brutal, Dubourdieu replied that 'the only brutal thing about the centrifuge is its cost'.[25] Dubourdieu also subjects his wine to a number of filtrations. I believe that these treatments do affect a wine's quality: I shall explain why in a later chapter.[26] Even if a wine is not treated brutally, and fermentation is stopped simply by chilling it, it still has to be either filtered or well-sulphured afterwards, to prevent its re-fermenting. After all, in the last century the fermentation of champagne was halted by transferring the casks to a cooler cellar – and in the spring the wine re-fermented in bottle without the addition of any more yeast or sugar.

Does this then mean that using Süssreserve is less adulterous than stopping fermentation? Or are Loeb and Prittie correct in their condemnation? They say that Süssreserve is worse than sugar because, by adding Süssreserve to a wine, its alcohol content is reduced – the wine is diluted. A wine is allowed to contain up to 10 per cent of unfermented grape-juice in the form of Süssreserve. Dilution is not a criticism which can be levelled at the addition of dry sugar, though it does apply to liquid sugar, the use of which is prohibited throughout the EEC, precisely because it involves adding water to wine. In time, this problem may be solved by concentrating the Süssreserve by freezing.

The major defect of Süssreserve lies in its misapplication. It does not have to come from the same vineyard or village, merely from the same region – but, if it does not come from the same vineyard, the addition of Süssreserve undoubtedly alters the character of the wine. One reason why different wines made by the same producer in Germany often taste more alike than wines from the same vineyard made by different producers is that the wine-maker has used the same Süssreserve for all his wines. Even as quality-conscious a firm as Deinhard use Süssreserve, not from each vineyard, but from each village. They have carried out experiments, and they say that there is no difference in taste. But this is tantamout to saying that there is no difference in taste between the wines from the different vineyards in the first case. If Deinhard's Bernkasteler Doktor and Bernkasteler Bratenhöfchen are made with the same Süssreserve, of course they are going to taste more alike than they otherwise would.

Frequently, Süssreserve is not even made from the same grape variety as the wine to which it is added. Many producers of Riesling wines make their Süssreserve from a less noble but earlier-ripening variety – one which attains higher sugar levels, such as Müller-Thurgau. A Riesling wine may comprise up to 15 per cent of Müller-Thurgau grapes without losing the legal right to describe itself as being made from Riesling. Admittedly, in order to produce a wine of a given level of sweetness, it is not necessary to add so much of a sweeter Müller-Thurgau Süssreserve as of a less sweet Riesling one. But the wine's quality is patently diminished thereby.

These misuses of Süssreserve blunt the principal distinction between its application and the addition of sugar to a finished wine. Whereas the sugar in Süssreserve is grape-sugar, added sugar owes nothing to the vine or to the soil in which it grows but is the produce of a vegetable (beet) or a grass (cane). The addition of non-grape sugar in any form after fermentation is prohibited in Germany. But it is permitted elsewhere within the EEC, as long as the sugar is not mixed with water. Two of France's most celebrated drinks are adulterated in this manner.

Sugar is added to cognac, as a substitute for proper ageing. Properly aged cognac does not need added sugar, partly because it does not have harsh edges which need to be rounded off, and partly because it has absorbed sugars from the hemi-cellulose in the wooden casks in which it has been matured. For this, up to twenty years' ageing is necessary, an expensive procedure, not least because a quarter of the spirit evaporates in this time.

The laws permit up to 8 grams per litre of sugar to be added to cognac. Much more than this is added to most champagnes. Champagne is allowed to contain up to 15 grams of sugar per litre and still call itself *brut*, and up to 20 grams and still be called *extra sec*, whereas, under EEC regulations, other wines can only be called 'dry' if they contain less than 9 grams of sugar per litre. Under the new Austrian wine laws, introduced in the wake of the di-ethylene glycol scandal, wines with more than 10 grams per litre of residual sugar have to be labelled 'sweet'. Many of the *bruts* produced by leading houses sail close to the maximum permitted sugar content: samples of Lanson, Laurent Perrier, Louis Roederer and Taittinger have been analysed and found to contain *around* 15 grams per litre. Though the sugar can certainly be tasted, champagnes do not appear, when drunk, to contain as much sugar as they do, because carbon dioxide gas and what is, by French standards, a relatively high level of acidity, diminish the taste of sweetness.

This all makes nonsense of Patrick Forbes' attempt, in his book on the region, to justify the addition of sugar to champagne by arguing that, because it ferments not once but twice (the second fermentation producing the sparkle), all the sugar in a bottle of champagne is converted into alcohol, making it drier than other wines.[27] Indeed, one might wonder why the addition of so much sugar, enough to produce an extra 1 per cent alcohol, does not cause champagne to ferment a third time. Champagne houses used to add brandy to their wines to stop this from happening, but the last two to do so, de Castellane and Louis Roederer, gave up in 1972, since it had been realized that the process of yeast decomposition during the secondary fermentation in bottle probably absorbs yeast nutrients necessary for fermentation to occur.

The addition of sugar to champagne has been described by Alain de Polignac, Pommery's wine-maker, as 'a kind of make-up'.[28] The fact that they do not need to tart themselves up in this way is the strongest argument in the wardrobe of those sparkling wine producers in Italy, California and Australia who seek to emulate champagne. This said, we would probably not be able to afford to drink champagne, so long would it have to be aged before sale, and so much would it have to cost as a result, were it not sweetened with substantial amounts of sugar in order to make it prematurely drinkable.

[1] Roy Andries de Groot, *The Wines of California*, 1982, pp. 194–5.
[2] Stephen Brook, *Liquid Gold: dessert wines of the world*, Constable, 1987, pp. 309–10.
[3] Ibid., p. 174.
[4] Fynes Moryson, *Itinerary*, 1617.
[5] Otto Loeb and Terence Prittie, *Moselle*, Faber & Faber, 1972, pp. 117–19.
[6] State Papers, 89 series, no. 53, quoted in Sarah Bradford, *The Story of Port*, 2nd ed., Christie's Wine Publications, 1983, p. 35.
[7] Martin Lister, 'A Journey to Paris in the Year 1698', in John Pinkerton (ed.), *Voyages and Travels*, vol. 4, 1809, pp. 50–53.
[8] William Turner, *A New Book of the Natures and Properties of all Wines that are Commonly Used here in England*, 1568, p. 84.
[9] Walter Charleton, *The Mystery of Vintners*, published in *Two Discourses*, 1669, pp. 195–8.
[10] Such a re-fermentation is still sometimes provoked in Chianti, as will be described in Chapter 10. Charles Estienne, *Maison Rustique*, 1572, p. 210; Christopher Merret, *Some Observations Concerning the Ordering of Wines*, published in *Two Discourses*, 1669, pp. 221–2, 226–7; *L'Encyclopédie*, 1765, vol. 17, pp. 300–31, art.: 'Vin muet'.
[11] M.-A. Puvis, *De la culture de la vigne et de la fabrication du vin*, 1848, pp. 205–6, 240–41.
[12] *Decanter*, September 1985, p. 25.
[13] Quoted in Jancis Robinson, *The Great Wine Book*, Sidgwick & Jackson, 1982, p. 149.
[14] Frederick A. Pottle (ed.), *Boswell's London Journal*, Heinemann, 1950, p. 297.
[15] Cyrus Redding, *A History and Description of Modern Wines*, 1833, p. 202.
[16] A. Henderson, *History of Ancient and Modern Wines*, 1824, pp. 220–21.
[17] Allan Sichel, *The Penguin Book of Wines*, 2nd ed., Penguin, 1971, p. 191.
[18] J. L. W. Thudichum and August Dupré, *A Treatise on the Origin, Nature and Varieties of Wine*, 1872, pp. 281–304, 548, 556–7.
[19] Allan Sichel, p. 186.
[20] J. L. W. Thudichum and August Dupré, *A Treatise on Wine, its Origin, Nature and Varieties*, 1894, p. 201.
[21] Quoted in Brook, p. 154.
[22] Michael Broadbent, *The Great Vintage Wine Book*, Mitchell Beazley, 1980, p. 316.
[23] Alfred Langenbach, *The Wines of Germany*, Harper & Co., 1951, p. 80.
[24] Ibid., pp. 84–7.
[25] Brook, p. 57.
[26] Chapter 16.
[27] Forbes, p. 329.
[28] Quoted in *Wine and Spirit*, March 1987, p. 49.

THE SUN IN SACKS

The one general, prevailing pattern which runs through the history of alcoholic drinks in the last two hundred years, is that of increasing lightness made possibly by modern technology. This can be seen in changes in the taste of beer. The dominant beer-style of the eighteenth century was porter – a bit like a more alcoholic version of today's Guinness stout. It proved commercially successful because it was suited to mass production, whereas Burton ale, the forerunner of today's bitter, was not. Unlike Burton ale, porter was able to withstand the high temperatures generated in fermentation vats of the size necessary if beer was to be mass-produced. Porter lost its technological advantage over Burton ale when temperature-controlled fermentation was introduced in the 1790s. The method was quite simple: a length of coiled wire through which cold water circulated was introduced into the fermentation vat. By the second half of the nineteenth century Burton ale had replaced porter as the dominant beer-style.

Has wine become lighter in the same way? It would seem so. In the eighteenth and early nineteenth centuries, wine used to be fortified with brandy. It was commonly believed that this was necessary in order to enable the wine to travel. Even after Gladstone had reduced the duty on light wines from France in 1860–61, and the middle classes had taken up unfortified wines with enthusiasm, it was still being argued that 'all wine whatsoever must be treated artificially before it will last more than one or two years'.[1] Today, though, few wines are still fortified. An exception is sherry, which is still treated like a liqueur and left half-consumed on sideboards for months at a time. It is possible that an open bottle of fino sherry will grow *flor* (a film of yeasts) if it is unfortified. Most sherry is still fortified before shipment to this country.

Many wines, however, receive a hidden fortification. Whereas some wines are sweetened with sugar after fermentation, to others sugar is added before and/or during fermentation – the modern equivalent of adding brandy afterwards. The process is called chaptalization, after Jean-Louis Chaptal, Napoleon's Home Secretary, who suggested the method in a book written in 1801. Sugar is added to the grape-must in order to increase the alcohol content of the finished wine. Adding 7.5 kilograms of sugar to a barrel of wine increases the alcoholic degree by 2 per cent just as surely as adding 15 litres of brandy after fermentation is finished. It has been said[2] that 25,000 tons of beet-sugar (I have no idea how much cane) are used for chaptalization in France each year. This is a pretty substantial adulteration. Is it really necessary? Have not sufficient technological advances been made to permit the production of unfortified wine?

Certainly, modern methods of vinification and storage render a wine much less liable to suffer decay from bacterial contamination or oxidation than was the case in the past. Fermentation is now frequently carried out in stainless-steel or epoxy-resin-lined concrete tanks rather than hard-to-clean wooden casks; and wines are no longer stored in casks for so long. Therefore, wines are in need of smaller quantities of preservatives than hitherto.

These preservatives are alcohol, acidity, tannin and sulphur. In order to satisfy popular taste, it is much more important to reduce the levels of tannin, acidity and sulphur than that of alcohol. We want to be able to drink wines young nowadays, and wines with high levels of acidity, tannin or sulphur taste unpleasant in their youth. Alcohol, on the other hand, makes a young wine seem riper and more appealing. Wine-makers who do not chaptalize as much as their competitors lose out in blind tastings, for example, Hubert de Montille, who makes outstanding Volnays and Pommards. His wines contain 12 per cent alcohol compared with the 13 per cent normal in Burgundy; he relies on a balance of acidity and tannin to preserve them. So they are hard to taste in their youth. As the wine merchant and wine writer Thomas George Shaw was told more than a century ago, red burgundies were chaptalized in order to give them an appearance of richness.[3]

Shaw and other wine merchants who travelled in Burgundy in the middle of last century were shocked to discover that chaptalization was practised. Certainly, the chaptalization of fine wines is a modern phenomenon. The treatment was invented only in the seventeenth century, when wine-makers discovered that what happened during fermentation was that sugar turned to alcohol. It was known in both Bordeaux and Burgundy in the eighteenth century, but hardly used before the nineteenth. Even then it did not become common, because sugar was a scarce commodity before the development of the sugar-beet industry in the 1840s, and because this was the heyday of fortification: it was estimated that at this time three-quarters of all wine exported from France had alcohol added. The best of wines made in this way had the alcohol added at the start of fermentation, just like sugar for chaptalization.[4]

It was feared that chaptalization affected the quality of a wine. In 1816 Lamothe, the manager of Château Latour, increased the alcohol content of the wine by chaptalization by only 0.5 per cent, yet found that the wine tasted tainted and concluded that 'when nature fails to provide the basic elements of a good-quality wine, man cannot make up the loss; he will never achieve anything greater than mediocrity'.[5] In Burgundy in the 1840s a committee of growers and merchants was set up in order to try and find out how to restore burgundy to its ancient prosperity; they came out against chaptalization, which, they said, took away a wine's bouquet, its delicacy, and its individuality.[6] The same was said of those Mosel wines of the same period which were improved by the addition of liquid sugar. Growers in the Rhine expressed their disapproval on the grounds that sugaring took away a wine's individual characteristics.

Certainly, excess chaptalization makes all wines very similar. Some wine writers believe that they can tell if a wine has been chaptalized. Either cane- or beet-sugar can be used; on the whole, cane-sugar is added to white wines, and either cane- or beet-sugar to red. Edmund Penning-Rowsell says that alcohol from cane-sugar is likely to taste different from that produced from grape-sugar, and produces a sweetish, glyceriny taste if overdone.[7] Pamela Vandyke Price says that she can tell whether a wine has been chaptalized, because the wine smells of beet from the beet-sugar used.[8] The smell of beet, or of boiled beetroot, is used by many people as a mnemonic for the smell of Pinot Noir, the grape variety from which most red burgundies are made. Are we in fact identifying red burgundies by their 'boiled beetroot' smell, because that is the smell, not of Pinot Noir, but of chaptalization? Certainly, red burgundy is the lightest and most shamelessly chaptalized of French red wines. I have identified wines from their beetrooty smell as burgundies which have turned out to be heavily chaptalized clarets from a light year. I remember being one of a tasting group where we all unhesitatingly identified a 1968 claret, Domaine de Chevalier, as burgundy.

Burgundies are frequently chaptalized beyond the limits permitted by the law. For example, sugar is added so as to increase a wine's alcohol content from 10 per cent to 13 per cent. Legally, burgundies cannot be chaptalized unless they attain a minimum potential alcohol content of 10.5 per cent (for a commune wine) or 11 per cent (for a *premier cru*). Moreover, the alcohol content is not permitted to be increased by chaptalization by more than 2 per cent, nor to be raised by chaptalization to more than 12.5 per cent alcohol. According to Anthony Hanson, the Fraud Squad turns a blind eye to such practices.[9] Charles Tovey wrote last century that 'these mixtures of sugar are almost poison to some constitutions. Men of sedentary habits and the victims of indigestion should avoid these compounds, as they irritate the stomach. How frequently do we hear the observation, "I cannot drink burgundy; it invariably upsets me." This would not be the case were the wine unsugared.'[10]

Over-chaptalized wines taste unbalanced. Just as sugar is said, nutritionally, to produce 'empty calories', so chaptalization produces 'empty alcohol': more alcohol from the added sugar but no more extract to balance it. There is no reason why very alcoholic wines should taste particularly alcoholic – but heavily chaptalized wines always do, even if they contain less alcohol. An over-chaptalized red burgundy of 13 per cent alcohol will taste far more alcoholic than a Châteauneuf-du-Pape which has naturally obtained 15 per cent.

Chaptalization does not disastrously affect the balance of a wine if only a little sugar is added, enough to increase the alcohol level by 0.5 per cent or at most 1 per cent. Such wines may not have enough alcohol to keep well, but there is no reason why red burgundy should have to be cellared for years, especially not if it is from a bad vintage. Gérard Potel, who makes benchmark red burgundies at the Domaine de la Pousse d'Or in Volnay, chaptalized his 1975s only to 11.5 per cent alcohol and instructed all those to whom he sold them to drink them young. The problem lies with those consumers who still expect red burgundies to be rich, full-bodied wines, when they are, in fact, more often light wines to be drunk young and cool – like Beaujolais. As the production of what is expected lies beyond the abilities of nature in most years the vital ingredient is provided by man out of sugar bags. To the Burgundians, these bags of sugar are known as 'the sun in sacks'.

Chaptalization has always been used in Burgundy in poor vintages. The climate of Burgundy is similar to that of Bordeaux in terms of average temperature, sunshine, rainfall and humidity, but it varies more from year to year.[11] There are more bad vintages, in which the wines need chaptalizing. But in fact burgundies are now chaptalized not only in poor years but in all vintages, bad and good, with the exception of occasional very hot years like 1983 and 1985.

In Bordeaux, chaptalization was rarely practised before 1925, when it saved the vintage. It was not legalized until 1938. It has been allowed every year since 1962, although many of the top châteaux did not start chaptalizing until the late 1960s. Château Latour, for example, did not chaptalize the terrible vintage of 1963. Nowadays, as in Burgundy, all the estates always chaptalize except in very hot vintages such as 1982.

Now this is very odd. Grapes are picked later, with a higher sugar content, than they used to be. Last century, when clarets were not chaptalized, grapes were picked before they were ripe, in order to avoid possibly cold and damp autumn weather which, in the absence of modern chemical and physical treatments, would have caused them to rot. Until the end of the century first-growth clarets, when analysed, were found to contain an average of only 7–9 per cent alcohol. Today they achieve a natural 11–12 per cent before chaptalization. Since overripeness is regarded as a virtue, the grapes are left on the vines after they are ripe, resulting in high levels of sugar and low levels of acidity, and wines which can be drunk young but whose ability to age remains a matter of dispute. In Burgundy, according to research carried out by the manager of the Domaine du Marquis de Laguiche, the average date of starting the harvest in the twentieth century has been three weeks later than the average date early in the nineteenth.[12]

In Bordeaux last century, not only did the harvest generally begin earlier, but different varieties were planted higgledy-piggledy, rather than in separate plots, and therefore unripe grapes were picked along with ripe. This still happens in Rioja. Even where one plot is planted in only one grape variety, not all the grapes in a bunch ripen at the same time. Away from the light, fruit does not take on colour, so a tightly knit bunch will have paler berries on the inside. Between 10 and 30 per cent of the grapes in any given bunch will be unripe; it is to give these berries time to improve that many wine-makers recommend delaying the vintage.

This delay has been made possible by the introduction in some regions of harvesting-machines. It used to be necessary to begin the harvest before the grapes were ripe and to finish when they were overripe. Since he invested in a harvesting-machine in 1979, Georges Vigouroux of Château de Haute-Serre in Cahors has cut his harvesting time from one month to ten days. The machine allows him to wait for ripeness, even for the best time of day. It shakes the vines: the green, unripe grapes don't drop off. Today, in Bordeaux, the majority of the harvest is machine-picked.

So why this sudden adoption of chaptalization? I do not think it is a coincidence that the adoption of wholesale chaptalization in Bordeaux and Burgundy coincides with a vast increase in yields – in the quantity of wine produced per vine – since the 1950s. Yields in Bordeaux remained very much at their nineteenth-century level until the end of the 1950s, since when they have doubled. Chaptalization compensates for overproduction. Sometimes this is quite necessary. Only with chaptalization are wine producers in the South Tyrol and Friuli in north-east Italy able to overcome the economic necessity of overproducing, on the grounds that they cannot get a fair return for their wines. Only by chaptalizing illegally has Alois Lageder, for example, been able to produce serious dry white wines at remarkably low prices.

The Italian methanol scandal of 1986 occurred as a consequence of trying to boost the alcohol content of thin, overproduced wine with a cheaper and more readily available means than sugar. In 1985 heavy fines were imposed by Piedmontese magistrates on sugar producers for selling sugar to wineries, which made the sugar business riskier. Adding ordinary alcohol (ethanol) was not an alternative, not just because this is illegal too, but because ethanol is taxed, and therefore its movement round Italy is controlled. Since 1984, however, methanol had been untaxed and its movement uncontrolled. So methanol was used instead of ethanol. So twenty-one people died.

A more valid justification of chaptalization lies in the necessity on some occasions of picking grapes before they are fully ripe and have reached their optimum sugar content. This is true for white wines, particularly if produced in warm climates. Whereas red wines are not always required to taste of the grapes from which they are made, and can very well be dominated by 'secondary' aromas produced during fermentation, in white wines fresh fruit flavours are always desired – that is, 'primary' aromas from the grape. These aromas are localized in the skin and underlying cells and appear very early, long before complete maturity, so that early picking can result in finer wines than late picking.

This will not serve, however, as an explanation for the wholesale chaptalization of white burgundies. Whereas the chaptalization of red burgundies is much talked of, that of white burgundies is not. Yet it is far more culpable. Producers of white burgundies need not worry too much about losing acidity if they wait for the grapes to achieve better levels of sugar, since they can always prevent the malolactic fermentation, which converts malic acid into lactic acid and carbon dioxide – as is done, for example, by Marcel Vincent, the leading producer of Pouilly-Fuissé, in hot years. This is not an option that is open to producers of red burgundies, as a red wine with high levels of malic acid can taste rather strange. Moreover, most white burgundies are drunk so young nowadays that lack of acidity is irrelevant as regards keeping qualities. Whereas black grapes do not always ripen in Burgundy, and therefore genuinely require chaptalization, white grapes almost always ripen. Chardonnay grapes usually achieve between 12 and 13 per cent alcohol naturally, so why chaptalize? Is it because now, as white burgundies have become so expensive that no one can afford to drink more than half a bottle, they are being made more alcoholic so that it is possible to get drunk on this small quantity? The alcoholic content is raised gratuitously to between 13.5 and 14 per cent. According to Percival Brown of the specialist burgundy importers Heyman Brothers, the alcohol levels of white burgundies are between 1 and 1.5 per cent higher than they were ten or twenty years ago.[13]

Nor is it possible to justify the chaptalization of sweet white wines when the vine grower is not prepared to wait for the grapes to achieve the necessarily high sugar content. Many leading Sauternes châteaux chaptalize their wines in order to ensure that when fermentation stops the wine is sweet. Because they do not want – or cannot afford – to risk the loss of their grapes because of bad weather in the autumn, they do not wait until the grapes contain enough sugar to produce a potential 18 per cent alcohol – enough to achieve the legal minimum alcoholic strength for the *appellation*, 13 per cent, whilst leaving 90 grams per litre of unfermented sugar. Whereas dry wines were developed in Sauternes in the 1960s because the sweet ones could not find buyers, the cooperative cellars in Jurançon introduced a dry wine after the last war on the grounds that this was preferable to the excessive chaptalization of the sweet version.

The most regularly, and legally, overchaptalized of French wines is champagne. This is ridiculous, considering that since the last century making a wine sparkling has been an *alternative* to fortification or chaptalization. Sufficient sugar is added before the first fermentation to increase its alcoholic content by 2 per cent, and enough before the second fermentation in bottle – which makes the wine sparkle – to increase its alcohol content by a further 1.25 per cent. Thus champagne is chaptalized, overall, from a natural 9 per cent potential alcohol to an actual 12.25 per cent. Bottle-fermented sparkling wines are not chaptalized in Italy, California or Australia, which supports the argument of the producers of top-quality sparkling wine in these countries that their products are more natural, if not better, than champagne.

Advocates of chaptalization argue that it prolongs fermentation. The best Burgundian wine-makers add sugar, not all at the beginning of fermentation, but gradually during its course. Frédéric Lafarge, who makes some excellent Volnays and a particularly good-value Bourgogne Rouge from vineyards outside the Volnay *appellation*, chaptalizes his wines gradually by between 0.5 and 1 per cent in order to prolong fermentation to about ten days and to improve keeping qualities thereby. But I do not see how a wine-maker achieves a longer and better fermentation by picking at 12 per cent and adding 1 per cent sugar gradually during fermentation than by picking late at 13 per cent. Moreover, there are plenty of other means of prolonging fermentation, in order to achieve better extraction of tannins and other flavouring molecules, such as lowering the fermentation temperature, though this reduces the colour and can produce some oddly flavoured red wines if taken to excess; or leaving the wine in the fermentation vat in contact with the grape-skins after fermentation has finished. This brings a danger of acetification, but, if the temperature is brought down to 20°C, it produces a rich wine with soft tannins.

Instead of chaptalizing, why do vine growers in Burgundy not wait until the grapes are ripe and then, if necessary, add acidity during fermentation to compensate? After all, the reason for burgundy's reputation lies in the length of the growing season. Chaptalization can never provide the taste that would have been achieved had the grapes been picked later.

The big difficulty with delaying a harvest is that it means risking the weather. Sometimes fortune favours the brave; sometimes it does not. But this is not the point. If their gamble pays off, those vine growers who wait are able to make a better wine; whereas those who risk nothing only ever achieve a mediocre one.

In 1985 Bordeaux suffered from drought in August and September, which retarded the ripening process, so that in mid-September Cabernet Sauvignon grapes contained enough sugar to produce only 10.5 per cent potential alcohol. This was reduced by dew and mists in late September to 9.5 per cent. Rain was predicted for the first weekend in October, so some picked at this point; others picked swollen berries after the rain; only those who had the courage to wait until dry weather returned harvested a crop with a good alcoholic degree and fair concentration. The weather held up throughout October; the best wines were picked mid-month. Though the best 1985s are the Saint-Émilions and Pomerols, where the early-ripening Merlot grape did not stop ripening on the cooler soils and was picked before the bad weather, there are some very good late-picked Médocs, such as Château Lynch-Bages and its second wine, Haut-Bages-Averous.

We should not, however, be misled by those recent vintages in Bordeaux in which victory has been snatched from the jaws of defeat into imagining that waiting longer always brings happy results. Certainly, like 1985, 1983 and 1978 were last-minute successes. A fortnight before the harvest in 1983 Michel Delon, the owner of Léoville-Lascases, said to his cellarmaster, 'We've lost the vintage. We have a 1972 on our hands.'[14] But 1964 was a last-minute failure. It was a wonderful summer, and in August Edgar Pisani, the Minister of Agriculture, proclaimed that it was going to be the 'vintage of the century'. A number of merchants bought wines *sur souche* – while the grapes were still ripening on the vines – in anticipation of demand exceeding supply after the vintage. Some very good wines were made, notably at Château Latour, who finished picking before 8 October, when it began to rain and did not stop for a fortnight. Those who had waited for a late harvest saw their wines ruined, most famously at Lafite and most disastrously at Mouton-Rothschild.

Late picking, however, can be taken to excess. The most celebrated estate in Burgundy, the Domaine de la Romanée-Conti, is one of the most fervent advocates of late picking. When he bought the estate in 1869, M. Duvault-Blochet published a book in which he stated that, except when bad weather or rot threatens to ruin the harvest, the grapes should never be picked until they have reached between 13 and 13.5 per cent potential alcohol. Today the Domaine de la Romanée-Conti picks between one and two weeks later than most other growers. I have never tasted their wines, so can only cite the opinions of others. Anthony Hanson considers that the wines are 'made with a heavy hand'.[15] Serena Sutcliffe thinks that 'the grapes are picked too late'.[16] Clive Coates agrees, adding that the wine also spends too long in contact with the grape-skins in the fermentation vat. On the other hand, he considers their 1983s and 1985s to be superb.[17]

The proprietors of the Domaine de la Romanée-Conti seem to believe that, by dint of late picking, they are immune to the forces of nature and are able to make wines worth the amazingly high prices asked even for off-vintages like 1963, 1975 and 1977. They have difficulty in persuading specialist wine merchants to demonstrate agreement on this point by purchasing the wines. In 1981 Serena Sutcliffe wrote to *Decanter* to say that she had seen the 1963 Romanée-Conti (the top wine of the Domaine) on sale at the Carrefour supermarket at Châlon-sur-Saône, scarcely an outlet which would normally have been allowed to stock so prestigious a wine. The Domaine's proprietors argue that the wines they make in lesser vintages take longer to develop than the produce of good ones, rather than less time, as one might expect; but, if they are right, how much longer would a purchaser have had to wait for this particular eighteen-year-old wine to blossom?

A number of Burgundian vine growers certainly did pick too late in 1985, as they had in 1983, as a result of which there is a taste of dry rot in many of the wines. They were responding to the demands of old-fashioned merchants who want high levels of alcohol, which in these two years could unusually be obtained without much in the way of chaptalization. Waiting does not pay off in the best years – the result is overripeness and dangerously low acid levels, and sometimes actually a sweet wine, such as the extraordinary 1985 Côte de Nuits-Villages from the merchants Lupé-Cholet. But it pays to delay the harvest in run-of-the-mill vintages, such as 1986. This had begun well in Burgundy, but it rained in mid-September, causing a great deal of rot. Many vine growers were panicked by the rot into picking early, when the grapes were still swelled by the rain; only those who waited until the end of the month made fine wine. Sugar levels fell by 1 per cent as a result of dilution of the grapes by the rain to reach a low point of 9 per cent in mid-September, but then gained 2 per cent alcohol in the next fortnight.

Traditionally, Burgundian wine-makers were said to equate acidity with bones and sugar with flesh, and to point out that it was easier to put on more flesh than to alter bone structure. In other words, it was better to pick early to safeguard acid levels than to pick late and acidify. This view has now been challenged by the new generation of Young Turks who have done a great deal to restore red burgundy to its former glory, and who believe that the balance of a wine is less affected by adding acidity than by adding sugar. Gérard Chave, the leading producer of Hermitage, agrees that it is better to pick on ripeness – and acidify if necessary – than to pick on acidity and then chaptalize. In 1986 the other growers in Hermitage began picking on 20 September; Chave picked between 2 and 12 October, after everyone else had finished. Perhaps the Domaine de la Romanée-Conti is right after all.

'Old-fashioned' Burgundian wine-makers have a problem today if they are not willing to improve the bone structure of the monster they create. It used to be said that red burgundy was a more acidic wine than claret. This is no longer true. Today Pinot Noir grapes suffer from disastrously low levels of acidity, the consequence of the heavy administration of potassium fertilizer in the 1960s, and of the planting in the same period of particular clones of Pinot Noir, called Pinots Droits, which naturally produce grapes low in acidity. As a result, in Burgundy every year growers either chaptalize if too cold or add acidity if warm. One vine grower in Savigny-lès-Beaune, who says that 'to make a good wine, you have to break the law' and would therefore probably prefer to remain anonymous, chaptalizes his wine most years, but did not in 1983 or 1985, when he added acidity. He adds the acidity after the wine has spent eight months in cask, saying that it affects the taste only for the next six to eight months in cask. His wines certainly do not taste of added acidity. In fact under EEC regulations the addition of acidity is permitted in 'exceptional' years: and in Burgundy any year in which they need to add acidity is an exceptional one. I am not clear, however, that wine-makers are aware of this.

Though many wine-makers believe that acidifying the must is better than adding acidity to the finished wine – just as chaptalization is preferable to adding alcohol afterwards – there is no evidence that we can taste added acidity, unless it is of a different type from that produced naturally by the grapes. Tartaric acid is produced by grapes and by no other fruit. Other acids, such as sorbic and citric, can give wine a strange taste. Citric acid is unstable and can decompose under the influence of malolactic bacteria to produce a diacetyl (buttery) odour. Sorbic acid is said to produce a 'geranium' taste if given time in the bottle. If some Australian wines taste as though acid has been added, it may be the result of adding sorbic or citric acid, or, in the case of red wines, which one does not expect to taste of malic acid, of preventing the malolactic fermentation from taking place. Certainly I have detected what I thought was added acidity – you taste the acidity after the wine – in Australian wines, only to be assured by the wine-makers that acid had not been added to these particular wines.

Even if the option of picking late and then adding acidity is not available, other alternatives to chaptalization present themselves. Concentration by heating merely replicates the natural process of overripening under a hot sun. When it has achieved its maximum sugar content, the grape ceases to receive substances from the plant, and begins to lose water. The same effect can be achieved by heating grapes for twenty-four hours at 40°C, causing a fall in the content of the harsh malic acids (but not the tartaric, which break down only at 57°C), slight concentration by evaporation of water, and an increase of 1 per cent in the wine's alcohol content. This method, however, produces a loss in bulk, which would have to be compensated by increased prices; and, like pasteurization, it alters a wine's chemical structure and thus affects its ability to age. A less harmful process is concentration by freezing. At below 0°C ice crystals form, composed of water: alcohol does not solidify at this temperature. By law, concentration by freezing must not produce a greater reduction than 25 per cent in volume nor a greater increase than 2 per cent in alcoholic strength.

These alternative methods are important, because the EEC is thinking of abolishing chaptalization. In order to drain the wine lake, at present 10,000 million litres deep and growing, chaptalization with sugar will be replaced – as it has already been, at least in theory, in Italy – by enrichment with grape-must concentrate, produced by heating the must in a vacuum. This would be fine, were it not that grape-must concentrate inflicts an undesirable taste on the wine. Even if produced from the same vineyard, if concentrated to more than 26 per cent potential alcohol it tastes 'cooked'. Commercially available musts have been concentrated to between 28 and 36 per cent potential alcohol. Certainly must can be 'rectified': indeed, this is obligatory in some regions of Italy, if not in others. But rectification of a must by passing it through an ion-exchanger does not rid it of its yeasts or bacteria; nor, though it can remove heavy metals and mineral salts, does it take away all its taste elements. Much of the grape-must concentrate used in northern Italy very substantially affects the taste of the wines to which it has been applied, because it is imported from the South. Moreover, even locally produced concentrate, even if kept to below 26 per cent potential alcohol, is effectively the same thing as liquid sugar. On the one hand, the use of liquid sugar is illegal, as it adds water to wine. On the other, depending on the region, it is permitted to use concentrate to increase a wine's volume by between 6.5 and 11 per cent.

Even those Italian wine-makers who care nothing for quality use sugar illegally rather than concentrate legally, though not because it produces superior wine. Concentrate costs more. To chaptalize one bottle's worth of wine with even the cheapest and nastiest form of unrectified grape-juice concentrate available, in order to increase its alcoholic degree by 2 per cent, costs 75 lire (about 3 p) more than doing the same thing with sugar. Three pence can make a lot of difference to your profit margin when you are selling wine at 40p a bottle. But then methanol was cheaper still. . . .

[1] Oswald Crawford, *Portugal Old and New*, 1880.
[2] Hallgarten, p. 63.
[3] T. G. Shaw, *Wine, The Vine and the Cellar*, 1863, p. 284.
[4] M.-A. Puvis, *De la culture de la vigne et de la fabrication du vin*, 1848, pp. 234–9.
[5] Quoted in René Pijassou, *Le Médoc*, Tallandier, 1980, p. 570.
[6] Puvis, pp. 225ff.
[7] Penning-Rowsell, p. 38.
[8] Pamela Vandyke Price, *Enjoying Wine*, Heinemann, 1982.
[9] Hanson, p. 100.
[10] Charles Tovey, *Wine Revelations*, c.1881, pp. 67–71.
[11] Hanson, p. 60.
[12] Hanson, p. 299. This comparison is not altogether confirmed by the dates for the start of the harvest in the eighteeth and nineteenth centuries given by M. J. Lavalle, *Histoire et statistique de la vigne et des grands vins de la Côte d'Or*, 1855, pp. 26–9, and M. R. Danguy and Charles Aubertin, *Les grands vins de Bourgogne*, 1892, pp. 118, 463–4, which suggest that in Burgundy harvesting used to take place only three or four days earlier than it does today. In Bordeaux the average date of beginning the harvest was 23 September in 1869–1914, and 28 September in 1945–87.
[13] Quoted in *Decanter*, September 1987, p. 42.
[14] Quoted in *Wine and Spirit*, August 1984, p. 24.
[15] Hanson, p. 217.
[16] *Decanter*, February 1984, p. 68.
[17] *The Vine*, January 1986, p. 32; February 1987, p. 34.

THE CHAMPAGNE GAME

Instead of heating or freezing it, or adding sugar or rectified grape-must concentrate before fermentation, a wine-maker can fortify a weak wine by blending a stronger wine into it. In the past, this sort of adulteration was the principal means of fortification. It has been said that, in the middle of the nineteenth century, virtually the entire Hermitage harvest was added to clarets, and practically the whole yield of Châteauneuf-du-Pape to burgundies.[1]

This bolstering is often spoken of as if it were something historic, which ceased as soon as *appellation contrôlée* laws were introduced to prohibit it. As we in Britain did not have to obey French wine laws until we joined the EEC in 1973, it is accepted that we continued the practice until then – carrying out the blending at home. We were given three years' grace when we joined the EEC, so not until the start of 1977 did we have to conform to European wine laws. For this reason it is certainly wise to be wary of pre-1977 British-bottled burgundies. For example, one well-known company used to make an excellent 'Nuits-Saint-Georges' from a blend of 85 per cent burgundy, 10 per cent Moroccan red, 5 per cent port and a little glycerine. I have tried concocting a similar blend, without the glycerine, and found it a very effective method of giving body to a light red burgundy without entirely destroying its character. These blends are still being produced. If we do not see so much of them, it is because very few burgundies are bottled in Britain any more. In 1982 some wine merchants found themselves stuck with large quantities of excellent Argentinian red wine. I know for certain that one highly respectable firm solved the problem by adding this wine to their own-label red burgundies. Moreover, according to one burgundy merchant, those merchants in Burgundy who used to add wine from Algeria or the South of France to their red burgundies have not stopped doing so. As Hanson has pointed out, giving up is pretty much impossible: once a merchant starts adding bolstering wine in off-vintages, he has to do so in good ones as well, or else they lack the richness of his lesser years.[2]

The illegal addition of a hefty dollop of blending wine from the South is the simplest and most effective means of producing full-bodied red burgundies. Table wine from the South is always at hand; Burgundy merchants already handle it. The practice of selling branded table wine, produced in the South but bottled in Burgundy in burgundy bottles and sent on its way with a nudge and a wink about including some 'declassified' red burgundy – of which there has in fact been no such thing in France since the 1974 nor in Britain since the 1976 vintage – has been explained on the grounds that the quantity of wine available for trading in Burgundy is small, so merchants fill up the empty spaces in their business calendars by selling table wines. But is the explanation not in fact the other way round? If Burgundy merchants have become involved in the business of selling branded table wines, might it not be because they were already involved in importing wine from the South for blending into their red burgundies? They only had to invent these branded wines in the 1920s, when the introduction of *appellation contrôlée* laws meant that they could no longer sell them under famous Burgundian names.

Certainly burgundy merchants have a problem on their hands. Whereas the climate is perfect for the production of white wine, it is frequently too cold for the production of red. The deep-coloured and full-bodied burgundies of popular imagination are produced only three or four times a decade – in the present decade only in 1983 and 1985. Adulteration is the best means of supplying these in lesser years; the Burgundians do not have open to them the option available to the Bordelais, of planting a number of grape varieties, all of which ripen at different times, as a hedge against the climate. They rely on a single black grape variety, Pinot Noir. It is true that a certain amount of Gamay, the Beaujolais grape, is interplanted in the vineyards, and that, blended with Pinot Noir, usually in the proportion of two-thirds Gamay to one-third Pinot Noir, it makes a wine called Passe-Tout-Grains. But the result usually bears more resemblance to an earthy sort of Beaujolais than to a red burgundy. Though there are exceptions – the great Henri Jayer produces a Passe-Tout-Grains which really does taste like red burgundy –

Passe-Tout-Grains could never be passed off as burgundy. The Gamay is too coarse and overbearing a grape, and the Pinot Noir too delicate, for the character of the principal grape to dominate – which is the purpose of such blends.

In the Médoc region of Bordeaux, wines made principally from Cabernet Sauvignon, the main grape variety, are given richness by blending with Merlot. This latter variety has long been cultivated in Saint-Émilion; and in the last century wine from Saint-Émilion, which did not yet enjoy a reputation of its own, was blended into claret from the Médoc, because, whereas Cabernet Sauvignon in the Médoc naturally achieved only 7–9 per cent alcohol, the earlier-ripening Merlot grape in Saint-Émilion reached 11 per cent. It was obviously a small step to introducing Merlot vines into the Médoc, and carrying out the blending in the vineyard. Because Merlot ripens earlier than Cabernet, it will produce a good crop even if Cabernet is spoiled by bad autumn weather, as happened in 1964. On the other hand, Merlot ripens earlier than Cabernet because it flowers earlier and is therefore susceptible to bad weather in early summer. The weather was bad in June 1984; the Merlot buds failed to set properly and dropped off; the later-ripening Cabernet was not affected. The châteaux of Saint-Émilion and Pomerol, where far more Merlot is planted than in the Médoc, having produced generally far better wines than those of the Médoc in 1964, made much inferior, and much less, wine in 1984. Those châteaux with the most equal balance of the two varieties escaped the worst excesses of either: Vieux Château Certan, for example, which cultivates 45 per cent of Cabernets Sauvignon and Franc, a relatively high proportion for Pomerol, made an outstanding 1964 but also a very good 1984.

Blending as a hedge against the weather explains one of the great mysteries of Bordeaux: why Cabernet Franc is grown alongside Cabernet Sauvignon. The wine they produce is so similar that experts have trouble in telling them apart. They think they can, but that is because Cabernet Franc ripens earlier and therefore is favoured by vine growers in relatively cool climates, such as the Loire valley. The taste which people think is typical of Cabernet Franc would in fact be equally typical of Cabernet Sauvignon if it were cultivated in similarly cool climates. In the South Tyrol Herbert Tiefenbrunner, unusually, cultivates Cabernet Sauvignon rather than Cabernet Franc, but I doubt if many people could identify blind the wine he makes as the produce of the former rather than the latter. Cabernet Franc is planted in Bordeaux because it ripens a little earlier, and so, even if the Cabernet Sauvignon crop is damaged by bad autumn weather, its relative Cabernet Franc will ensure that the wine retains a Cabernet character.

But is this blending economically necessary? The leading châteaux of Bordeaux are now charging enormous sums of money for their wines, and making huge profits every year: the break-even point for them would be achieved by selling their wines at a mere 30 francs a bottle. They can afford the occasional failure of their Cabernet Sauvignon vines to produce healthy grapes. Burgundians rely for their red wine entirely on Pinot Noir, which is more susceptible to disease than Cabernet; given bad weather, they just have to make the best of a bad job. Yet they can still afford to drive around in smart cars – if not in public. There is a story current in Burgundy of a grower in Gevrey-Chambertin who is making much more money than he wants the tax authorities to know about. He has bought himself a Maserati, which he garages fifty miles away. He drives around Gevrey-Chambertin in an old DCV, but every weekend drives up to the place where he has garaged his Maserati, and takes it for a spin round Beaune, where no one recognizes him.

It would not bankrupt the Bordelais if they pulled out all their other vines and cultivated only their best variety, Cabernet Sauvignon. Certainly this was what, a century ago, Auguste Petit-Lafitte, Professor of Agriculture in the Department of the Gironde, thought they should do. He believed that it was right for the makers of ordinary wines to plant a mixture of varieties to insure themselves against the vagaries of the weather, as they depended economically on producing a good quantity of wine each year, being unable to charge premium prices for their products. The producers of fine wines, on the other hand, had no need to mix different varieties of vine in their vineyards, because they were able to charge high prices. For them, the aim had to be to produce the best possible wine. Petit-Lafitte cited Deuteronomy 22:9: 'Thou shalt not sow thy vineyard with divers seeds: lest the fruit of thy seed which thou hast sown, and the fruit of thy vineyard, be defiled.'[3]

There is, however, a very good reason why the Bordelais will never pull out their other vines and cultivate only Cabernet Sauvignon. In an interview in 1963, Ronald Barton, the late, highly respected proprietor of Château Léoville-Barton, in explaining why clarets were not as good as they used to be, gave four main reasons why most of them are made from a blend of grape varieties. Even in the Good Old Days before the war, the best clarets were blended wines. Quality-conscious vineyards contained 70–80 per cent Cabernet Sauvignon with 20–30 per cent of the other four species – Cabernet Franc, Merlot, Petit Verdot and Malbec. 'Some vineyards favoured one and some another and this gave each its own character.'[4] That is to say, each château cultivated the secondary varieties in different proportions in order to create a house-style for itself. What individuality would they have if they all cultivated 100 per cent Cabernet Sauvignon?

Admittedly one estate's Cabernet Sauvignon is not the same as another's. Different clones are planted in different vineyards, and they produce very slightly different wine. Equally, wines differ according to the strains of yeast used, the temperature at which they are vinified, the proportion of new oak barrels used for their cask-ageing, and the length of time they are kept in these barrels. Nevertheless each château of Bordeaux – each brand – cultivates a different mixture of grapes in order to be able to offer an individual product. For example, the two leading châteaux in the village of Saint-Julien are Léoville-Lascases and Ducru-Beaucaillou. The wines are not made in precisely the same way: Ducru tends to be more oaky because it spends a bit longer in cask. The principal distinction between them, however, is that Lascases is a more austere wine than Ducru, and takes longer to develop. The reason for this is that it contains a higher proportion of Cabernets Sauvignon and Franc and a lesser proportion of Merlot. Lascases is 80 per cent Cabernets and 15 per cent Merlot; Ducru 70 per cent Cabernets and 25 per cent Merlot.

So important is this uniqueness of taste that, in years when one particular grape variety suffers from adverse weather conditions and therefore produces very little wine, many châteaux prefer to maintain their usual balance of varieties, even though this necessitates a drastic reduction in the amount of wine they are able to commercialize. One-third of the vineyard area of Château Pichon-Lalande is planted in Merlot. In 1984 one-third of their Merlot crop failed; this would, in the natural way of things, have produced a much harder wine, with only one-fifth Merlot. In order to maintain a normal balance, however, the château 'declassified' one-third of its Cabernet; that is, included it, not in the wine commercialized under the Pichon-Lalande label, but in the château's second-string wine, Réserve de la Comtesse. As a result, Château Pichon-Lalande 1984 was very typical of Pichon-Lalande, and not at all typical of the generally unsatisfactory 1984 vintage.

Producing wine in this way, regardless of vintage conditions, reduces wine to the level of beer. For a brewer, the great challenge is to produce a consistent end-product from continually changing raw materials. For a wine-maker, one might have thought, it is to give expression to a natural product. One leading Italian wine-maker, Emidio Pepe, who makes an outstanding Montepulciano d'Abruzzo, has described consistency in wines from year to year as not only undesirable but actually dishonest.[5]

In Valencia in eastern Spain, all the wine for export is produced by merchants who buy and blend the same wine from the same cooperatives. Vinival's top wine, Torre de Serranos, is made by blending in 10 per cent Rioja. (Ironically, the wine tastes tired and over-oaked as a result.) Carlos Garrigos, the son of the owner, explained that 'if this wasn't allowed, everybody's wines would taste the same'. The same is true of Dão in Portugal. Only one estate-bottled wine is commercially available; the majority of Dãos are bottled and marketed by merchants who are not allowed to make wine from grapes which they have not themselves grown. All the merchants buy most of their wine from the same ten cooperatives. The results would taste more alike than they do if it were not common practice to blend in wine from Bairrada. That is why the Bairrada region was not demarcated until 1979: merchants needed the wine for their 'Dãos'.

In fact, most Bordelais châteaux do their best to give expression to the character of individual vintages within the confines of the requirement to maintain their house-styles. Only occasionally do they indulge in the blending of vintages. A number of Bordelais châteaux overproduced Merlot in 1983, which came in very handy when much of the Merlot crop failed in 1984. Bernadette Villars of Château Chasse-Spleen has admitted that she added to her 1984 some 1983 press-wine, made by pressing the residue of skins left over after fermentation and therefore very rich in extract, colour and tannin. Others did likewise, but are more cagey about disclosing the fact. After all, it is illegal: all French *appellation contrôlée* wines bearing a vintage date must have been produced solely from the fruit of that vintage.

Champagne houses, however, make no effort to give expression to the character of individual vineyards or vintages. Like the Bordelais, they each combine the same grapes in different proportions, in order to create – in theory – a unique and individual taste. Thus Bollinger, which contains 70 per cent Pinot Noir and 20 per cent Chardonnay, is altogether 'bigger' than Lanson, which contains 45 per cent Pinot Noir and 45 per cent Chardonnay. But here we are talking not about the planting of different varieties in the same vineyard, but the blending of wines from different regions – as though classed-growth clarets were still produced by blending Cabernet Sauvignon from the Médoc with Merlot from Saint-Émilion. In Champagne, the house-styles are not expressed in the context of different vintages and villages.

Vintages are irrelevant in Champagne. Classed-growth clarets are sold to be laid down, not to be drunk at once, so vintage dates are important. Champagne, however, is sold to be drunk immediately, on the spur of the moment, for a celebration. It is sold, theoretically, ready-aged: non-vintage champagne tends to be three years old at time of sale, and vintage champagne five or six. Apart from a few connoisseurs, no one lays it down, and therefore vintage dates are irrelevant. Vintage champagne, it is true, does taste of the vintage in question as well as of the house-style of the producer. But, as far as most consumers are concerned, it is simply a smarter, more expensive version of non-vintage champagne. We do not buy a champagne because it comes from a particularly good vintage. We buy a bottle because it has a vintage date – any date – on it. We simply buy whatever vintage is currently available.

In the champagne boom of Edwardian England, virtually all champagne bore a vintage date. Today 80–90 per cent is non-vintage: that is, a blend of vintages. For champagne producers, a vintage label is more of a hindrance than an advantage, because it detracts from their purpose of ensuring that, every time someone buys a bottle of their particular product, it tastes the same as it did on the previous occasion. What they seek to produce is a consistent and reliable product. Therefore they blend wines together in order to overcome their natural variability, in order to damp down the character of the individual vineyards, villages and vintages. As Rémi Krug has put it, 'Champagne bears the stamp not of geography but of its maker.'[6] The maker's mark is usually a bland and characterless wine which is offensive to as few people as possible, and therefore can be sold to as many people as possible.

We are often told that blended champagnes are superior to champagnes made from single grape varieties in single villages. It may have been necessary in the past to blend together different grape varieties, but the reasons for doing so no longer exist. In the seventeenth century, champagnes from different vineyards were blended together in order to make them drinkable in poor vintages. But in those days champagne was a still wine. The climate of the Champagne region, though frequently too cold for still-wine production, is perfect for the production of the considerably more acid grapes needed to produce sparkling wine. There is no vintage so bad in Champagne that excellent sparkling wine cannot be produced.

In the eighteenth century, when sparkling champagne became fashionable, it was found that the addition of white grapes to a wine hitherto made only from black grapes made it sparkle better. But in those days champagne was made sparkling by a method different from the one used today. It fermented only once, and its degree of effervescence depended on how much of the fermentation was incomplete when the wine was bottled in the spring. Today champagne is fermented not once but twice, and the bubbles are produced by adding yeast and sugar before the second fermentation. The type of grapes used does not affect the amount the wine sparkles.

The blend of black and white grapes which had been found to produce the best bubbles also, however, established a particular taste. People came to imagine that good champagne *had* to taste the way it usually did. Champagne as a whole became a brand; just like the individual houses, it developed its own 'house-style' – at the expense of the individuality of the wines produced within it. Even champagnes made entirely from white Chardonnay grapes were looked down upon a generation ago as being 'too light'.[7] Today they are highly esteemed and sought after, partly as a consequence of the fashion for white burgundy, which is made from 100 per cent Chardonnay, and partly because they don't taste any different from

– in other words taste equally bland as – most standard blends. But champagne made from 100 per cent black grapes does have an individual taste: too individual to be acceptable to all consumers. Therefore very little is produced, except by those growers who cultivate only black grape vines and therefore have no option. Even pink champagne is usually made, not by fermenting black grapes briefly in contact with their skins, but by blending red and white grapes in the usual way and then adding a little red wine. Yet for anyone interested in drinking champagne for its taste rather than just for its image, the great virtue of champagne made from 100 per cent black grapes is that it does actually taste of something. Outstandingly good – and inexpensive – pure Pinot Noir champagnes are made by the brothers Pierre and Michel Arnould in the *grand cru* village of Verzenay. I am told that they are not on speaking terms, but their wines are so good, and so similar, that I am tempted to suspect that they are the same.

The produce of different vineyards also once needed to be blended together in order to ensure that the wine sparkled consistently. One hundred and fifty years ago, sparkling champagne cost twice as much as a white burgundy such as Meursault, whereas today it costs two-thirds as much. It was expensive because the method of making it effervesce – bottling it before the first fermentation had finished – was hit-and-miss. Between 10 and 40 per cent of any particular batch of bottles exploded; probably just as many failed to sparkle properly. No wonder that at this time the majority of champagne made was still. The problem of inconsistency was gradually solved during the course of the nineteenth century, in a number of ways. One solution was found by Mumm, who imported from Germany some colossal 12,000-litre tuns in which to ferment the wine. These huge vats produced wine which sparkled consistently, and were rapidly taken up by other producers as a result. They also produced wines which tasted consistent, and it was this new consistency which made possible the mass marketing of sparkling champagne.

The people who tell us that blended champagnes are superior to champagnes made from single grape varieties in single villages are interested parties. The big champagne houses, who seek by means of vast public relations expenditure to indoctrinate us with this belief, began as, and still are, merchants, who buy in grapes or wine from various growers and blend them together. Only two of them,

Bollinger and Louis Roederer, themselves grow more than 50 per cent of the grapes they need; several houses, including Alfred Gratien and Piper-Heidsieck, own no vineyards at all. Thus, if they say champagne is a blended product, it is because their business lies in selling blended products. To sell champagne under the names of individual vineyards or villages would weaken the brand image which they have worked so hard to promote.

The same is true of port. Blended, branded port achieved its apotheosis when Cockburn's failed to declare the 1977 vintage, as they needed the grapes to improve the quality of their non-vintage ruby port, Special Reserve. This was an act of folly, especially considering that their 1983 and 1985 vintage ports are perhaps the finest of those years, and serve greatly to enhance the image of the company and its products as a whole. But even classic vintage ports such as these are a blend of wine from several different vineyards. Need they be? So we are told by Cockburn's and other leading British shippers of port. But then, until recently, they had no vineyards in the Douro. The first port-shipping house to start buying vineyards up-river was Offley in the middle of last century. Although, in the last ten years or so, some of the shipping houses, such as Taylor's, have tried to manoeuvre themselves into a position in which all the grapes for their vintage port at least are produced in their own vineyards, it is too late: the belief that vintage port must be blended from vineyards in different places already runs in their blood. Moreover, for the shippers to countenance single-estate vintage port would be to encourage farmers to set themselves up in rivalry. Export regulations prevented farmers who lacked offices in Oporto from exporting their own vintage port before the 1982 vintage. Now an increasing number of single-estate vintage ports from growers are becoming available. The best is probably Quinta do Cotto from Montez Champalimaud, an ex-playboy who had to start to earn a living after the revolution.

Vintage ports, like vintage champagnes, are produced on average only three or four times a decade. In lesser years the fruit of the best vineyards has hitherto been used by merchants to improve the quality of their standard blends. In middling years the port houses, having purchased all these new vineyards, have started to commercialize their produce under the name of single-*quinta* ports. In theory these come from single estates (*quintas*) but here, as elsewhere in the port trade, the absence of strict regulations enables the shipping houses to do what they like. Unlike in France – where to call a wine Château Quelque Chose there has to be a château – nothing in the Portuguese wine laws compels them to use only the produce of a single *quinta* in a so-called single-*quinta* port. Only the vintage port, not the other qualities marketed by the port firm Quinta do Noval, is made from the produce of the estate from which the company takes its name. More confusing still, Graham's Malvedos is not a single-*quinta* port but simply the same sort of blend as their vintage port from a less good year. Malvedos is a brand name; it is purely coincidental that Graham's own a *quinta* called Malvedos. Graham's Malvedos, however, has often been listed by wine merchants as Quinta do Malvedos, and is twice described by Robin Young in his *Really Useful Wine Guide* as a single-*quinta* port,[8] so clearly someone is getting confused. Are Graham's bothered? Or do they, along with all the other houses who release 'single-*quinta*' ports in years which are not quite good enough to declare a vintage, want us to believe that in these years the best wine they can produce is the unblended produce of a single farm? If so, this conflicts with the doctrine that the best vintage ports are a blend of wine from several different vineyards.

Likewise, the best champagne is the unblended produce of the best vineyards. Though they do not admit as much by word, the champagne houses confess this by deed. In 1984 Krug launched Clos du Mesnil 1979, at the top of their range, at twice the price of 'ordinary' vintage Krug, a ridiculous £60 a bottle retail, despite the vines being only six years old. By this act they gave the lie to their and their colleagues' protestations. Here was the most esteemed firm of champagne-blenders admitting that the best wine they could produce came from a single grape variety in a single vineyard in a single year.

A priori, the best champagnes must be those made from single grape varieties in single vineyards in single years. To argue otherwise would be to suggest that the best burgundies should be made, not only from a blend of vineyards or vintages – as is currently the case only for lesser burgundies – but from a blend of red and white grapes. For the grape varieties in Champagne are the same as those in Burgundy; indeed, they were introduced into Champagne from Burgundy, probably in the fifteenth century. The idea of making pink burgundies from three-quarters red and one-quarter white grapes went out in the eighteenth century. No one nowadays produces a burgundy comprising 60 per cent Mâcon Rouge (half Gamay and half Pinot Noir), 30 per cent Mâcon Blanc, 5 per cent Gevrey-Chambertin and 5 per cent Meursault – and then sells it at the price of Gevrey-Chambertin or Meursault. Yet this is precisely what happens in Champagne. It is patently absurd that tasteless blended champagnes, containing a great deal of indifferent grapes, should retail in this country for £15 a bottle, more than it costs to buy champagnes made by growers from the best grapes in the best vineyards.

One of the many reasons why the superiority of single-variety over blended champagnes is not appreciated is that champagnes are drunk young, and champagnes made solely from Chardonnay or Pinot Noir do not start to develop their complexity until they are six or seven years old. Most champagnes on sale in 1988 are made predominantly from the 1985 and 1986 vintages. One purpose of blending is to render wines ready for drinking earlier than they might otherwise be. In his interview in 1963, mentioned earlier, Ronald Barton said that, as a result of the increased proportion of Merlot, clarets are ready to drink earlier than they used to be. Before the development of modern methods of controlling fermentation temperatures, and of extracting colour and flavour without tannin, one of the best means of satisfying popular demands for wine to drink young was by blending the main variety of the region with something softer: in Bordeaux, softening Cabernet Sauvignon with Merlot.

Blending for this reason is carried out in many other regions. The 'traditional' mix of grapes which go into Chianti was invented by Baron Ricasoli, who took over his family estate at Brolio in Chianti Classico in the 1830s. He developed a blend of 80 per cent Sangiovese, 15 per cent Canaiolo and 5 per cent of the white grape Trebbiano, with the explicit purpose of satisfying the demands of Tuscan consumers for a wine which could be drunk young. Even when Florence briefly became the capital of Italy in the late 1860s, the wines served in polite society were French ones, not Chianti, which was still thought of as an everyday wine for drinking young, not a fine wine to keep. It is perhaps surprising that Ricasoli should have thought it necessary to develop this new blend, when historically Chianti had been made principally from Canaiolo, a grape which produces a much less tannic wine than Sangiovese; and in fact, in the 1930s, his family firm were producing Chianti from 40 per cent Sangiovese, 40 per cent Canaiolo and 20 per cent white grapes. But the introduction of white grapes into red Chianti had been Ricasoli's idea, and was fossilized when, in 1963, *denominazione* regulations were drawn up, making it obligatory for growers to plant a minimum of 10 per cent white grapes in their black grape vineyards, while failing to create a *denominazione* for white Chianti. In 1984 the minimum of white grapes was reduced to 2 per cent. Those Chianti producers who have been trying to create the reputation of their region as a source of fine wine for ageing have steadfastly ignored these requirements. Many of them now make their best wine entirely from Sangiovese grapes, such as Badia a Coltibuono's Sangioveto, though these are not entitled to the Chianti *denominazione*.

What happened in Chianti was not unique. In several regions of France white grapes were in the past included in the red wine, but in most cases this ceased last century, when consumers became willing to buy wines that needed time to mature. Nevertheless, Burgundian wine-makers are still allowed to include up to 15 per cent of the white Pinot Blanc and Pinot Gris grapes in their red wine, and producers in the Northern Rhône are still permitted to introduce up to 15 per cent of the white grapes Marsanne and Roussanne into red Hermitage, and up to 20 per cent of Viognier, the grape variety responsible for Condrieu, into Côte-Rôtie. Though white grapes are never, so far as I know, added to red burgundies, which tend to be pale enough as it is, and rarely to red Hermitage, which is usually considered to be a big, tough wine, they are frequently included in the blend for Côte-Rôtie, particularly by vine growers with holdings on the 'blonde' side of the slope, in order to give their wines delicacy. René Rostaing's Côte Blonde *cuvée* includes 15 per cent Viognier; Guigal's La Mouline, a vineyard in the Côte Blonde, contains between 10 and 12 per cent, though no one would describe this as a light wine.

A blended wine is usually ready for drinking sooner than a single varietal. One might expect it to be the other way round, and that a blended wine needed longer to marry. In fact, using a mixture of varieties gives a complex flavour much more rapidly – the different tastes of the different varieties – whereas wine made from a single variety will be no more than fresh and fruity when young. Only as it ages will complexity develop. Few of the chemical reactions which occur during bottle-ageing have as yet been identified. It is, however, believed that it is the tannins in red wines which are principally responsible for the virtues of maturity. Since tannins are found in the skins of the grapes, the eventual quality of a bottle-aged wine clearly depends on the quality of the grape variety. In each particular region, the best grape variety produces the best wine – if you are prepared to wait for it to develop.

Those clarets which, in the last century, had a little Hermitage added to them, to make them fuller and richer, had a much shorter life than pure clarets, even though the latter were lighter and lower in alcohol. It was said that the practice of 'hermitaging' clarets 'gave the appearance of body, but deadened the flavour; and, after a few years in bottle, the wine became of a brownish hue, hard and flavourless'.[9] Much the same happens to those red burgundies which are today produced by blending different vintages. This would be legal if the wines did not boast a vintage date: but they do, so it is illegal. Both 1976 and 1983 were abnormally hot years, producing grapes with very high sugar and tannin levels. Sensibly enough, many wines in both vintages were blended with the produce of lighter years – 1982 in the case of the 1983s. This blending was successful when carried out during fermentation, but not when done afterwards. That is why some 1976s have already fallen apart, without ever coming round.

The use of softer varieties to make a wine ready to drink sooner necessarily implies blending with higher-yielding varieties in order to increase the size of the crop, since one reason why, in Bordeaux, Merlot is softer than Cabernet is precisely that it gives a higher yield and therefore is less concentrated. As Ronald Barton said in his 1963 interview, 'Since the war, the Merlot has come into favour because in certain years it produces more.' Even those producers who achieve sufficiently high prices to justify making wine entirely from a top-quality but low-yielding variety have recourse to high-yielding varieties which have no real taste of their own but can serve as a cheap, neutral base for a better variety. Whereas Merlot in Bordeaux imposes a definite character of its own on the wine, Pinot Meunier – the little-discussed third grape in Champagne – does not.

The most pervasive of these neutral, high-yielding blending varieties is Trebbiano, known in France as Ugni Blanc. It comes in very useful in central Italy. Since Frascati is not generally considered to be the sort of wine on which it is worth forking out large sums of money, £7 or £8 a bottle, it is not really economic to make it from Malvasia, which yields only half as much juice per hectare as Trebbiano. So Malvasia is blended with Trebbiano. In many cases, the blend is something like 10 per cent Malvasia and 90 per cent Trebbiano, which probably explains why most Frascatis bear a marked resemblance to a solution of 12 per cent ethanol in water. The only mass-produced Frascati which I know to be made solely from Malvasia is the one sold by Colli di Catone in unattractively frosted bottles; it is good, but hardly cheap. Trebbiano serves a similar purpose in Umbria, where it comprises up to 65 per cent, and the relatively low-yielding Grechetto no more than 30 per cent of any wine bearing the Orvieto *denominazione*. The best white wines of Umbria are consequently not Orvieti but 100 per cent Grechetto *vini da tavola*, such as Bigi's remarkable Marrano, which is fermented and matured in new oak casks, and, from Perugia, thirty miles north-east of Orvieto, the Grechetto of Arnaldo Caprai.

The alternative to blending with higher-yielding varieties in order to increase the size of the crop is blending with wine from elsewhere. In some instances, this is permitted by the laws. Whereas, in Burgundy, a 1985 Vosne-Romanée les Malconsorts must be 100 per cent Pinot Noir, 100 per cent from the 1985 vintage and 100 per cent from the Malconsorts vineyard – and similar rules apply throughout France – in the Mosel, a 1985 Wehlener Sonnenhur Riesling Kabinett may be only 85 per cent Riesling, may contain 15 per cent from another vintage, and 15 per cent from other vineyards, not merely from other parts of the village of Wehlen, but from anywhere within the Mosel-Saar-Ruwer region.

In Italy the position is more complicated. Spanna in the Novara-Vercelli hills in northern Piedmont is not a DOC – *denominazione d'origine controllata*, the Italian equivalent of *appellation contrôlée* – but it is the local name for the Nebbiolo grape and therefore, under EEC regulations, any wine sold as Spanna must comprise at least 85 per cent of that grape variety. This requirement is frequently ignored. Some of the finest wines of the region are produced by blending in an unspecified quantity of Aglianico from Basilicata,

500 miles to the south; Spanna on its own can be rather thin. Antonio Vallana's once-wonderful Spannas were rumoured to have been produced by just such judicious blending; have they fallen off since the early 1970s because he now makes them solely or largely from local grapes?[10] On the other hand, Barolo, the most celebrated Nebbiolo wine of Piedmont, is a DOCG – *denominazione d'origine controllata e garantita*, one step up on DOC, with a compulsory tasting test – and local regulations do not permit any blending at all. A number of 'very distinguished' Barolo producers nevertheless use Gaglioppo grapes from Ciro in Calabria for the same reason as Spanna producers use Aglianico from Basilicata. But, unlike the Spanna-makers, who are allowed their 15 per cent, Barolo producers have to do it in secret.[11]

Until it was elevated from DOC to DOCG in 1984, the 85/15 per cent rule applied also in Chianti. Now wines from Chianti Classico and the two other officially recognized sub-zones (Chianti Rufina and Chianti Colli Fiorentini) must comprise only locally grown grapes. They are no less in need of beefing up with a quantity of Montepulciano from the Abruzzi than before, but it is now illegal. In the rest of the Chianti region, however, it is still permitted to blend in not only 15 per cent of wine from elsewhere, but also grape-must concentrate, which often contributes a 'cooked' taste. This is usually produced in the south of Italy, but not from the noble Aglianico or Gaglioppo grapes. The use of concentrate in Chianti has *increased* in recent years as a result of the general abandonment of the traditional *governo* process, whereby vine growers dried grapes on trays and added their concentrated juice to the finished wine at the end of the year, causing it to re-ferment, producing a richer, slightly sparkling wine (like the old use of Süssreserve). Growers say that they have given up the *governo* because wines thus produced do not have the ability to age. Nonsense. Fabrizio Bianchi of Monsanto, who makes one of the best and longest-lived Chiantis, used the *governo* until 1968; he made superb wines by this method, and some of them are still available. The American wine writers Sheldon and Pauline Wasserman believe that producers have abandoned the *governo*, not for reasons of quality, but because of the extra labour costs involved: adding concentrate from the South instead is so much cheaper.[12]

Thus, in Chianti at least, most blending, legal or otherwise, worsens the quality of the wine.

The suffering of wine-drinkers at the blenders' hands should, however, be seen in perspective. Tea-drinkers, for example, are badly misled. Although the best Darjeeling tea, like the best champagne and the best port, is the unblended produce of a single estate – in which condition it can be bought from a few specialist tea merchants such as Whittards – for commercial reasons it is not merely blended but shamelessly adulterated. There is simply not enough genuine Darjeeling to supply international demand. A statistic, of unknown origin, which is much quoted by members of the tea trade, is that Darjeeling exports only 12 million kilograms of leaf annually, yet 40 million kilograms of Darjeeling blends are sold every year round the world. At least these 'Darjeelings' often include *some* genuine Darjeeling leaves. A lot of what is sold as 'Keemun' is ordinary blended China Black tea, *none* of it from the Keemun region. Although tea is not affected by specific labelling regulations, these practices might well be held to constitute making a false description contrary to the provisions of the Trades Descriptions or Food Act. They take us back to the wine trade of the 1960s when, according to John Mahoney, the Secretary of the Wine and Spirit Association, merchants' labels described the wine and not the area of production. 'After all, you do not expect Brussels sprouts to come only from Brussels.'[13]

Those days are not gone for ever. Though the term *vinho verde* is applied colloquially by the Portuguese to any young white wine, the only region of the country permitted to market its produce as Vinhos Verdes is the Minho, in the north. The districts allowed to produce Vinho Verde have been officially demarcated. Not a great deal of Vinho Verde is made here, and an increasing proportion of it is bottled and commercialized by the growers themselves. Some of them make fine, dry, fragrant, frequently still wines, which are well worth buying. Paço do Cardido, from João Pires, is outstanding. Certain suppliers of branded 'Vinho Verde' cannot fulfil the needs of customers from the produce of the small estates of the Minho, especially in conditions of increasing demand and declining supply. They therefore buy the light white wine produced by cooperatives in Oeste, north of Lisbon, 200 miles away, and import it into the Minho, where they add a bit of sugar to soften it and some carbon dioxide to make it prickle, and send it on its way as 'Vinho Verde'. These wines are no more genuinely the produce of the Minho than are 'British-made' cars, assembled here from components imported from abroad, genuinely the product of Britain.

[1] H. Warner Allen, *A History of Wine*, Faber & Faber, 1961, p. 214.
[2] Hanson, p. 120.
[3] Auguste Petit-Lafitte, *La Vigne dans le Bordelais*, 1868, p. 189.
[4] Anthony Hogg (ed.), *Wine Mine*, Peter Dominic Ltd, 1970, pp. 132–7.
[5] Burton Anderson, *Vino*, Macmillan, 1982, p. 377.
[6] Quoted in Jancis Robinson, *The Great Wine Book*, Sidgwick & Jackson, 1982, p. 128.
[7] Forbes, p. 378.
[8] Robin Young, *The Really Useful Wine Guide*, Sidgwick & Jackson, 1987, pp. 90, 162.
[9] T. G. Shaw, *Wine, The Vine and the Cellar*, 1863, p. 171.
[10] Sheldon and Pauline Wasserman, *Italy's Noble Red Wines*, Blandford Press, 1985, pp. 145, 152.
[11] Nicolas Belfrage, *Life Beyond Lambrusco*, Sidgwick & Jackson, 1985, pp. 255–6.
[12] Wassermen, pp. 171–2.
[13] *The Times*, 29 November 1966, p. 9.

THE LAW IS A ASS

Why do wine laws not prohibit adulterations such as those described in the previous chapter? Essentially, adulteration is permitted if the most powerful wine producers in a particular region want it to be. Looking at the different views of adulteration taken by the wine laws of various countries, it is clear that what they do is impose the practices of the majority of producers on the rest, whether they like it or not. For example, the addition of sugar to fully fermented wine is allowed in France but not in Germany. It was legal in Germany between 1886 and 1971, but, once it was no longer used by the majority of wine-makers, who had adopted Süssreserve instead, it was made illegal by the new wine laws of 1971. Thus the sugar scandals of the early 1980s, in which 2,500 wine-makers were prosecuted for adding liquid sugar to their wines, are a consequence of a change in the law, not of any change in the methods used by wine-makers. On the other hand, chaptalization is permitted in Germany for wines below Kabinett quality, and in the northern half of France but not in Italy, where the political lobbying power of vine growers in the South has managed to get enshrined in law their insistence that growers in the North who need to chaptalize their wine should do so with concentrated grape-must produced in the South.

Likewise, wine laws prohibit a number of seasonings while permitting some others which are no less adulterous but which the majority of producers want to use. In the Middle Ages table wines used to be flavoured with herbs and spices; though this is no longer permitted, they are still used to preserve unsuccessful wines – it is just that the result is now called vermouth. The up-market French vermouth Lillet, which is produced in the Sauternes region, was created late last century as an attempt to do something with Sauternes from a bad harvest. Today, except in the case of retsina, pitch and pine resin may no longer be added to wines. In Roman times they were widely employed, and Pliny waxes lyrical about the different varieties used, saying that the best resin comes from Cyprus and the best pitch from Calabria – just as a wine writer today might express his preference for oak from Limoges and Nevers.[1]

Not all wine producers whose wines taste of oak, however, have derived that flavour from cask-ageing. For a barrel to bestow a remarkable taste of oak, it has to be new – but new casks cost £200 a time for the 225-litre size they use in Bordeaux. Allowing for interest charges, profit margins, transport costs and taxes, this means that ageing a wine in new oak casks can add an extra £1.50–2 a bottle to the price by the time it arrives in Britain. The alternative is to age the wine in much older oak casks for a much longer time, as is done in Rioja. This is dangerous – the wine is likely to lose fruit and develop excessively high levels of acetic acid. Perhaps that is why there is all too often a lack of correspondence between the oaky flavour of a Rioja and the length of time it has spent in casks which really are too old to have given it much oak flavour. There is no doubt that many wineries in Rioja add commercial oak essences or oak chips, though they are not candid about it. In Portugal many companies are much more open about their practices. Certainly the large Portuguese firm of Caves Aliança freely admit to treating their best Dão wines with oak strips.[2]

To age cognacs in oak takes twenty years or more. It is far more cost-effective to sweeten a young cognac with sugar in order to conceal its rough edges and to add *boisé* in order to give an appearance of age. *Boisé* is a tannin solution made by adding wood chips to boiling water, straining it and adding the liquid to young cognacs. However, adding wood to a spirit is not just as good as maturing the spirit in a wooden cask. Reactions occur during cask-ageing, involving, among other things, the lignin in the wood, which naturally improve the taste of the spirits.

It is no coincidence that many consumers prefer whisky to cognac on the grounds that an excess of cognac produces a terrible headache the morning after the night before. The headache is caused by the higher alcohols, also called fusel oils – *Fusel* in German means, colloquially, 'rot-gut' – and it is the purpose of long cask-ageing to break these down. No cognac is required to undergo long cask-ageing. Even VSOP cognac need only be four and a half years old. Attempts have been made to 'mature' whisky and brandy with carbon to remove the fusel oil, but without complete success. The carbon removes not only the bad but also the good tastes. It absorbs everything: that is why it is used in gas masks. That is why, too, vodka is passed through carbon, so that the end result is as close to a solution of pure ethanol in water as possible.

Boisé is perhaps the least surprising of the various substances which are added to brandies. It is alleged that some cognac houses add artificial flavours which they have purchased from Dutch perfume manufacturers.[3] Early last century, much of the brandy sold as 'cognac' derived its character from having almond cake kept in it for a long time – which was considered even then to be adulteration. Yet almonds are widely used to flavour Spanish and Portuguese brandy today. In Jerez, Terry, who are owned by Harveys, steep each 30,000 litres of brandy in 1,000 kilos of almonds for six months.[4] Prunes are also used. Can these adulterations be justified on the grounds that flavour is thereby improved?

A product is adulterated if the consumer is thereby deceived into believing that it is different, or of another quality, from what it claims to be. It is a criminal offence under section 2 of the Food Act 1984 to 'sell to the purchaser's prejudice any food [which in this context includes drink] which is not of the nature, or of the substance, or of the quality of the food demanded by the purchaser'. The flavouring of brandy with fruit and nuts is certainly adulteration – we expect brandy to be distilled *wine* – but not, perhaps, a very serious one, as there is no evidence of an intention to deceive, as there was, for example, in the minds of those producers who, early last century, kept chilli peppers in the brandy for a month to give it a hot pungent flavour, and therefore an appearance of strength.[5]

By this criterion, the addition of caramel to brandies and whiskies is a very serious adulteration, because the customer is thereby deceived. Since long cask-ageing turns a spirit dark in colour, because of the oxidation of the tannins, a dark colour is associated with a longer-matured, and thus superior, spirit. Producers of whisky and cognac who colour these spirits with caramel might well defend their practice on the grounds that consumers want this colour, but do not necessarily want – or at least cannot afford – to pay for a product which has acquired this colour naturally. But this argument can hardly be pressed by port producers who add caramel to tawny port, since the raw product to which this treatment is applied is sometimes table wine from the Dão region. With a bit of judicious colouring and sweetening with caramel, this can very successfully be passed off as tawny port. If the addition of caramel to port comes to be prohibited as a result of Portugal's entry into the EEC, perhaps the practice of passing off Dão wine as tawny port will cease too.

Not only does its use deceive the consumer, but caramel (E 150) is not necessarily safe. Burnt sugar is fine, but commercial caramel is not made by burning sugar. Certain caramels have been found to include 4-methylimidazole, which is toxic to mice, rabbits and chickens. Some forms of caramel are banned in some countries. Even if the labelling of the ingredients contained in drinks products were made compulsory, we would not necessarily be told which products contained caramel, because, if it is used as a flavouring, as opposed to a colouring, it does not have to be specified. A safe alternative is malt extract, but that costs twice as much.

Like darkness in spirits, a deep colour in a red wine is considered to be a positive feature, since we associate it with the produce of a hot summer and with a product that offers a concentrated flavour. Frequently nature fails to provide this colour, and it has to be added. In the days before industrial technology, vegetable dyes such as logwood, beetroot or elderberry juice were used. England's monastic vineyards in the Middle Ages found it easier to produce white than red wine; they then coloured this with elderberry juice to produce the blood-red wine that was required for their religious services. Many of the ports of the first half of the eighteenth century owed their vibrant purple colour also to the virtues of elderberry juice. In this case, however, the blending was carried out surreptitiously; and, after the 1750s, it became a felony punishable by transportation for life to have an elder tree growing on a property within the port region. Nevertheless, the use of elderberry juice did continue, if not to the extent alleged by Mr Lytton, the Secretary to the British Legation at Lisbon, when he said that, up until 1865, all the port exported to England was 'composed almost quite as much of elderberries as of grapes'.[6]

The first artificial dyes, derivatives of coal tar, were produced in the 1850s. Their vibrant, permanent colours transformed the textile industry. One of the first of these dyes was magenta (originally called fuchsine), produced by the action of arsenic acid on aniline.

This came into use in the 1870s, when phylloxera devastated the French vineyards, and *piquettes* and raisin wines had to be commercialized. *Piquettes* were made by adding water to the residue left over after making wine and fermenting the result; raisin wines, by adding water to raisins imported from abroad and fermenting this. Neither looked very pretty: *piquettes* were a dirty pink, raisin wines a dirty white colour. Red colouring therefore had to be added. The exposure of this practice caused a big scare in Britain, not least because it was stated by an authority that 'all the French wines are suspicious'.[7] Quite apart from its arsenic content, fuchsine, like all coal-tar dyes, is a suspected carcinogen and mutagen. It is no longer used in foodstuffs. Its role has been taken over by Red 2G (E 128), also derived from coal tar, and also possibly unsafe. This is widely used (in Britain at least) in cold meats, sausages, chocolate-flavoured sweets, taramasalata, etc. It is not a permitted additive to wine, but I would not be surprised if it were sometimes used. Certainly a number of lager, cider and brandy producers add the yellow coal-tar dyes tartrazine (E 102) and sunset yellow (E 110) to their products.

Pink champagne is a fad which comes and goes. Ironically, though much champagne, which is made from red grapes, is naturally a pink wine, it is difficult to produce pink champagne to order. The degree of pigmentation of the grapes varies according to the warmth of the summer; and in any case, most of the colour falls out during the double fermentation which champagne undergoes to make it sparkling. Whenever pink champagne is in vogue, therefore, two versions tend to be available: pink champagne made properly by the maceration method, that is, leaving the juice in contact with the skins of the black grapes for a while, to pick up some red colour from them; and pink champagne made by adding red colouring matter. In the early nineteenth century there was *vin de Fimes*, coloured with elderberry liqueur; in the middle of the century pink champagne was coloured with cochineal (E 120). In the second half of last century, this was replaced by synthetic dyestuffs, whose colour lasted better. (In any case, cochineal is made from cactus beetles, and is therefore too expensive to be used widely today.) Most pink champagne is made nowadays by adding 10–12 per cent of the still red wine of the region to white champagne. It is the only *appellation contrôlée* wine in France permitted to be made from a blend of red and white wine. Yet it costs more than white champagne. Patently, a pink champagne made in this way is a rip-off; but the method whereby the champagne has been coloured is not indicated on the label. Only on tasting can you tell if a pink champagne has been made from black Pinot Noir grapes, vinified briefly on their skins. By then it may be too late.

The attitude of wine laws to seasoning and adulteration can only be understood if it is appreciated that they were introduced to protect wine producers against the adulteration of their products by unscrupulous rivals – not to protect consumers against the adulteration by wine-makers of their own products. Wines have always been adulterated, but the development of technology in the Industrial Revolution made methods of doing so more sophisticated. Factories were set up for the faking of wine. It was said that, at the port of Sète in the Languedoc, 'All the wines in the world are made. You only have to give an order for Johannisberg or Tokay – nay, for all I know, for the Falernian of the Romans or the nectar of the gods – and the Sète manufacturers will promptly supply you . . . The great trade of the place is not so much adulterating as concocting wine; they will doctor you up bad Bordeaux with violet powders and rough cider, colour it with cochineal and turnsole, and outswear creation that it is precious Château Margaux, vintage of '25.'[8] Adulteration became the order of the day after the French vineyards were devastated by the phylloxera louse in the 1870s. In Paris in 1905, out of 600 samples tested at random in various warehouses, 80 per cent had been adulterated. It was said that it was as rare to find pure wine in the city as a virgin of twenty-one summers. In 1882 the *Pall Mall Gazette* stated that most of the 'cognac' entering England 'comes out of potatoes and not out of grapes'.[9] No wonder the English upper classes turned to whisky instead.

As demand increased and adulteration with it, reliance on the reputation of a brand name became increasingly important. But the brand name needed to be protected in law. By 1819 Le Chambertin was 'producing' 3,000 casks a year, of which only 100 were genuine. As a result of this and similar adulterations, pressure was brought to bear by the political representatives of fine-wine districts, resulting in the introduction in 1845 of legal protection for brand and place names. The establishment in the second half of the nineteenth century of today's brands of whisky, cognac, champagne, port and sherry, would not have been possible without the legal enforcement of the exclusive use of brand names. The registration of trade marks and brand names was introduced gradually: in France in 1857, in Britain in 1875, and internationally in 1890, though not by the Germans until they were forced to in 1919. The present century has seen the gradual introduction in France of *appellation contrôlée*, which is intended to safeguard the reputation of wine regions as a whole.[10]

But has *appellation contrôlée* succeeded in preventing the abuse of famous names? In his book on Burgundy, Anthony Hanson points out that, before the 1979 vintage, burgundies did not have to be tasted before being allowed to bear the name of the *appellation*. A wine produced within the *appellation contrôlée* rules therefore had the right to a famous name, regardless of how disgusting it tasted. As a tasting test now applies to all wines from regions entitled to the *appellation contrôlée*, all wines should, in theory, at the very least be typical of their region. But patently they are not. How else could red wine still be coming out of Burgundy and tasting as though it has been bolstered with wine from the South of France? Is that how the official tasters think burgundy ought to taste? Or are they simply not doing their job? Certainly some growers can evade the tasting test by submitting samples of a good wine twice, and then using the second certificate for a poor *cuvée* which would not otherwise have been passed. An enormous amount of tasting has to be done in growers' cellars in the few months after the vintage, before the wines disappear into merchants' blends. In practice, only random sampling is carried out, and only in growers' cellars. No one seems to mind what the merchants do with the wines they buy.

Control is even more lax in Germany. Ninety-five per cent of wines applying for an AP (*Amtliche Prüfung*) number are awarded it. This indicates that the wine has passed an official blind tasting and chemical analysis. Patently, undeserving wines are passed – the liquid sugar scandals reveal that, as does the di-ethylene glycol scandal, when German wines were found to be contaminated because their makers had illegally blended in substantial quantities of Austrian wine.

Anyway, it is easy enough to fake an AP number. In 1984 it was reported that a wine producer from Franconia was being investigated for the suspected illegal labelling of unexamined wine as quality wine; that he had used fake AP numbers on his labels from 1979 until 1983; but that 'the investigators are having a difficult time'.[11] Moreover, once a sample of wine has been passed and given its AP number, the grower can print as many labels as he likes. There cannot be any control over the quantity of wine allowed to be bottled with a particular AP number, because in many parts of Germany there is as yet no control over yields. How can Germany expect its wine laws to be treated with respect, when, despite its irregular and often excessively cold climate, 95 per cent of its wines – all those in receipt of an AP number – are entitled to the designation 'quality wine'? In Italy, which enjoys a much more favourable climate, the figure is 10–12 per cent. In England, which does not enjoy a much worse climate, the figure is 0.

But then, in France, the *appellation contrôlée* regime, though it successfully ensures that no more wine is sold than has been produced, does not make certain that the wine sold with the *appellation contrôlée* label is the same wine as that which was produced under the *appellation contrôlée* regulations and submitted for the tasting test. One may wonder why merchants were so frightened when compulsory bottling in the area of production was introduced in Alsace in 1972. It was feared that this was the thin end of the wedge – but it has not proved to be, despite the support of growers throughout France. I doubt that the reputation which Alsace enjoys throughout the wine trade for offering sound, reliable wines – the sort you might order in a restaurant, even if you had not heard of the producer – is a coincidence.

Bottling a wine in the region of production has always been an effective means of preventing adulteration. For example, Chianti had become very popular in England by the beginning of the eighteenth century. As it was exported in cask, merchants found little difficulty, in 1710, in supplying particularly large orders by blending it with other, inferior wines, so the decision was taken by a number of producers to ship the wine in flasks which could not be tampered with in the same way.[12] In the early nineteenth century, when Lafite was so much the snob name that even Latour was being passed off as Lafite in England, Goudal, the manager of the château, suggested that Lafite should bottle all its wine itself in good vintages. In fact château-bottling was not adopted by the five first-growth clarets until the 1920s, and then only for part of their production.

Since the 1972 vintage it has been compulsory for all the classed-growth châteaux of the Médoc, which may help to explain why they are no longer adulterated to the same degree as burgundies.

In Australia, laws of *'appellation'* exist in only two regions: Margaret River in Western Australia and Mudgee in New South Wales. In both cases, a wine may claim to have been produced in the region only if 100 per cent of the grapes were grown there. Elsewhere, wine producers act as if there were no laws to restrict their blending activities, mixing wines from various regions, partly to provide consistency of taste, partly in order to hold down prices, and selling the result as the produce of a single region. They are breaching the Pure Foods Act, which stipulates that, if a grape variety or district is specified on the label, at least 80 per cent of the wine must have been produced from that variety or district. In 1985 the State of Victoria introduced an Authentication Scheme. A member of the Authentication Sub-Committee said, 'We wanted to introduce authentication in order to stop the big boys from cheating. But I'm afraid we're already too late.'[13]

Adulterations usually come to light only by chance. The addition of methanol to cheap Italian wine was exposed in 1986 when a two-litre bottle of wine claiming to have been made from the local Barbera grape was bought in a Milan supermarket and caused the deaths of the three people who drank it. This bottle cost 1,790 lire (about 75p). It had been an open secret for some time that such wines must have been fraudulent. After all, the production costs alone of a genuine two-litre bottle of Barbera were about 2,000 lire. It was well known that Piedmont sold more than twice as much wine as it produced. It had been pointed out on many occasions that wines could be bought in big stores in Italy at prices which indicated either that the producer was making a loss or that he was doing something illegal. Yet the only reason why the truth about methanol emerged was that the producer of this wine, Giovanni Ciravegna, made the mistake of adding too much methanol to a particular batch of 'Barbera'. Otherwise he and his fellow adulterators would probably have gone on selling their wines for years. People might have died from methanol poisoning, but too slowly for it safely to be attributed to any one source.[14]

The Austrian 'anti-freeze' scandal was revealed only because Siegfried Tschida, a wine producer in Pamhagen, was greedy enough to claim VAT refunds on the di-ethylene glycol he had added to his wine.[15] Yet the most appalling adulterations had been going on in Austria for years before this scandal was exposed, including the production of artificial wine, which owed nothing to the grape, and the addition of dangerous preservatives to stabilize sweeter wines. At the end of 1985 Erwin Klenkhart was arrested and charged with adding gunpowder to his wine to make it sparkle. Wine laws existed, but they were not enforced. Enforcement lay in the hands of the regional governments, who were not willing to pursue matters which might have embarrassed their political supporters. According to an article in the wine-trade magazine *Wine and Spirit*, in 1981 an inspector was refused permission to instigate a prosecution against one of the country's leading wine houses.[16]

In Germany, the most eminent of the wine-makers to be prosecuted in 1983 for adding liquid sugar to their wines was General Werner Tyrell, former President of the German Viticultural Association, and sole proprietor of the celebrated Eitelsbacher Karthäuserhofberg in the Ruwer. During his trial it was revealed that the official chemist, Brigitte Holbach, had known since 1979 that Tyrell had been sugaring his wine, but had been prevented by her superiors from informing the Public Prosecutor of her findings.[17] But then, as long ago as 1975 it had been noted by a German trade paper that more wine of Spätlese quality was being sold than had actually been produced in some vineyards, and that this wine was sold for two marks a bottle although genuine Spätlese cost five marks to produce. This wine could only have been produced by illegal sugaring.

Adulterations are sometimes brought to light for political reasons. In 1974 the Cruse scandal destroyed public confidence in the integrity of Bordelais merchants, and impelled a collapse in the market for fine clarets. Because of a dramatic rise in the prices of Bordeaux wines, Pierre Bert, a small merchant, had found himself unable, without losing money, to fulfil a contract he had made to supply wine. Therefore he purchased wine from the South of France, and altered *appellation contrôlée* documents covering white Bordeaux in order to pass off this wine as red Bordeaux. He sold this wine to the firm owned by the prominent Cruse family. Bert and the Cruses were found out, prosecuted, and given prison sentences. During his trial, Bert told Anthony Terry of the *Sunday Times* that he could not understand 'why on this occasion the inspectors did not just ring up as they have done in the past and say they had some information. The matter was then settled with a handshake and a few thousand francs across the table. After all, everyone has been doing it in one way or another for years and the inspectors have learnt to live with the facts of life.' The reason why the Fraud Squad did proceed for once, Anthony Terry was told by a Bordeaux merchant, was that the Cruse family were related to Jacques Chaban-Delmas, whom Giscard d'Estaing had just defeated in the Presidential election. There was no suggestion that Giscard had ordered the Fraud Squad to investigate the Cruses' activities, but rather that the Fraud Squad Inspector in charge of the case thought that Giscard would be delighted to get one over on his erstwhile opponent.[18] That would certainly explain why only the Cruses, and none of the other merchants who had bought wine from Pierre Bert, were prosecuted.

Most scandals, however, are brought to light because jealous rivals have sneaked on a colleague. At the time of writing (1988), the Fraud Squad is proceeding against René-Claude Martin, the owner of the Muscadet firm of Martin-Jarry, for allegedly blending table wine from the Entre-Deux-Mers and Loire-Atlantique regions, and selling it as *appellation contrôlée* Muscadet. René Martin maintains that the allegations were made by three rival companies who were jealous of his success. Indeed, they had been jealous for years – it was simply that no one had got round to doing anything about it. According to the allegations, René Martin, like Pierre Bert before him, juggled *appellation contrôlée* certificates so that he could sell cheaper wines as more expensive ones. Like Pierre Bert, no one ever complained about the quality of the wine he was selling.

For Frascati, too, demand exceeds supply, as the expansion of the Roman suburbs puts pressure on land which might otherwise be used for vineyard expansion. No problem: the wine is produced beyond the generous maximum yield of 108 hectolitres per hectare, and the excess production is attributed to vineyards which are buried under tons of concrete apartment block. It has been suggested that this opportunity for deception will be removed by an official census of vineyard sites.[19] Will it? In the Douro region of Portugal, in order to be allowed to turn grapes into port, a producer must possess a *cartão de beneficio* – a permit which states that the grapes have been produced in a site which is classified for port production, and which indicates the quality of the site and the price paid for the grapes, varying on a scale from A to F. Not all the land classified for port grape production is still vineyard land. For example, the football pitch at Regua is classified to produce grade A port grapes. Not surprisingly, there is a booming trade in *cartãos de beneficio*. Armed with these permits, a producer can go down to the Dão region and buy wine there for use in his 'tawny ports'.

In the long term, wine laws can only become effective through the development of scientific techniques of detecting adulteration. The technology exists: it is a matter of using it. Di-ethylene glycol was added to some Austrian wines from 1976 onwards, and its presence could have been detected long before 1984 if anyone had thought of putting the wines through a gas-chromatograph in order to analyse their constituent components. Gas-chromatography was developed in the 1960s, and does not require particularly expensive equipment, so there can be no excuse for failing to use it.

It may, before too long, prove possible to check a wine's geographical origin and vintage date by analysing the proportion of different isotopes of oxygen atoms in the water – which is the principal constituent of wine. These atoms do not all weigh the same, and can be divided into the isotope ^{16}O and the isotope ^{18}O. Since ^{18}O isotopes are lost by evaporation, a wine produced in a region where rain falls will contain more of them than one produced near the coast. They can therefore be examined to determine a wine's region of origin. As different amounts of rain fall each year, it should also be possible to use ^{18}O isotopes in order to test a wine's vintage.

The grape variety from which the wine has been made can then be checked by 'fingerprinting'. If a wine is put through a gas-chromatograph, its aroma can be separated into several hundred individual components, and the quantity of each of these can be measured. By comparing the aroma compounds of a suspect wine with the 'fingerprints' of one that is known to be genuine, its veracity can be determined. This method still has a long way to go, because only 400 out of wine's approximately 800 aroma compounds have so far been identified, and detection is proceeding at a rate of only three or four a year. It is hoped that eventually, by attributing specific aroma compounds to particular trace elements in the soil, it will be possible to identify the vineyard from which a wine originates.

On the other hand, the American oenologists Amerine and Roessler do not believe that one can differentiate grape varieties by examining the results of fermentation, because the processes which occur during fermentation are not properly understood and are affected in different ways by various strains of yeasts and bacteria.[20]

In any case, consumers would not necessarily be assisted by more effective laws. Already the Italian government has spent a quarter of a million pounds on its first nuclear magnetic resonance spectrometer, which has come into use with the 1987 vintage, and it is being predicted that illegal chaptalization with sugar in Italy will become a thing of the past. This instrument is capable of determining whether alcohol has been derived from sugar or from grapes, because alcohol obtained from sugar has a different molecular structure from that originating from grapes, and, by means of nuclear magnetic resonance spectroscopy, it is possible to work out a molecule's structure. But forcing wine-makers to use grape-must concentrate instead of sugar for chaptalization is a political decision, not a qualitative one. The problem for the consumer is not merely that wine laws can readily be avoided or manipulated, but that wine laws exist to protect the interests of producers, and in some cases themselves manipulate consumers.

The yields permitted for the production of quality wine in many wine regions far exceed those which are commensurate with quality. In France, until 1974, the cascade system existed. This permitted a wine-maker to sell the same wine under several different *appellations*, as each one set down a different maximum yield. If, say, a grower in the village of Pauillac in Bordeaux produced 80 hectolitres per hectare when the maximum permitted crop for a Pauillac was only 40 hectolitres per hectare, he could sell 40 hectolitres per hectare as Pauillac, 5 hectolitres per hectare as Médoc (the limit for this *appellation* being 45 hectolitres per hectare), 5 hectolitres per hectare as plain Bordeaux (for which the limit was 50 hectolitres per hectare), and the other 30 hectolitres per hectare as *vin de table*. Today the excess production over the limit permitted for each *appellation* has to be sold off for distillation. The wine-maker can choose between, at one end of the scale, making a Pauillac and sending half his production to be distilled, and, at the other, making a *vin de table*, in which he is permitted to include all the wine he has made.

It is remarkable how many members of the wine trade believe that the cascade system is still in operation, and claim that the table wine they are selling is the 'excess production' of some *appellation* or other. Such bargains, if that is what they were, no longer exist. Outstanding *vin de table* can, however, occasionally be found in the form of the produce of vines in famous regions which are less than four years old and therefore not permitted to bear grapes for *appellation contrôlée* wine. An example is Domaine Corsin's white *vin de table*, from the Mâconnais. The availability of such wines cannot be relied upon, as it depends on vines having recently been planted.

In 1974 the old maximum yield for each *appellation* became its basic yield (*rendement de base*). This figure could now be reviewed annually, to take account of especially bad or especially good vintages. The yield for the year (*rendement annuel*) in question was to be proposed by the local vine growers' union and determined by the Institut National des Appellations d'Origine. The *rendement annuel* usually exceeds the *rendement de base*. The actual maximum yield (*plafond limite de classement*, or PLC for short) is 20 per cent above the permitted annual yield, providing that growers ask for it before the harvest. This extra 20 per cent is defended on the grounds that a vine grower asking for it has to submit his wine to a tasting test, and if it fails, his entire production of that *appellation* has to be declassified into *vin de table*. What casuistry! This tasting test applies to all wines claiming *appellation contrôlée* status, not just to those wanting an extra 20 per cent PLC. The basic yield in Vosne-Romanée is 35 hectolitres per hectare. However, in 1986 an annual yield of 50 hectolitres per hectare was requested, and granted. Add on 20 per cent PLC, and you arrive at a maximum permitted yield of 60 hectolitres per hectare, substantially more than was allowed for such relatively humble appellations as Côtes du Rhône-Villages. No wonder so many red burgundies taste watery.

In Champagne the new law, though it permits generous enough yields, is *legally* broken. In 1973 the maximum yield (PLC) was set at 86 hectolitres per hectare. A bumper harvest in 1982 produced an *average* yield of 92 hectolitres per hectare. No one wanted to waste this bounty, even though it was – theoretically – an illegal one. The

Institut National des Appellations d'Origine allowed the Champenois to keep it in reserve, to be used to top up vintages which did not reach the maximum yield. The 1983 harvest was even bigger, so a further quantity of wine was put into reserve. By this point reserve stocks of illegally overproduced wine amounted to 75 million bottles' worth. These were used to top up the rather smaller vintages of 1984 and 1985. In 1986 producers, happy with a system of legalized illegal overproduction, set aside a new reserve of 10 per cent of their total crop. This system of 'blocking' stocks was one of the scandals about Bordeaux revealed by Pierre Bert in his book, *In Vino Veritas*: that growers who exceeded the legal maximum yield of 40 hectolitres per hectare simply kept their excess production in reserve and declared it as part of the next harvest, if that turned out to be a small one.[21]

As has already been mentioned, in much of Germany the laws do not at present attempt to impose any brake on overproduction. The reason for this is that the Germans do not consider the quality of their wines to relate to their concentration of flavour – which depends on the lowness of the yield. They dismiss years like 1984, when yields were very low and the wines had good depth. They look for a fragrant balance of fruit and acidity, which can be achieved with enormously high yields. In 1983, allegedly a great year, yields were two to three times higher than those achieved in the 'mediocre' 1984 vintage. Without yield control, the German authorities will never come to grips with the problem of illegal sugaring or illegal AP numbers. Even the Austrians brought in a legal maximum yield after the di-ethylene glycol scandal, which owed its origins to the need to give more body and richness to thin, overcropped wines. It is now being suggested that, at long last, the Germans will do so too. Maximum yields have already been introduced autonomously by the States of Baden-Württemberg (95 hectolitres per hectare) and Bavaria, which includes the Franconian vine-growing region (100). This is one reason why these regions produce dry wines with body which stand up to food better than their counterparts in the Rhine or Mosel, such as the Silvaner and Rieslaner *trockens* produced by the princely estate of Castell (Fürstlich Castell'sches Domänenamt) in Franconia. But, as dry wines grow in importance in the Rhine and Mosel, the need to restrict their yields becomes ever more pressing. In 1987, the German Viticultural Association agreed to introduce maximum yields by 1989; the limit will vary throughout the country, but will average 100 hectolitres per hectare. This limit is intended to be absolute, with no possibility of overproducing and selling the result as table wine. I shall believe it when I see it.

In some instances wine laws, instead of trying to make things easier for consumers, help producers to pull the wool over their eyes. In Burgundy, *appellation* laws have officially ennobled lesser wines by allowing them to append the name of the village's most famous site to the name of the village. Thus the wines produced in the village of Gevrey can bask in the reflected glory of their greatest wine by passing under the appellation of Gevrey-Chambertin; those of Chassagne can call themselves Chassagne-Montrachet, and so on. Something similar has also occurred in Bordeaux. By the early 1920s twelve châteaux in the Graves had hyphenated the name Haut-Brion on to their own. André Gibert, the new owner of Château Haut-Brion, took ten of these châteaux to court, and in four instances won his action. The court ruled, however, that Haut-Brion was a place and not a brand name, and therefore might be appended to the names of châteaux which shared the Haut-Brion plateau. Larrivet-Haut-Brion, which was not on the plateau, was allowed to continue using the name Haut-Brion on grounds of long usage, but it was forbidden to print 'Haut-Brion' in larger type than Larrivet, as it had done previously.

In the Glenlivet case, the court was more generous to the appropriators. Glenlivet had once sarcastically been known as 'the longest glen in Scotland'. In 1880 George Smith, the owner of The Glenlivet, brought a case to establish that only whisky made from the water of the Livet burn could bear the name, but he succeeded only in forcing neighbouring whiskies to use a hyphen. Whereas Tamnavulin-Glenlivet is situated in Glenlivet, Aberlour-Glenlivet is a Speyside whisky and does not even taste like a Glenlivet one. Dufftown-Glenlivet is in Glenfiddich; Glenfiddich could call itself Glenfiddich-Glenlivet if it wanted.

At the southern end of Burgundy's Côte d'Or, three little-known villages, Cheilly, Dezize and Sampigny, have enjoyed the right to add to their names that of their most famous vineyard, Les Maranges. In fact they are so obscure that the wines have hitherto been sold largely under the generic *appellation* of Côte de Beaune-Villages. But in 1987 a new *appellation* was created; or rather, an existing one was enlarged. All three villages are now able to sell all their wines, not just with the name of their most famous vineyard, Les Maranges, appended, but under that name alone. It is as though all the wine produced in Gevrey could sell itself as Le Chambertin, or all the wine in Chassagne as Le Montrachet – which is precisely what has happened in Germany.

The German wine laws were overhauled in 1971. Famous vineyard names were turned into names covering, not just a whole village, but a whole district; Scharzberg, hitherto a single site, became a generic name which every single wine produced in the Saar is entitled to use. The single-vineyard site Scharzberg no longer exists. It is as though every single red burgundy produced, not merely in the village of Gevrey, but in the whole of the Côte de Nuits (which is about the same size as the Saar) were allowed to call itself Le Chambertin.

Many other of Germany's most famous sites, though not abused to the same extent, were in 1971 enlarged so far as to lose all meaning. Whereas in Burgundy the *grand cru* vineyards, however variable the wine made from them, at least in most cases enjoy a unity of potential, in Germany single-site names now encompass a wide variety of soils and exposures. Thus one man's Piesporter Goldtröpfchen or Wehlener Sonnenhur is not merely less well made than another's, but, even if it were equally well made, it would not be equally good. That is why it has been suggested that, whereas Burgundy enjoys a classification of the best vineyards into *grands* and *premiers crus*, based on their potential quality, in Germany such a classification would not work. Given the current legalized abuse of famous site names, the only valid classification would be one of growers.

All of which is particularly unfortunate, since the law which applied in Germany before 1971 was considerably less misleading than that now applying in Burgundy. Any wine grown in the borough of Piesport could be sold as Piesporter, but only wine from the Goldtröpfchen vineyard could be called Piesporter Goldtröpfchen. (Given their practice, mentioned above, of appending the name of its most famous vineyard on to the name of each village, the Burgundians would have given the name Piesporter-Goldtröpfchen to all wines produced in Piesport.) It did not matter too much that there were 30,000 different site names, as it was indicated from which village a wine came. But nowadays there is no way of knowing from which village a wine comes. It may sound ridiculous, but any wine originating within the same *Grosslage* – a generic denomination covering several villages – can use the name of any village within it.

The French have not deprived themselves of this peculiarly Germanic form of self-abuse. There are a number of instances of the enlargement of the area of vineyard entitled to famous names beyond the soils to which the reputation is due. The wines of Saint-Joseph in the Northern Rhône have become fashionable in the last couple of years, following upon those of Hermitage, Côte-Rôtie and Cornas. Some outstanding wine is produced within the *appellation* of Saint-Joseph, particularly in and around the village of Mauves. Growers such as Pierre Coursodon, Emile Florentin and Roger Blanchon produce mini-Hermitages. But the *appellation* of Saint-Joseph covers a total of twenty-six villages, few of which contain vineyard sites with the potential to produce fine wine. Apparently, when the boundaries of the *appellation* were drawn up, some of the leading growers, complacent about the outcome, failed to attend the crucial meeting.

In Madeira there is a substantial demand for wines made from the noble grape varieties: Malmsey (Malvasia), Bual and Sercial. But consumers are not prepared to pay the necessary price. For example, the ten-year-old Malmseys from Blandy's and Rutherford and Miles cost as much as twenty-year-old tawny ports (though even at that price they are undervalued). Therefore the majority of madeiras, though pretending to the names Malmsey, Bual and Sercial, are made from the less noble Tinta Negra Mole grape. In his book on madeira, Noël Cossart says that, when this practice began, between the wars, his cousin Sidney Cossart would 'spit with fury' when he saw an inexpensive madeira labelled 'Malmsey'. What's wrong with 'Rich'?[22] This practice misleads us into thinking that Malmsey, Bual and Sercial madeiras are everyday wines which it would not be a crime to use in madeira sauce. Following Portugal's accession to the EEC, this practice will become illegal in 1992.

On the Portuguese mainland the wine laws favour producers of branded wines, who, in concocting their blends, ride roughshod over different regions. After seventy years of discussion, Bairrada was finally demarcated for the production of quality wine only in

1979, the wines having hitherto been used to satisfy the blending needs of merchants in Dāo. Yet there is no question that, of the two regions, the future of Bairrada is the brighter.

The vineyards of Dāo are planted in a mish-mash of grape varieties, many of them bad, and most of them diseased. By law, a minimum of 20 per cent of each red Dāo should be made from Touriga Nacional, the best black grape variety in Portugal and the oustanding constituent of vintage port. But how can this law be observed when plantings of Touriga Nacional in Dāo fall far short of 20 per cent of the vineyard area and are in decline, and when peasants bring to the cooperatives grapes of different varieties, both black and white, mixed together? On the whole, Dāo is being stifled by bureaucrats – a common enough experience in post-Revolutionary Portugal. Wine production is supervised by the Federação dos Vinicultores do Dāo, whose inspectors seal the openings of casks with white tape and red sealing-wax. If a merchant wants to draw a sample of wine from a cask to check its progress, he has to notify the Federação in advance, so that they can send an inspector to break the seal. This requirement is, I suspect, more honoured in the breach than in the observance. Wines may not be commercialized until they have passed a tasting test. This would be fine, were it not that tasting panels prevent wines, both red and white, from being put on the market whilst they are still young and full of fruit; they seem to prefer wines which have spent too long in cask and dried out.

Whereas the vineyards of Dāo, an isolated region almost surrounded by mountains, are split up between 40,000 peasants, the Bairrada region runs north from Coimbra, and a number of relatively wealthy landowners own substantial vineyards whose produce they commercialize themselves. That of Luis Pato is superb. If the reputation of the table wines of Bairrada has been eclipsed by that of the port wines of the Douro over the last two centuries, it derives only in part from the potential quality of the produce, and partly from the fact that, in the 1750s, the Marquês de Pombal, the effective dictator of Portugal, decreed that the majority of Bairrada vineyards be uprooted, in order to protect the growing port wine trade from competition.

Even less well known in Britain than Bairrada is Reguengos de Monsaraz in the Alentejo, which is not yet demarcated, as it is still needed to give richness to *garrafeira* blends. Yet, according to Antonio Franco, president of the merchants J. M. da Fonseca, this region probably offers greater potential than any other in Portugal. In 1986 his firm sold most of their shares in the company which produces Lancers (which Americans who are new to wine drink instead of Mateus Rosé) in order to finance the purchase of the estate of José de Sousa Rosado Fernandes. The red wines produced by this estate are sold at a price which makes them perhaps the greatest bargains in the world of wine today, though they do need a few years' ageing in bottle to show of their best.

Many wine laws protect famous regions against the attempts of other regions in the same country to attain the same status by restricting the cultivation in those other regions of grape varieties to which the famous regions have staked a proprietorial claim. In France, for example, growers wishing to enjoy the right to inscribe the word *appellation contrôlée* on their wine labels are usually prohibited, outside Bordeaux, from cultivating Cabernet Sauvignon, and outside Burgundy, from cultivating Chardonnay or Pinot Noir. It is not that these varieties are not 'local' elsewhere – until last century Pinot Noir was the dominant black grape variety in the northern half of France – but that the two famous regions wish to enjoy the exclusivity of their use. Vine growers claiming the right to the *appellation* of Châteauneuf-du-Pape may cultivate as many as thirteen different grape varieties, and some producers use all of them. But Jacques Reynaud, the proprietor of Château Rayas, arguably the leading estate of the *appellation*, grows other varieties as well, including Chardonnay and Pinot Noir. His father, Louis Reynaud, who planted the vineyard in 1922, once famously declared that '*appellation contrôlée* is the guarantee of mediocrity'. To a degree, it is right that it should be so. The function of laws is to protect the status quo, not to encourage experimentation. Wine laws exist partly in order to protect the individuality of different regions. I don't think anyone would want all the vine-growing regions of the world to jump on the bandwagon and convert to growing Cabernet Sauvignon or Chardonnay, the fashionable varieties of the moment. Protecting the status quo, however, is one thing; looking backward is another. According to Mario Consorte, oenologist at Sella e Mosca in Sardinia: 'The function of DOC has been to preserve the memory of historic wines, not to reflect the actuality of the market.'[23] For example, DOCG laws require Barolo to be aged in oak for a minimum of two years. Many producers consider this to be too long, and, quite sensibly, ignore the law on this point. Roberto Voerzio, who obeyed the laws until 1982, says that the wines he used to produce now make him sick.[24]

The security of a famous name offers a negative virtue. The most celebrated wine-producing regions acquired their reputation by offering quality; but today a famous name denotes, at best, nothing more than lack of abuse. Improvement is frequently impossible within the confines of wine legislation. Italian wine laws, by supporting the biggest producers with the most muscle, penalize quality-oriented wine-makers. Mario Pojer and Fiorentino Sandri, who make an outstanding Müller-Thurgau and an excellent Chardonnay in Trento in northern Italy, believe that DOC is a disadvantage for producers of top-quality wine, since it enables 'industrial' producers to use the sanction of official denominations to enhance the status of their mediocre wines, causing consumers to expect lesser wines from a particular region than they might otherwise have done, and thus making it more difficult for the better producers to obtain adequately high prices.[25] That is why they sell all their wines as table wines (*vini da tavola*). Many of the greatest wines of Italy – from the 100 per cent Cabernet Sauvignon Sassicaia to Avignonesi's sublime Vin Santo – are also *vini da tavola*. Indeed, hardly any of the Vin Santo produced in Tuscany – including Avignonesi's – is entitled to DOC status. Yet, unlike such sanctioned wines as Chianti, Vino Nobile di Montepulciano or Brunello di Montalcino, this semi-maderized dessert wine made from dried grapes preserves the taste of the most celebrated wines of Roman Italy.

[1] Pliny the Elder, *Natural History*, AD 77, Book 14, Chapter 25.
[2] *Wine and Spirit*, February 1985, p. 48.
[3] Nicholas Faith, *Cognac*, Hamish Hamilton, 1986, p. 118.
[4] *Wine and Spirit*, August 1986, Sherry and Spanish Brandy Supplement, p. 5.
[5] Anon., *Wine and Spirit Adulterations Unmasked*, 3rd ed., 1829.
[6] Quoted in anon., 'Wine and the Wine Trade,' *Edinburgh Review*, 1867, pp. 179–204.
[7] Professor L. Grandeau of Nancy, quoted in *Brewers' Guardian*, 1876, pp. 309, 336, 373.
[8] 'A popular writer' – I know not who – quoted by James L. Denman, *Wine and its Adulterations*, 1867.
[9] Quoted Faith, p. 73.

[10] The best account of the introduction of *appellation contrôlée* is given by Hanson, pp. 40–54.

[11] *Wine and Spirit*, October 1984, p. 25.

[12] G. Cosimo Villifranchi, *Oenologia Toscana*, 1773, quoted in A. Marescalchi and G. Dalmasso, *Storia della Vite e del Vino in Italia*, 1931–7, vol. 3, pp. 563–4.

[13] Quoted in *Wine and Spirit*, August 1985, p. 67.

[14] *The Times*, 21 April 1986; *Wine and Spirit*, December 1987, p. 10.

[15] *Observer*, 11 August 1985, p. 9.

[16] *Wine and Spirit*, April 1986, p. 45.

[17] Hallgarten, pp. 68–9.

[18] *Sunday Times*, 20 October and 3 November 1974.

[19] Nicolas Belfrage, *Life Beyond Lambrusco*, Sidgwick & Jackson, 1985, p. 227.

[20] M. A. Amerine and E. B. Roessler, *Wines: their sensory evaluation*, W. H. Freeman, 2nd ed., 1983, p. 73.

[21] Pierre Bert, *In Vino Veritas*, Albin Michel, 1975, p. 65.

[22] Noël Cossart, *Madeira*, Christie's Wine Publications, 1984, pp. 111–12.

[23] Quoted in Belfrage, pp. 48–9.

[24] Quoted in *Wine and Spirit*, April 1987, pp. 49–51.

[25] Quoted in Belfrage, p. 188.

VARIETAL WORSHIP

Why should wine laws need to prohibit the plantation of noble but foreign grape varieties in order to ensure that individual wine regions retain their uniqueness as far as possible? Why, for instance, should Tuscan vine growers want to desert the intrinsic character of Chianti, which is derived from the local grapes, Sangiovese and Canaiolo, by planting the Bordeaux grape, Cabernet Sauvignon? The laws restrict plantations of Cabernet Sauvignon to a maximum of 10 per cent of any Chianti vineyard; but some Chianti producers make quasi-Bordelais blends, only entitled to *vino da tavola* status, such as Antinori with their Solaia, 75 per cent Cabernet Sauvignon and 25 per cent Cabernet Franc. Antinori, who are part-owned by Whitbread, do so in order to satisfy an international taste. The taste of every grape variety is different, and takes time to acquire. For historical reasons wine-drinkers are used to the taste of claret (red Bordeaux) and white burgundy.

The long history of British partisanship for the wines of Bordeaux began in 1152, when the region became part of the domain of the English king as the result of the marriage of Henry II to Eleanor of Aquitaine. The *per capita* consumption of Bordeaux wine in early fourteenth-century England was five to six litres per adult per year – a figure not again equalled for *all* wines until the 1980s. Claret fell out of favour in the eighteenth and early nineteenth centuries but regained its popularity when Gladstone reduced the duties on light wines from France in 1860–61, after which 'wine consumers seemed to care for nothing else'.[1]

Admittedly, the taste for white burgundy is a newer one: although it was widely drunk in Britain last century, it was, with the exception of Le Montrachet, not as highly esteemed as champagne, Rheingau wines or sherry. The present elevated reputation of white burgundy derives largely from the gradual falling by the wayside of its rivals: sherry at the turn of the century, German wines on account of the two world wars, champagne because, apparently, it was tarnished by its association with 'profiteers' in the 1920s;[2] these wines are no longer drunk with meals. Bordeaux is associated with the Cabernet Sauvignon grape, Burgundy with Chardonnay – and vice versa. This is the consequence of the French system of *appellations*, which has succeeded in claiming proprietorship over certain grape varieties, in identifying certain varieties with certain regions. Claret (at least in the Médoc) is made predominantly from Cabernet Sauvignon; therefore Cabernet Sauvignon is associated with Bordeaux. It was not always so.

The reputation of the fine wines of Bordeaux was created by wealthy local businessmen who planted their estates in vines largely in the period from 1670 to 1725. In some cases, they uprooted white grape vines and replaced them with black. One of these black grape vines was the Cabernet Sauvignon. It was highly regarded, but yielded little; therefore it spread only slowly. Not until the 1850s and 1860s were the leading estates sufficiently in demand and thus sufficiently profitable to be able to convert a predominance of Cabernet Franc into one of Cabernet Sauvignon.[3] Thus in Bordeaux the fame of the grape derives from the fame of the region, and not vice versa.

It is possible that the growth in the reputation of white burgundy in the course of the last hundred years has owed something to the rise to prominence of Chardonnay. It is not, however, clear when white burgundies began to be made predominantly from Chardonnay rather than Pinot Blanc or Pinot Gris. These varieties have probably been cultivated in the region for longer than Chardonnay, since they are mutations of Pinot Noir, which is a descendant of a variety of wild vine native to France, whereas Chardonnay is an (admittedly ancient) import from the Lebanon. No one knows when Chardonnay replaced the Pinots Blanc and Gris; and no one will admit that it has not yet entirely done so. Vine growers have sought to excuse their 'confusion' by claiming that the leaves of Chardonnay vines are indistinguishable from those of Pinot varieties; they are similar but they are not identical. Because Chardonnay today enjoys a better image than Pinot Blanc, vine growers in Burgundy and Champagne claim that their Pinot Blanc vines are Chardonnay. They tell you that they could not have any Pinot Blanc vines, because it is not legal to plant them; but they do, and it is. Indeed, *appellation contrôlée* regulations for Champagne name Pinot Blanc as a permitted variety but make no mention of Chardonnay! Certainly the majority of white grape vines in both regions are Chardonnay; but I defy anyone, in a blind tasting, to distinguish a white burgundy professedly made from Pinot Blanc, such as Lequin-Roussot's Santenay Blanc, from one made from Chardonnay.

In all probability white grape vineyards were converted from a predominance of Pinots Blanc and Gris to one of Chardonnay in the middle of last century. But the authorities contradict each other. In 1816 Jullien stated confidently that the main white grape variety for fine wines in Burgundy was Chardonnay.[4] Yet forty years later Lavalle described the Pinot Blanc as the fine-wine white grape in Burgundy. He was a botanist, and can hardly have been ignorant of the difference between Pinot Blanc and Chardonnay.[5]

Until the 1940s no one spoke of grape varieties, of Cabernets and Chardonnays, but of clarets and white burgundies. Wines produced in Australia or California from good-quality grapes – as likely Sémillon or Syrah as Chardonnay or Cabernet Sauvignon – were called 'white burgundy' or 'claret' if they resembled these wines in any respect. This practice led to abuses. In California, after Prohibition, producers of ordinary-quality wines appropriated the names champagne, chablis, burgundy and claret, and lessened their image in the eyes of the consumer. Therefore producers of fine wines took up naming their products after their unique feature – the grapes from which they were made. Thus the labelling of wines as Chardonnay and Cabernet Sauvignon began as a *faute de mieux* way of saying 'white burgundy' or 'claret'.

Today wine-makers sell blended wines as Chardonnay or Cabernet Sauvignon. In California, until 1983, a Cabernet Sauvignon wine need have been produced from no more than 51 per cent Cabernet Sauvignon; that figure has now been increased to 75 per cent. Ridge's brilliant York Creek Cabernet Sauvignon, for instance, contains between 5 and 15 per cent Merlot, depending on the vintage. The names Cabernet Sauvignon and Chardonnay have become known and are being cultivated the world over as a result of the success of the Californians in their explicit efforts to 'beat' the flagship French wines. Initially they were so keen to do this that they didn't bother about planting these grapes in the right soils or regions. They planted them in the Napa Valley – which is probably not the area of California best suited to the cultivation of Chardonnay, and possibly not to that of Cabernet Sauvignon either. The cooler Carneros Valley, where the vines enjoy a climate more comparable to that of Atlantic and Continental France, had been planted in the nineteenth century, but not again in earnest until the 1960s. The gap, according to the locals, came because academics at the University of California at Davis wanted to prove that Cabernet Sauvignon and Chardonnay could produce great wine under Californian, not quasi-French, conditions; and they wanted wines which would win tasting competitions in their youth, not ones which were austere and uncompromising for the first five or six years of their life. The American bicentennial tasting organized in Paris by Steven Spurrier in 1976, in which Cabernets and Chardonnays from the Napa Valley 'beat' those of Bordeaux and Burgundy, proved the Davis academics' point.

It is hard to berate Californian vine growers for cultivating Cabernet and Chardonnay. They have no good native grapes of their own; any variety they planted would have to be imported from Europe. This gives them, like the other vine-growing regions of the 'New World' – Australia, New Zealand, South Africa et al. – an advantage. They do not have gradually to transfer from one vine variety to another as occurred in Bordeaux and Burgundy in the nineteenth century. They can start with a clean slate; and with only the best variety. The planting of the Napa Valley over the last generation has been compared by Hugh Johnson to the planting of Bordeaux in the period from 1650 to 1750.[6]

The Italians, the Spanish and the Portuguese, on the other hand, have great native grapes. Noble black grape varieties native to Italy include Nebbiolo, Sangiovese, Montepulciano, Gaglioppo and Aglianico; in Spain they include Grenache, Tempranillo, Mencia and Graciano; in Portugal, Touriga Nacional, Barroca, Baga, Ramisco and Periquita. Noble white grape varieties are fewer but still include Aleatico, Greco, Grechetto, Arneis and Nosiola in Italy; Malvasia and Verdejo in Spain; Arinto, Alvarinho, Louriero, Trajadura and Fernão Pires in Portugal. The enormous potential of some of the more obscure of these varieties will be evident to anyone who has tried the Arneis delle Langhe from Castello di Neive in Piedmont. Why should vine growers in these countries need Cabernet Sauvignon and Chardonnay?

These local varieties suffer from a negative image. According to Nicolas Belfrage, in the 1940s and 1950s the Italians found themselves having to decide which way they were going to point their wine industry. They decided that, since France had already captured the fine-wine sector, Italy's future could only lie in taking up the low and middle ground. This worked well until the early 1970s, when wine consumption began to fall. The wine lake grew. Because the wines which were no longer wanted were those mass-produced from native Italian grapes – Soave, Valpolicella, Chianti, etc. – other wines made from Italian grapes were caught in a 'negative image trap'. Vine growers who wanted an up-market image therefore had to plant grape varieties with an up-market image: French ones.[7]

Rather like a new pop singer seeking to establish himself by recording 'cover versions' of a song made famous by someone else, the planting of French grapes by vine growers in other countries will achieve the desired effect only if, the reputation having been established, the singer/wine-maker starts producing his own material. That is the route of long-term fame. It is one reason why the Rolling Stones achieved superstar status in the mid-1960s but the Animals did not.

It is particularly tempting to plant Cabernet Sauvignon and Chardonnay because they are very hardy, disease-resistant vine varieties, which even in the hands of a bad wine-maker will usually produce an acceptable wine. Moreover, Chardonnay, if not Cabernet Sauvignon, regularly produces large yields. Many of the good native grape varieties in Italy, Spain and Portugal, on the other hand, have not been clonally selected to produce the best, most disease-free and highest-yielding varieties. Clones are different varieties of the same plant; the best clone of a particular variety can be found by careful examination of individual vines over a number of years. Cuttings from the healthiest and most productive vine then provide the source of all new plantings. The problem with clonal selection is that, at present, it takes twenty years to tell if the vines which appear superior really do produce better wine. It is hoped that, in time, by taking chemical 'fingerprints' of the aroma compounds of a grape by means of a gas-chromatograph, it will be possible to make a judgement as to the eventual quality of the wine from which it is made. It should, therefore, no longer be necessary to wait ten years for newly cloned vines to reach maturity, followed by a further ten whilst the wine made from grapes from ten-year-old vines reaches maturity. A grape from a three-year-old vine would suffice. Clonal selection will also be accelerated by the use of test-tube vines. If the tiniest particle of the growing-tip is incubated in a test-tube, a healthy baby can be produced from a diseased mother, because, if the mother vine grows fast enough, the virus does not keep up with the growing-tip. One day it may even prove possible, through genetic engineering, to alter cell material in order to bring about specific changes in the resulting new vine. But all these developments are some way off.

It was precisely because of their hardiness and reliability that Cabernet Sauvignon and Chardonnay came to dominate the vineyards of Bordeaux and Burgundy in the nineteenth century. In the first half of the century, according to Wilhelm Franck's book on the Médoc, the two best varieties were Cabernet Sauvignon and Carmenère, which produced wine of the same quality.[8] In the second half of the century Carmenère lost its popularity. This was not so much, I suspect, because of its susceptibility to floral abortion – Merlot and Malbec, which are still popular, had the same problem – but because it yielded so little. It was said in 1868 that, whereas Cabernet Sauvignon (itself a low-yielder) produced 27 hectolitres per hectare, Carmenère grown in the same spot would yield only half as much.[9] Following the devastation of their vineyards by the oidium fungus in the 1850s and the phylloxera louse in the 1870s, the Bordelais could no longer afford quite such a voluntary reduction of their crop. At the same time as Carmenère gave way to Cabernet Sauvignon in Bordeaux, Pinot Gris fell out of favour in Burgundy because of its tendency to degenerate and its unwillingness to produce a reliable crop.

In the same period, and for the same reason, vine growers elsewhere in Europe planted Cabernet Sauvignon. In the Ribera del Duero in Spain, Vega Sicilia was planted in 1864 with Cabernet Sauvignon, Merlot and Malbec cuttings brought from Bordeaux. The owner was disillusioned with local varieties; he wanted varieties which he knew would produce good wine. This wine is today made 40 per cent from Bordelais grape varieties, and 60 per cent from the local Tinto Fino, which, under the name Tempranillo, is also the predominant grape in good-quality Rioja.

There is nothing new about the craze for Cabernet Sauvignon in Italy. The grape was brought to Piedmont in the 1850s, where it was cultivated in small quantities until phylloxera, after which growers planted Barbera. Angelo Gaja, the leading producer of Barbaresco, was simply proposing to reverse this process when he told Nicolas Belfrage that he was thinking of uprooting his Barbera vines and replacing them with Cabernet.[9]

Chardonnay was brought to Australia in the 1830s, possibly earlier. One of the best of the wines produced in the Hunter Valley in New South Wales during the 'wine rush' of the 1840s was a 'white burgundy' made at the now-abandoned Kirkton vineyard from 'white Pinot' grapes. When Murray Tyrrell, a great lover of white burgundies, wanted to revive the production of varietal Chardonnay, he planted cuttings taken from Chardonnay vines which had been 'discovered' in Mudgee in the mid-1960s and had been in Australia since before the 1930s, at the very least. Tyrrell produced his first vintage of Vat 47 Chardonnay, still an outstanding wine, in 1971.

If you are looking for a copy of a claret or a white burgundy, you will not, however, find it in hot-climate wines. According to Bill Jekel, 'white burgundies are not to every American consumer's taste'; he said, in 1981, that Californian wine-makers were trying, with Chardonnay, to produce a wine with more fruit than white burgundy, by picking grapes with a higher sugar and lower acid content.[11] Attempts in the early 1980s to produce wines which are more 'French' in style have met with considerable criticism. Robert Parker believes that Californian wines enjoyed their heyday at the end of the 1970s, and that they have fared less well in the early 1980s, not because of a stronger dollar or better European harvests, but because, in search of greater elegance, wine-makers produced wines with perfect balance but little flavour. With the bigger 1984 red wines, he believes that they have learned the error of their ways.[12]

In any case, it is not so much the grape varieties used as the style of wine-making and ageing which produces a copycat wine. It is often said that wine-making methods in Rioja today are a fossilization of nineteenth-century Bordelais practice, on which they were modelled: for example, several years' ageing of the wines in old 225-litre oak casks, compared with the eighteen to twenty-four months' storage in a mixture of new and nearly new oak casks which is general in Bordeaux today. During the 1840s Don Luciano de Murrieta, a refugee from the Carlist Wars, had settled in London and acquired a taste for fine French wines. On his way back to Rioja in 1850, he made a thorough study of the latest practices in Bordeaux, and then reorganized the cellars of the Duque de la Victoria on the same lines. The wines, matured in oak casks, won enormous acclaim. In the 1850s and 1860s French merchants turned to Rioja when their own vineyards were devastated by oidium and phylloxera, and the new demand for their products encouraged other Rioja producers to take up Bordelais methods. But very little Cabernet Sauvignon was ever planted in Rioja, because it yielded too little. Bordelais techniques were applied to the produce of the native Tempranillo, Graciano, Carignan and Grenache grapes.

New oak casks on the modern Bordelais model have become very popular in Italy since the early 1970s. Particularly successful wines are now being made in Tuscany from the native Sangiovese grape but employing Bordelais methods of maturation. The resulting wines certainly taste of Sangiovese – but I am not clear that all amateurs of claret could discern the taste of Sangiovese from that of Cabernet Sauvignon. Claret-lovers distinguish their preferred wine by its style and structure – and in terms of structure Tuscan wines such as Avignonesi's I Grifi, made 80 per cent from Sangiovese and 20 per cent from Cabernet Franc, and aged for one year in new oak casks, resemble nothing so much as claret.

For most producers and consumers, all these questions of copying, of losing one's national identity, are irrelevant. All that matters is whether Cabernet Sauvignon and Chardonnay produce good wines outside Bordeaux and Burgundy. Indeed, are they as good as – or even better than – clarets and white burgundies?

There is nothing intrinsically superior about Champagne, Burgundy and Bordeaux; there is no reason why wines of the same quality cannot be produced elsewhere. If these French wines achieved fame, and others did not, it was the result of political geography and superior wine-making; it had nothing to do with the climate or soil.

Since Roman times, the great wines of France have been produced by the bourgeoisie of the cities. The wines with the greatest reputation under the Romans were those produced by the cities of Vienne, Bordeaux, Autun and Paris. These remain the great wines of France today: respectively, those of the Northern Rhône (Hermitage, Côte-Rôtie and Condrieu), Bordeaux, Burgundy and Champagne. The French bourgeoisie derived personal pride from serving their own wines at their tables, and civic pride from the production of wines so good that they were thought to be worthy of export. In the most famous wine law of the Middle Ages, in 1395, Philip the Bold, Duke of Burgundy, ordered the uprooting of Gamay vines, which he considered to be 'wicked and disloyal'. Plantations of Gamay had increased at the expense of the noble Pinot Noir because the Pinot vine required much more attention and produced many fewer grapes, and there was a shortage of vineyard workers following the Black Death of 1349. This was disastrous to the ambitions of Philip the Bold, who was at the time more powerful than the French king, a point he wanted to rub in by staging magnificent festivities at his palace in Paris. He had to be sure that the wine he offered was up to scratch. When he described Gamay as disloyal, he really meant it. He may have failed to achieve a political position which would enable his grandson to acquire a crown, but he succeeded in creating the reputation of burgundy as the greatest wine of France and the one that, for the next 300 years, everyone else, including the Champenois, tried to copy.

In Australia, vine growing is still in the process of emerging from the historic plantation of vines last century close to the major cities. The traditional vine-growing area of Western Australia is Swan Valley, in the suburbs of Perth, which was first planted in 1859. It is rather hot for fine-wine production. Twenty years ago the government agronomist Dr John Gladstones applied to Western Australia the growing season temperature classification developed by the University of California at Davis and found the most suitable area to be the Margaret River, which had never before been seriously proposed as suitable for commercial viticulture, not least because it is 200 miles south of Perth. The first serious estate here, Vasse Felix, was planted in vines in 1967 by the Perth heart specialist Dr Tom Cullity. Vasse Felix Cabernet Sauvignon is still the most celebrated of a number of top-quality wines now being produced in the region.

In medieval France, Vienne, Bordeaux, Autun and Paris were not the only cities whose bourgeoisie produced great wine. But these were the cities which enjoyed the easiest access to the wealthy markets of northern Europe, where wine sold at the highest prices. Before the coming of the railways in the mid-nineteenth century, the only way of reaching these markets was by sea or river, or by one or two land routes suitable for heavy carts. (Burgundy, being not too far from Paris, was where Parisians went when their harvest failed.) We have heard of the wines of Sancerre and Saumur, but not of those of Bourges and Oiron. The difference is not one of soil or climate. Sancerre and Saumur exported their wines, because they are on the Loire; Bourges and Oiron did not, because they are not. Yet in terms of quality, the red Vin de Thouarsais produced from Cabernet Franc by Michel Gigon, the only vine grower remaining in Oiron, loses nothing to the majority of the red wines of Saumur and Saumur-Champigny.

If we have always bought fine wines from France, it is because it was more accessible than, say, Italy. The wine merchants who tried to import Chianti into England in the seventeenth century found that it frequently went off on the way. By the time the railways were built in the middle of last century, it was too late. The supremacy of France was already established.

The quality of the site was not particularly important. The land round Bordeaux is poor and flat: so much so that the Portuguese who came to Pomerol in the twelfth century, looking for areas to settle, rejected the site of Vieux Château Certan as it was too arid and dry, and gave it its name – *sertão* means wilderness in Portuguese. The soil was so poor that its peasants were exempted from paying local taxes. It did not matter that the soil in Bordeaux was not particularly suitable, as wines could be made superior by taking greater care over cultivation and vinification, providing there were consumers willing to pay for them. After all, that is the principle on which many of the great Californian wines of the 1970s were produced. No one has attributed the differences between these principally to the nature of the soil – so why do so with the wines of Bordeaux?

What can be said is that the climate of Bordeaux and Burgundy ideally suits the grapes which are grown in each of the regions. That is because Cabernet Sauvignon in Bordeaux, and Chardonnay and Pinot Noir in Burgundy, lie at their limits of cultivation; and it is true of all fruits that the longer the growing season, the closer they are grown to their cultivable limits, the better the quality of the product. The longer the growing season, the greater the extraction of nutriments from the soil, the more complex the flavours that are produced. On the whole, Spanish oranges are better than North African, French olives are better than Spanish, and English apples are better than French. The best tea is grown in relatively cold conditions, such as Darjeeling in the foothills of the Himalayas and high-grown Ceylon from the hills in the centre of the island. So is the best coffee, such as Jamaican Blue Mountain, Kibo Chagga from the lower slopes of Mount Kilimanjaro in Tanzania, and the Colombian coffee produced on the foothills of the Andes.

Different grape varieties have different limits of cultivation. The Mourvèdre used to be cultivated all over Provence, but since being grafted on to American root-stock after the vineyards were devastated by the phylloxera louse a hundred years ago, it ripens later, and can only be grown near the Mediterranean coast, principally in Bandol. The wines produced under this *appellation* must by law comprise a minimum of 50 per cent Mourvèdre, which here, at its cultivable limit, produces a superb red wine. The leading estate is Domaine Tempier, though their wines are expensive, and I have been more struck by La Bastide Blanche, which the Wine Society sell under the name Les Restanques. The region as a whole maintains very high standards, with the Bandol produced by the La Roque cooperative offering particularly good value.

The Riesling does best in the Rhine and Mosel valleys, which in some parts are little warmer than southern England. Alsatian Riesling lacks the delicacy of the best German Riesling; it is never of the same quality; nor is wine made from Riesling elsewhere – in most cases illegally – in France. It is just too warm.

It should even be possible to match southern England to its ideal variety. Many different grape varieties have been crossed by German viticultural stations in order to produce new varieties which will achieve more regular ripeness in their marginal climate. Müller-Thurgau was developed a century ago, allegedly a crossing of Riesling and Silvaner; in fact, in German conditions, it ripens earlier than both of them and lacks the class of either. But then it is not at its cultivable limits in Germany. In England it is, and can produce very elegant, lean, dry wines, of which the best is made by Breaky Bottom in Sussex.

Viticulture throve in medieval England. Then it died out, not to be revived on a commercial scale until the 1970s. Why? Was it the weather? Possibly not. In the early Middle Ages all monasteries cultivated vines, regardless of soil or climate, because they needed wine to celebrate mass, and could not rely on international trade to supply their needs. Vines grew in totally unsuitable places, even in Ireland and South Norway. Viticulture in England became impracticable when the monastic workforce disappeared after the Black Death.[13] Moreover, after the English Crown annexed Aquitaine in 1152, it was more profitable – not least for the king – to produce corn and import wine from Bordeaux. Imported wine could easily be taxed; home-produced wine could not. There was no great expansion of vineyards after this point.

The late, great, Edward Hyams believed that the climate in Britain, Flanders and North Germany did not preclude viticulture but simply made it relatively unprofitable. The extent of vineyards north of 50°N is therefore only ever a function of general agricultural prices. Hyams believes that a rise in cereal prices as a result of population growth was the main reason for the retreat of vines from northern Europe in the sixteenth century, not the late medieval cooling of the climate.[14]

On the other hand, the climate would certainly seem to have fluctuated in time with the rise and fall of English viticulture. Vines do not start growing until the mean air temperature reaches 10°C, a level usually reached in southern England some time between mid-April and mid-May. A fall in the average temperature of 1°C will delay the start of growth by ten days one year in two, and sometimes longer; moreover, the autumn will be cooler, preventing the compensation of a later harvest. During the medieval warm epoch which lasted from 950 to 1050 and from 1150 to 1300, the average temperatures in England between April and September were between 0.7 and 1°C higher than the average temperatures this century. The climate in summer this century nevertheless represents a substantial improvement on that achieved in the last one, and the temperatures which prevailed between 1933 and 1952 were as high as those of the early Middle Ages.[15] It surely cannot be coincidental that vine growing in England was revived during this warm period.

Even if our summers are not becoming warmer, even if the climate of southern England cannot be matched to an ideal grape variety, nothing stands in the way of the production of sparkling wine. The suitability of the English climate for sparkling wine production can be understood by comparing the climate of Champagne with that of Burgundy, where the same grape varieties – Chardonnay and Pinot Noir – are grown. Champagne, which Tom Stevenson has described in his book on the region as a 'viticultural twilight zone',[16] is 150 miles north of Burgundy, and its climate is influenced by the Atlantic, which has a cooling effect in the summer. Grape varieties which ripen fully in Burgundy do not achieve full ripeness in Champagne. They are therefore ideally suited to sparkling wine production. To make a sparkling wine by a double fermentation, you need a base wine which is low in alcohol and high in acidity. That is because the addition of sugar before the second fermentation increases the alcoholic degree and the process of fermentation reduces the acid level by the precipitation of tartaric acid crystals and the degradation of some of the malic acid by the action of yeasts. A base wine with 10.7 per cent alcohol produces a champagne with 12 per cent, and with acid levels between a quarter and a third lower.[17]

If at present champagne is better than bottle-fermented sparkling wines from California, Australia and Italy, it is because the latter are grown in warmer climates. In order to produce a fine wine, it is necessary that a grape should enjoy a growing season of about 100 days. The grapes for the majority of Californian sparkling wines are picked after only two-thirds as long. Even Iron Horse, possibly the best of them, though it does enjoy a full hundred-day growing season because of its foggy situation ten miles from the sea, still picks riper grapes than they do in Champagne – at 10 compared with 8 or 9 per cent potential alcohol – and makes a softer style of wine as a result. Champagne, which is, if anything, too cold for the production of table wine, is ideally suited to the production of sparkling wine. The same is true of England. When the bottle-fermented English sparkling wines which are presently being developed are put on the market, it may be demonstrated that champagnes are not necessarily superior. Most producers of English sparkling wines are using the same grape varieties as in Champagne, as these best suit the yeasty taste of wine made by the 'champagne method'. At the time of writing, the first sparkling wines have just been produced by New Hall in Essex and Lamberhurst in Kent. The one problem lies in the price: they are as expensive as champagne – the yields are only one-third as large – but lack its exclusive image.

A precedent exists for the production of sparkling wine in England. In the early eighteenth century, the gentleman farmer Charles Hamilton planted a vineyard in Cobham in Surrey in two grapes, both of them, I believe, clones or mutations of Pinot Noir. The first wine he made was red, but he was not pleased with it.

> The wine was so harsh and austere that I despaired of ever making red wine fit to drink; but through the harshness I perceived a flavour something like that of small French white wines, which made me hope I should succeed with white wine. That experiment succeeded far beyond my most sanguine expectations; for the first year I made white wine, it nearly resembled the flavour of champagne; and in two or three years more, as the vines grew stronger, to my great amazement, my wine had a finer flavour than the best champagne I ever tasted; the first running was as clear as spirits, the second running was *œil de perdrix*,[18] and both of them sparkled and creamed in the glass like champagne. It would be endless to mention how many good judges of wine were deceived by my wine, and thought it superior to any champagne they ever drank; even the Duc de Mirepoix preferred it to any other wine; but such is the prejudice of most people against anything of English growth, I generally found it most prudent not to declare where it grew, till after they had passed their verdict upon it.[19]

The travelling French connoisseur P. J. Grosley passed a less favourable verdict: 'to the eye, it was a liquor of darkish grey colour; to the palate, it was like verjuice and vinegar blended together by a bad taste of the soil.'[20] But he knew what he was tasting, and perhaps his prejudice got the better of him.

If every region is matched to its ideal grape variety, then only in climates comparable to those of Bordeaux and Burgundy can Cabernet Sauvignon and Chardonnay be regarded as suitable – at least as challengers to claret and white burgundy. Quasi-Burgundian Chardonnays are produced, not in the Napa Valley, but in those parts of California which enjoy a climate comparable to that of Burgundy. Summer temperatures in Carneros Valley, at the southern end of Napa, are on average 6°C lower, thanks to cooling breezes from San Francisco Bay. Hot air rises from the Napa Valley and is replaced by air from the ocean, which blows through Carneros first, because the hills west of Carneros are lower than those further north or south. ZD, who make an excellent, elegant Chardonnay, buy in grapes from three vineyards, two in the Carneros Valley and one in the similarly cool Santa Maria Valley in Santa Barbara, 350 miles to the south. In three years out of seven their Chardonnay grapes have been harvested in November – a month after the harvest in Burgundy has finished.

The argument that the finest wines are made in marginal climates has its detractors – not least among those wine-makers who seek to cultivate cool-climate grapes in warm regions. One of these is Miguel Torres, whose firm's Cabernet-based Gran Coronas Black Label won the 1979 Gaut-Millau 'Wine Olympics'. He argues that, if it was thought in the past that great wines could be produced only in those areas of Europe which enjoyed an Atlantic (e.g. Bordeaux) or Continental (e.g. Burgundy) climate, this was only because Mediterranean areas were too hot during September and October. The grapes were too warm when brought in to the winery, and fermentation was too rapid, at too high a temperature.[21] Moreover, grapes ripen very fast in hot climates, turning from underripe to overripe in a matter of hours. The problem of fermentation temperatures has been overcome by the introduction of temperature-controlled vats; that of fast ripening of the grapes has been solved by the development of harvesting machines. Torres says that in 1985 his Cabernet Sauvignon grapes were picked by machine in peak condition in three to four days; by hand it would have taken two weeks and the second week's fruit would have been 'lousy, totally overripe'.[22]

What Miguel Torres has to say is a Mandy Rice-Davies of an argument. If he cultivates cool-climate grapes in a warm region, then he would say that, wouldn't he? If wine-makers prefer warm climates, it is because the risks are less and the rewards no less. If wines produced from cool-climate grapes in warm regions 'win' comparative tastings against clarets and white burgundies, it is because they have more alcohol and more opulent fruit. This is not to decry Torres' red wines, particularly his 'ordinary' Gran Coronas, a classic example of a warm-climate wine.

It is possible to find a cool microclimate in a warm region, simply by going uphill. Torres grows Chardonnay and Riesling up in the mountains, at 2,500 feet. In the South of France, Aimé Guibert produces an outstanding, if no longer underpriced, Cabernet Sauvignon-based wine at Mas de Daumas Gassac, twenty miles north-west of Montpellier, in a part of the country which is generally far too hot for the cultivation of Cabernet Sauvignon. But the estate lies at the limits of vine cultivation, just below the moorland, hot by day but cold by night, at 700 feet but with the climatic equivalent of 1,600. The grapes are harvested early in October, at the same time as in the Médoc – not least because the vineyard faces not south, as is usual, but north-west. In warm climates it is often necessary to plant cool-climate grapes on north-facing slopes in order to produce fine wine. Angelo Gaja in Barbaresco, Antinori in Orvieto (for their 'Cervaro della Sala') and Jacques Reynaud at Château Rayas in Châteauneuf-du-Pape all cultivate Chardonnay vines on north-facing slopes.

The effect of the climate also depends on the nature of the soil. A warm soil mitigates a cool climate. Dark soils, such as the slate of many Mosel vineyards, absorb heat more quickly than light ones and radiate it more rapidly. A cool soil mitigates a warm climate. The ripening of grapes in Carneros Valley is retarded, not merely by a breeze from San Francisco Bay, but by the cooling effect of a clay soil. One might not think of Pomerol as hot, but its clay soil lengthens the ripening period of the early-ripening Merlot grape sufficiently to produce a fine wine.

For the successful cultivation of Cabernet Sauvignon, the soil has to have the right structure. Many growers in Coteaux d'Aix-en-Provence have planted Cabernet Sauvignon in the belief that a noble grape will automatically produce a good wine. But Cabernet needs unfertile ground; in Coteaux d'Aix-en-Provence there is too much fertile topsoil above the underlying gravel, so Cabernet produces a wine with deep colour and high alcohol but thin and harsh. At Mas de Daumas Gassac, there is a unique outcrop of glacial debris, four to six metres deep, covering 20 hectares, which provides the right soil conditions for Cabernet Sauvignon.

It is a matter of intense dispute whether, beyond physical effects such as these, the chemical and biological constituents of the soil greatly affect the nature of the wine made from vines growing on it. On the one hand, most soils contain all the chemical elements a vine needs; and, to those that do not, the necessary chemicals can be added. It is as ridiculous to imagine that there exists any chemical difference between nitrogen or phosphorus pre-existing in the soil and the same chemicals added in a pure form, as it is to imagine that there is any chemical or gustatory difference between acidity which occurs naturally in the grape and the same tartaric acidity which is added to the must before or during fermentation. Of course, if chemical fertilizers are added to excess, the vine produces too much fruit or vegetation, and the wine suffers; but one cannot blame the chemicals for a vine grower's abuse of them.

Can one quantify the relative importance of the microclimate and soil in making a fine wine? It depends on what side of the fence a wine-maker is standing. Whereas many Californians might say that a fine wine is 20 per cent soil and 80 per cent wine-making, a Frenchman is just as likely to say the opposite. Certainly the French make a great deal of noise about the uniqueness of the soils of the classed-growth châteaux of Bordeaux and the *grands* and *premiers crus* of Burgundy – but then they have to. Only by convincing people that the soil which produces their finest wines endows them somehow with unique properties can they possibly justify the prices they charge for them, or win the argument as to whether the wines they produce can be equalled elsewhere in the world. It is, however, a little difficult to fathom how the soils of the classed-growth châteaux of Bordeaux can be unique when they keep moving. As it is the brand names of the châteaux which have been classified, not their vineyards, many of them have got away with swallowing other, lower-rated or unclassified châteaux. There is nothing to prevent the grapes from all being vinified together, and the less good vats sold under the name of the lower-rated château. In those cases in which this is done, it patently contradicts the belief of the classed-growth châteaux in the superiority of their soils: for how can it be said that Château Rausan-Ségla, which heads the second growths in the 1855 classification of the leading châteaux of the Médoc, possesses the finest vineyard soil in the commune of Margaux after Château Margaux itself, when it has absorbed the humble *cru bourgeois* Château Lamouroux?

This said, much of the flavour of wines *does* come from the soil – from mineral substances taken up through the roots of the vine. These form what is called the sugar-free dry extract of the wine. In 1978–9 the University of Piacenza in Lombardy studied wines made from the black Vernatsch grape from nineteen different sites in the South Tyrol, and established that the colour, acidity and aroma substances of the wines were all fundamentally affected by the mineral content of the soil. It is not fanciful, for instance, to taste minerals in the wines made from the Schlossböckelheimer Kupfergrube vineyard by the Nahe State Domain. *Kupfergrube* means 'copper-mine', though early this century it was reshaped and turned into terraced vineyards by convict labour. Mas de Daumas Gassac is made 80 per cent from Cabernet Sauvignon, but it does not taste like claret. Aimé Guibert, the owner, points out that 'the *terroir* [soil] is so strong that it makes Pommard with Cabernet.'

One reason why Cabernet Sauvignon and Chardonnay in some new plantations in Australia and California have failed to produce fine wine is that the soil is too fertile: in most of the great vineyards of Europe the soil is meagre, and the vine has to dig its roots deep in search of nutriments. Another reason is that the vines in many parts of the New World are too young. As vines become older, they delve deeper, and a wine which initially tasted very much of the grape variety, but not much else, comes to taste uniquely of the soil of the region in which it is made. In time it ought to be possible to discern an Italian Chardonnay from a New Zealand one.

Young vines, however, offer the advantage of producing wine which often shows prematurely well in its youth. Cabernet Sauvignons and Chardonnays made from young vines in the New World often 'beat' those from Bordeaux and Burgundy in blind tastings for this reason – the fruit is more immediate. Young vines can produce excellent wine in good vintages, but the produce of old vines is much better in bad ones. Old vines have deeper roots, particularly if the soil is porous and therefore they have to reach down to the water table to find permanent water supplies. This not only enables them better to withstand drought, but also makes them less susceptible to rot. When rain follows drought, vines with only surface root-systems – young vines and those planted on poorly drained soil – take up water so fast that the skins of the grapes split, and rot results.

One cannot, however, write off as a consequence of the youth of vines in other countries the fact that Bordeaux and Burgundy are still producing wines from Cabernet Sauvignon and Chardonnay which are the envy of the world. The vines are not necessarily younger. The coming of prosperity to Bordeaux in the 1970s has enabled many proprietors to replant their vineyards: in 1979 57 per cent of the Cabernet Sauvignon vines in Bordeaux were less than ten years old. They produce their best and most concentrated grapes between the ages of twenty and thirty. The vineyards of Bordeaux and Burgundy are planted in a mixture of old and young vines and a mixture of clones. In the New World, on the whole, each grower has planted his vineyards in a single clone, and the same clone is cultivated by different growers in the same region – one reason why their Cabernets and Chardonnays taste more alike than they might otherwise have done. Moreover, Bordeaux and Burgundy have been provided with superior clones of Cabernet Sauvignon and Chardonnay by 300 years of natural selection. A vine grower in the New World can certainly buy a good clone of Chardonnay from a nursery – but he cannot tell how that clone will mutate once he has planted it in his soil. All plants will mutate to suit local climatic conditions. Chardonnay has changed its nature a great deal since it began life thousands of years ago in the Lebanon as the Obaideh grape. Certainly Chardonnay produces better wine in Burgundy than it does in the Lebanon. But it might well have produced worse. According to Attilio Scienza, principal of the Institute of Agriculture at San Michele all'Adige, the Chardonnay clones grown in north-east Italy – where they have been cultivated for 100 years or more – are of a type which produces more neutral wine than those grown in Burgundy. Because they cannot attain such high prices as the Burgundians, vine growers here overcrop, making the resultant wine more neutral still; then, in the excellent 1985 vintage, they overfined their wines with casein. As a result, a number of 1985 north-east Italian Chardonnays had to have their neutrality corrected by the addition of Muscat.

[1] Charles Tovey, *Wine and Wine Countries*, 2nd ed., 1877, p. 87.
[2] Evelyn Waugh, *Wine in Peace and War*, 1949, pp. 18–19, 50
[3] A. d'Armailhacq, *De la culture des vignes, la vinification et les vins dans le Médoc*, 1855; Jules Guyot, *Etude des vignobles de France*, 1868, vol. 1, pp. 455–6.

4 A. Jullien, *Topographie de tous les vignobles connus*, 1816, p. 107.
5 M. J. Lavalle, *Histoire et statistique de la vigne et des grands vins de la Côte d'Or*, 1855, pp. 164–5.
6 Hugh Johnson, *Wine Companion*, Mitchell Beazley, 1983, p. 51.
7 Nicolas Belfrage, *Life Beyond Lambrusco*, Sidgwick & Jackson, 1985, pp. 13–14.
8 Wilhelm Franck, *Traité sur les vins du Médoc*, 2nd ed., 1845, pp. 32–3.
9 Guyot, loc. cit.
10 Quoted in Belfrage, p. 169.
11 *Decanter*, August 1981, p. 42.
12 The *Wine Advocate*, no. 45, June 1986, p. 2.
13 Desmond Seward, *Monks and Wine*, Mitchell Beazley, 1979, pp. 126–38.
14 Hyams, pp. 191–4.
15 H. H. Lamb, *Climate Past Present and Future*, Methuen, 1977, vol. 2, pp. 435, 476.
16 Tom Stevenson, *Champagne*, Sotheby's Publications, 1986, p. 48.
17 Figures given by Jean Ribéreau-Gayon et. al., *Sciences et techniques du vin*, Dunod, 1976, vol. 3, pp. 475–82.
18 'Partridge-eye', i.e. pink.
19 Quoted in Sir Edward Barry, *Observations, Historical, Critical on the Wines of the Ancients and the Analogy between Them and Modern Wines*, 1775, pp. 471–5.
20 P. J. Grosley, *A Tour to London*, translated by Thomas Nugent, 1772, vol. 1, p. 83. The verjuice to which he refers was the juice of unripe grapes, which was used in cooking and for making mustard.
21 Miguel A. Torres, *The Distinctive Wines of Catalonia*, Hymsa, 1986, pp. 50–51, 66–8.
22 Quoted in *Wine and Spirit*, December 1985, p. 57.

OLD WINE IN NEW BOTTLES

I have already suggested that young vines produce wine which often shows particularly well in its youth. Does this make wine of this sort especially desirable? It is often said, after all, that we drink wines younger than we used to.

To some extent we drink young wines, not because we want to, but because we must. Updating, thirty years ago, the *Book of French Wines* he published originally in 1928, Morton Shand ascribed a *volte-face* in public taste after the First World War to our national failure to extract an indemnity from the Germans as part of the Treaty of Versailles. In order to defray the expenses of the war, money had to be raised by increasing taxation, which for the first time became a serious imposition on the pockets of the wealthy; one of the first luxuries to be abandoned as a consequence was the replenishment of private cellars. Moreover, wine merchants' stocks had been exhausted during the war, so they had to sell their customers wine from recent, unready vintages – which they did by claiming that, contrary to what had previously been believed, fine wines could be drunk young. 'Before we were half-way between the two World Wars people in Britain were already becoming accustomed to consuming what up to the First World War would have been dismissed as barbarously raw or wholesomely immature wines.'[1]

Is the present-day taste for young wines the result of a similar exploitation of their customers by wine merchants, who can no longer afford to tie up capital in holding stocks and are therefore anxious to turn them over as quickly as possible? In fact, although few people own houses with large cellars any more, we have not stopped laying down wine. In the last few years consumers have bought a great deal of wine *en primeur* – after it has been made, but before it has been bottled – to lay down. In return for helping the wine-maker to finance the high cost of ageing his wine in a substantial proportion of new oak casks, the purchaser *en primeur* pays a lower price than he would have done once the wine has been bottled and shipped. The *en primeur* market has spread from claret to Californian wine. This development is encouraged by wine merchants, producing a ridiculous situation in which consumers have taken over the traditional role of the merchants and are acting as stock-holders for them. If a wine merchant today is asked to find some 1970 clarets, he buys them at auction, where they have been sent by a private consumer, who may well have bought the wine from him in the first instance.

There is a further reason for the consumption of ever younger wines nowadays, a matter not so much of economics as of wine-making. Admittedly the two cannot be divorced, as it is in the financial interest of wine-makers to produce wines which can be sold, and drunk, young: they are paid for them sooner. But many people have always preferred the taste of young wines: the taste of fruit and the effect of alcohol. The big obstacle has always lain in finding the means to ensure that the sort of wines which are good to drink young are also microbiologically stable.

In the past wines contained more sulphur, acidity and tannin than they do today. The great German wines of the past contained up to one gram of sulphur per litre, compared with legal limits today of 350 milligrams per litre for Auslesen and 400 milligrams per litre for Beerenauslesen. They had to be kept for twenty years before drinking, in order that the sulphur content should diminish by 50 per cent. Even today German wines and Sauternes continue to be criticized for being 'over-sulphured' – when actually they are only young. That is one reason why the best wines, which contained enough sulphur to carry them through long ageing, were placed bottom of the *Which? Wine Monthly* tasting of German wines in 1987.

In the last century claret was far more acidic than it is today. Much more of the Petit Verdot variety was cultivated, even though this rarely ripened, and, even when ripe, contained one and a half times as much malic acid as Cabernet Sauvignon, and three times as much as Merlot. Since the last war, plantings of Merlot have greatly increased. On the one hand, the higher levels of acidity were necessary so that the wines could withstand long ageing in cask until they were sold; on the other, the long cask-ageing was necessary in order to soften wines which were picked earlier and were therefore more acid than they are today. In the Rheingau, until the introduction of the selective picking of ripe grapes (Auslesen) in the middle of the last century, wines had to be kept in barrel for between ten and twenty years, in order that their acidity should diminish.[2]

In the past, claret contained a level of tannin found today only in a few traditionally made Barolos. It contained a higher proportion of more tannic grape varieties; the fermentation temperature was not controlled; and the wine was kept in the fermentation vats after fermentation was complete, in contact with the grape-skins, for three or four weeks, compared with one or two today. The last vintage to have been made generally in the 'old-fashioned' way was 1945. By all accounts, neither the Château Latour nor the Château Mouton-Rothschild of that year is yet ready for drinking.

Until the recent introduction of heat-exchangers and stainless steel vats (which can be cooled by running water down their sides), there was no means of accurately controlling the fermentation temperature: wine-makers simply threw lumps of ice into the vats. Yet it is the length and temperature of fermentation which determine the character of a red wine. Red wine is different from white because of the colouring matter and tannins contained in the skins of the grapes. The longer and higher the temperature of the fermentation, the more substances are extracted from the skins of black grapes – both desirable and undesirable. Wine-makers must choose between a shorter, hotter fermentation, which extracts more tannin, and a longer, cooler one, which produces more aroma molecules. The tannins are responsible for the development of most of the flavours which we consider to be desirable in a bottle-aged fine wine; only a red wine which is intended to be drunk young is fermented at a relatively cool 25°C, at which temperature not too many tannins are extracted.

As a result of the influence of Emile Peynaud, Emeritus Professor of Oenology at Bordeaux University, who now acts as consultant wine-maker to a number of Bordelais châteaux, fermentations have become longer and cooler in the last twenty years. Peynaud says that for a fine wine the ideal fermentation temperature is no more than 30°C, irrespective of grape variety. He says that it is dangerous to ferment a wine at a temperature higher than this, because the yeasts work faster, tire more quickly, and are therefore more likely to stop reproducing, causing fermentation to cease, perhaps with some unfermented sugar left in the wine.[3] Not everyone is prepared to adopt such a defensive attitude to wine-making. The red wine at Domaine de Chevalier is vinified at a high 32°C. It used to be lower but in 1974 one vat was accidentally fermented at 34°C and found to be better than the rest. There are those who find a certain sameness in wines which have been *peynaudisés*. According to one story, a Bordelais proprietor, no lover of Peynaud's methods, was given a glass of wine by a visitor and asked to identify it. He tasted it and said, 'I cannot tell you where this wine comes from but, tell me, was it made by Emile Peynaud?' The wine was Greek, Château Carras. The consultant wine-maker to Château Carras is Emile Peynaud.

Certainly, Peynaud's influence has been substantial. After all, wine-making is not a process which changes rapidly. A wine-maker, unlike a chef, or even a brewer, does not get much chance to experiment. A chef cooks at least one meal every day; a brewer produces beer continuously; a wine-maker makes a vintage only once a year. Even today, a lifetime encompasses only fifty vintages; it was many fewer in the eighteenth and nineteenth centuries, when people died much younger. This may help to explain why there was little in the way of technological or scientific improvements in wine-making itself until this century, and why it took so long, for instance, for temperature-controlled fermentation to be introduced. When Château Latour installed stainless steel vats in 1964, there was an outcry: the new English owners were accused of turning the château into a dairy. Yet brewers have used temperature-control mechanism ever since the 1780s.

The most important technological improvement before the present century was the development of bottle-making. In theory, this should have enabled wines to be produced which did not need to contain the high levels of sulphur, acidity and tannin necessary to withstand long ageing in cask. Yet, even after 300 years, the full implications of the invention have not been realized.

Though bottles were manufactured from the first century AD onwards, until the end of the seventeenth century they were used, for the most part, only as decanters for serving wine, not as vessels for its storage. The late introduction of bottling is often ascribed to the fact that the cork was not 're-discovered' until the end of the seventeenth century; but I do not find it credible that a substance native to the Iberian Peninsula can have been an object of mystery to medieval Europeans. If wine was not bottled until the end of the seventeenth century, it was because the glass was too fragile. The origin of the straw-covered Chianti flasks which were so popular in the 1960s lies in the fact that, from the fifteenth century on, flasks containing Chianti were covered with straw to stop their breaking in transport. These bottles were not strong enough to withstand the corking process, and were therefore sealed with oil in the same way as Roman amphorae had been. This did not prove convenient, as foreign customers did not take the care nor have the equipment to remove the oil and often drank the wine mixed with the oil. Nevertheless, at least the Chianti exported to England in flasks at the beginning of the eighteenth century did not go off as previous consignments in cask had done.

The corking of bottles became possible thanks to the introduction of lead crystal glass in England by Ravenscroft in 1675. This was precipitated by the needs of the navy. Admiral Sir Robert Mansell was concerned at the destruction of forests by glass-makers and persuaded James I to prohibit the use of wood in glass-works furnaces. Coal was employed instead, and found to be better. It is the invention of lead crystal bottles which explains the invention of sparkling champagne in England at the end of the seventeenth century. At that time only the English had bottles strong enough to withstand either the corking process or the pressure of the carbon dioxide.

Champagne was put into bottles because it was too delicate a wine to survive in cask. Bottling enhanced the natural tendency of champagne to sparkle, on account of the high chalk content of the soil. (The same was true of Burton beer, which was made with chalky water.) Moreover, champagne did not complete its fermentation in the cold Champenois winter, and therefore refermented when the weather warmed up again in the spring. If put in bottle in March, and corked to prevent the carbon dioxide from escaping, it would become sparkling.

Like the fact that champagne sparkled if it was put in bottles at the start of spring, the fact that wines improved in bottle was discovered quite by accident. By the beginning of the eighteenth century champagne was valued for having a bit of bottle-age: one of King William III's old Dutch friends used to keep back some five-year-old champagne for his visits. As red burgundies, too, began to be aged in bottle, their style changed during the course of the eighteenth century. Deep colour and toughness came to be prized rather than despised; and, in order to achieve this result, the white grape vines, which earlier in the century had been interplanted in the black grape vineyards in order to achieve a lighter style of wine, were pulled out.[4]

Various factors, however, slowed down the development of bottle-ageing. Traditionally wine was kept in cask until it was sold. Bottling was carried out by the purchaser, in England or wherever, not by the producer. Thus, in the early nineteenth century, the first-growth clarets were aged in cask for five years, whereas today they spend only about two years in wood. There are still some producers in the South of France who keep wine in cask until it is sold. I have tasted seven-year-old Châteauneuf-du-Papes and Côtes de Provences which have only just been bottled.

The need to preserve wines while waiting for customers also influenced the style in which they were produced. In Burgundy the so-called *méthode ancienne* was invented because of a fall in demand at the end of last century. Long skin-contact produced rich, tannic wines of which Anthony Hanson famously remarked, 'If this is how the ancients did it, I am all for progress.'[5] In fact, before this, red burgundies had been light wines. In the early eighteenth century the best burgundy was considered to be Volnay, a *vin de primeur* which lasted only a year. This, like champagne, was a pink wine, the colour of a partridge's eye (*œil de perdrix*).[6]

Madeira may have been first fortified with brandy for the same reason. According to Noël Cossart, madeira began to be fortified in the first half of the eighteenth century when disturbed sea conditions caused ships to call at the island less often, leading to stockpiling, and therefore surplus wine was distilled into brandy, in order to fortify and preserve stocks.[7]

Futhermore, only in the present century has the difference between the chemistry of cask-ageing and that of bottle-ageing been realized. Empirically, the distinction is obvious. Compare, for example, a twenty-year-old tawny port, which will have been aged in cask for about twenty years, with a 1966 or 1970 vintage port, which will have been bottled after two years in cask. If the two ports come from the same shipping house, they will have been produced from the same quality and style of base wine. But last century no one understood exactly what the difference was. Last century Pasteur got it completely wrong when he said, 'It is oxygen which makes wine; it is by its influence that wine ages.' Certainly it is oxygen which controls the ageing of wine in cask. But, once the wine has been bottled, any oxygen dissolved in it combines rapidly with other substances. The ageing of wine in bottle owes very little, if anything, to the presence of oxygen, since only an insignificant amount enters through the cork. This is a fact of which a number of members of the wine trade appear to remain unaware: on several occasions I have been assured that all that happens during bottle-ageing is that the wine breathes through the cork.

Given this degree of scientific ignorance, the only way of finding out whether a better wine is produced by more or less cask-ageing has been a lengthy process of trial and error. As a result, the swing from ageing wine in cask and then bottling it when it is ready to drink to ageing a wine very little if at all in cask – perhaps only enough to give it a bit of extra flavour – and expecting it to do its maturing in bottle has been a very gradual one. This transformation is not yet complete. Will fine wines one day spend no time in cask at all? An oak flavour, if it is desired, can perfectly well be provided artificially – so what does cask-ageing do for a wine?

There is no simple answer to this question. We are told, on the one hand, that wines are aged in new barrels in order to increase their tannin content, and, on the other, that wines are matured in cask in order that they should become less tannic. Authorities appear to contradict each other – and even themselves – in this matter. In his book on wine-making, Emile Peynaud, quoting from the work of his mentor Jean Ribéreau-Gayon, says that the amount of tannin extracted from a cask is 'not negligible', and can be as much as 200 milligrams per litre from a small new oak cask in the first year.[8] Yet, in an interview in 1984, he said that it was a mistake to think that the wood of the cask gives tannin to a wine, and that the reason for using new oak casks was not to give more tannin but to give spice to the wine.[9]

Cask-ageing causes a wine's tannin content both to increase and to decrease. On the one hand, new oak gives tannin to the wine; on the other, oxygen enters the wine through the staves in the cask and oxidizes the tannins in the wine, causing them to bind into longer molecular chains which eventually become too large to remain soluble and so fall out of solution. Often the two processes cancel each other out. Figures given by Pascal Ribéreau-Gayon show that a wine aged in a new wooden barrel contains only 5 per cent more tannin than one aged in stainless steel, and that one aged in an old wooden barrel contains the same amount.[10] Is either effect of cask-ageing necessary? High levels of tannin are no longer needed in order to preserve wines during long barrel-storage. A wine's tannin content can be decreased by ensuring the absence of the tannic grape-stems from the fermenting vat, by vinifying at a lower temperature, and by draining the wine off the grape-skins before fermentation has finished. A wine's tannin content can be increased by doing the opposite.

As Peynaud says, new oak casks are used, not to give more tannin, but to give spice to the wine. In fact in many cases, the end-product tastes of spice rather than of wine. The taste of new oak is as pervasive today, and sometimes as destructive to fine wine, as that of resin was in Roman times. Consumers consider new oak to be a mark of quality; wine-makers believe that it confers prestige on their product. Many Italian Chardonnays, produced from under-age vines which are overcropped, lack the body to stand up to the application of new oak, and are all too often subsumed by its flavours. The fact that Meursault is aged in new oak does not mean that all Chardonnays are suited to this treatment. This is bad enough, but I have also encountered some examples of oak-aged Trebbiano. Perhaps producers have persuaded themselves that, because Trebbiano on its own tastes of nothing much at all, the admixture of new oak will improve it. It does not. An excellent example of an overpriced mouthful of new oak is the Vin de Pays des Côtes de Gascogne, Cuvée Bois, produced by the Grassa family, whose 'straight' version, at half the price, is considerably better.

If the fad for new oak is a modern one, the long-established practice of ageing vines in old oak continues today precisely because it has been going on for so long. Just as necessary fortification developed a taste for strong wines which is satisfied today by chaptalization, so necessary ageing in oak developed a liking for wines with a taste of oak – or, at least, what people think is a taste of oak. I am not sure that even expert tasters can necessarily detect it. One of the features of a long post-fermentation maceration of a red wine in contact with the grape-skins is that, once the temperature has fallen to 20–22°C, it brings a taste of soft, ripe tannins which many people confuse with that produced by ageing in new oak casks. We also associate a certain taste with wines which have spent a long time ageing in old casks. This is the result, not of cask-ageing *per se*, but of the 'old-fashioned' wine-making methods employed by the sort of people who imagine that it is a good idea to keep their wine in cask for a long time. There are wines made in this style without cask-ageing at all – Bairrada in Portugal is probably the best example. This said, the outstanding producer of Bairrada, Luis Pato, has, experimentally, aged some of his 1985 in oak.

In *Vino*, which, when it was published in 1980, was the pioneering English-language work on fine Italian wine, the expatriate American wine writer Burton Anderson describes how Luciano Usseglio-Tomasset, Professor of Oenology at Alba, having shown that a Piedmontese red wine after barrel-ageing had its basic elements deteriorate through oxidation and excessive presence of sulphates from cleaning operations, declared that, 'In my judgement, conservation in wood is without doubt detrimental to the quality of great red wines.' One maker of top-class red wine who would agree with him is Emidio Pepe from the Abruzzi in central eastern Italy. He ages his outstanding Montepulciano d'Abruzzo in bottles, and decants the wines off their sediment into fresh bottles before sale. Pepe justified his methods to Burton Anderson by saying that 'I want to keep my wine young as long as possible.'[11] He might not, perhaps, be described as a man of wide experience, since he only drinks his own wine, but he is not alone among the leading wine-makers of central and southern Italy in resisting oak-ageing: others to do so include Duchi di Castelluccio, also in the Abruzzi, and Salvatore Ippolito in Ciro in Calabria, down in the deep south where the hot climate causes wine to evaporate all too rapidly, and to put it in barrels is to invite oxidation. It was in these parts of Italy, not in the north, that the great wines of Roman times were made, and these were never aged in cask, but in earthenware amphorae.

It is, however, easy to dismiss oak-aged wines because, despite the oxidation of the tannins, they can take longer to mature than wines which have not spent time in oak. They are stabilized by cask-ageing, made resistant to further change. The more a wine has gradually been oxidized by ageing in oak, the better it will withstand further oxidation. An oak-aged white wine, such as the white Tondonia Rioja from Lopez de Heredia, which spends up to five years in cask, will not go off if left for a week or so recorked and half-consumed in a refrigerator; a 'modern', unoaked white wine, which has been fermented at low temperature, will sometimes go off within hours, because the shock of a first contact with air is too much for it. The ultimate demonstration of the longevity of barrel-aged wines is given by madeiras, which are aged in cask for up to thirty years – admittedly after having been heated to 40°C for six months. At a tasting in 1985 of old vintage madeiras from Cossart-Gordon, it was clear that none of the wines from 1920 and younger vintages were yet ready for drinking; the 1863 Bual seemed to be just about at its peak. Noël Cossart, however, ascribes the longevity of madeiras to the volcanic soil in which the vines grow rather than to the method of processing the wines.[12]

Wines lose their individuality with age, particularly if they have been aged in oak. After all, similar physical and chemical processes occur in all fine wines, irrespective of grape variety. Old Hermitage and Côte-Rôtie can be very similar to old claret; old Zinfandel can taste like old Californian Cabernet Sauvignon; old Australian Semillon and old white Rioja can be indistinguishable from old white burgundy. Mature vintages of the white Rioja from Marqués de Murrieta are commercially available, if anyone wants to go to the expense of testing this theory. Yet it is usually necessary to wait for fine wines to age. For reasons which are not yet understood, they 'close up' for a certain period of their lives. The worst time to drink a fine wine is at about five years of age – which tends to be when you think of broaching the first bottle to see how it is getting on. The finer the wine, the longer the period during which it will remain closed up. Having tasted a range of Gérard Chave's white Hermitage back to 1929, I would suggest either drinking the previous year's vintage or one of at least twenty years earlier – anything in between will be a disappointment.

The Holy Grail of wine-making today is to have the best of all possible worlds – to make a wine which tastes good when young, does not go through a dumb phase, and improves with age. This is not undiscoverable. It has been found, for instance, by the Châteauneuf-du-Pape estate of Domaine du Vieux Télégraphe, who, like many other producers in the region, have changed their style in recent years. With the installation of a new winery in 1979, several changes have been made to the vinification and storage, of which the most important is the use of a new pneumatic press. This presses the grapes very lightly without crushing their stalks, so that the wine no longer has a herby taste and green tannins as it did in the past. Whereas the 1978 is still tough and unyielding, *all* later vintages are attractive to drink now.

Other estates in Châteauneuf-du-Pape are producing a lighter, early-drinking wine by the adoption of *macération carbonique*. This is a method of vinification in which a certain proportion of the grapes ferment internally whilst still unbroken, before the alcoholic fermentation. It gets round the problem of drawing out colour and flavour from black grapes without extracting too much tannin, and produces wines with a reduced level of acidity. Figures given by Peynaud of an analysis four months after harvesting of a claret made from Malbec grapes, some of which have been vinified normally and some by *macération carbonique*, show that the wine made by *macération carbonique* contains two-thirds the tannins, two-thirds the acidity and two-thirds the extract of the wine vinified normally.[13] *Macération carbonique* is most famous for being used in Beaujolais; but it has been employed to greatest effect in the Midi, where it has transformed such wines as Minervois. Whereas in Beaujolais, the Gamay grape produces fruity wines, low in tannin, and attractive in their youth, whether vinified by *macération carbonique* or not, the wines of the Midi have suffered from being made from a grape, Carignan, which is very tannic when young, but not worth the effort of ageing.

There is, however, nothing new about *macération carbonique*. It simply involves the return by modern science to an ancestral process. In the past, grapes were poured into fermentation tanks without being crushed, or else trodden by foot, in which case crushing can hardly have been complete. Until Bordelais methods were introduced in the second half of the nineteenth century, the red wines of the Rioja were made by proto-*macération carbonique*. These are still made by small growers in Rioja Alavesa for consumption locally or in Bilbao. Recently, larger producers have adopted modern methods of *macération carbonique*, so traditional and modern methods are being used side by side. Since small growers in Rioja are not allowed to export their wines, we are able to try only the modern version of *macération carbonique*, such as Artadi from Cosecheros Alavesas.

The return to *macération carbonique* is symptomatic of a return to considering the production of red wines for drinking young as nothing to be ashamed of. In fact wines made by this method can last. If Beaujolais Nouveau has fallen apart within a year in the past, it has been the result of excessive filtration to try to produce a clear and stable wine within a month of the harvest, not because the wine is intrinsically incapable of ageing. Patently, it is in the interest of Beaujolais producers and merchants to encourage the belief that their wine has to be drunk young, as it does wonders for their cash-flow. Gérard Brisson, who makes an excellent Morgon, though not by *macération carbonique*, says that the Beaujolais merchants try and stop him from saying that his wine improves with age. Unless it has been filtered over-enthusiastically, Beaujolais Nouveau is no different from other versions of Beaujolais, whether made by *macération carbonique* or not, except that the malolactic fermentation is hastened, in order to ensure that it has occurred before the wine is bottled in early November.

In Châteauneuf-du-Pape, Domaine de Nalys, who use *macération carbonique*, claim that their wines can age, and even Robert Parker, who is not a fan of what is going on in Châteauneuf, admits to tasting a good 1967. I have tasted only the 1985, which seems to have the structure to last. Perhaps, however, it is because of the use of *macération carbonique* that Baron Le Roy of Château Fortia thinks that Châteauneuf-du-Pape is 'going to hell'.[14]

The great drawback of *macération carbonique* is not so much that wines made by this method are incapable of ageing gracefully as that the wine tastes more of the process by which it is produced than of the grapes from which it is made. Beaujolais made by *macération carbonique* is more closely comparable to Rhône wines or Rioja made by *macération carbonique* than to Beaujolais not made by *macération carbonique*. Georges Duboeuf, the most celebrated exponent of *macération carbonique* Beaujolais, also produces a Côtes du Rhône which I suspect many people would identify blind as Beaujolais.

Alternative means of extracting good colour and fruit flavour from a wine, without too much tannin, include must-heating and recycling of the pomace of skins in the vat. Heating the must is an extension of the principle that fermenting at a higher temperature produces a wine with better colour. Whereas, by vinifying at normal temperatures, a wine-maker extracts only 30 per cent of the colouring matter of the grapes (the rest is lost in the pomace), if he heats the whole grapes to 70°C the cells of the skin are killed, so that when the grapes are crushed they rapidly release into the juice the substances they contain. Recycling the pomace simply speeds up the extraction of colour, and is used to great effect by Masi to make their Valpolicella Fresco, which spends only a day in contact with its skins, and as a result offers the sort of tannin-free, vibrant fruit which makes one realize why Valpolicella became famous. Although Château Léoville-Lascases and a number of other leading châteaux in Bordeaux, all of whom produce very long-lived wines, employ a form of must-heating in order to obtain an intense, dark colour, they do not heat the must until after fermentation. They mix together, at a high temperature, some of the wine with the pomace of skins left over after fermentation, and add this back to the rest of the wine. As a general rule, neither must-heating nor recycling of the pomace produces wines capable of ageing. For this reason, wines made by these methods are sometimes described in France as *vins putains* – they are seductive when young, but do not age well.

To lighten a wine capable of ageing, it is probably best just to add water to the finished product. According to Noël Cossart, the relatively light Rainwater style of madeira originated in the eighteenth century when some pipes of Verdelho were left on the beach overnight before shipping to America; by mistake they were left unbunged, and some water seeped in. The style was very much liked by the American purchaser, who described the wine as 'soft as rain water'. Little did he know![15]

Although EEC rules today prohibit the addition of water to wine – which is why the use of liquid sugar in Germany is banned – it is used, both directly and indirectly. In Burgundy in 1983 the grapes came in with very high sugar levels, enough to have produced Meursaults with 16 per cent alcohol. Local oenologists advised the addition of twenty litres of water to each 228-litre barrel. I have no idea how many wine-makers carried out their advice. In California a number of leading producers achieve excessively high sugar levels most years, and therefore regularly add water to their wine. But then, many of those who condemn this practice water their wines indirectly, by irrigating the vineyard. The result is the same; it is simply that in the one instance the water is added to the finished wine; and in the other it is taken up into the grapes through the roots. One of the reasons for the excessive yields obtained by the leading Bordeaux châteaux at the turn of the century, causing a decline in their reputation, was that, at Château Latour, for instance, the vineyard was irrigated by spraying. This made nonsense of the fact that the quality of the wine derived at least in part from the porosity of the topsoil, which forced the vine's roots to dig deep to find water, and thus to extract more mineral flavours from the soil. [16] Certainly it is sometimes necessary for a vine grower in a hot summer or a dry climate to irrigate his vines in order to ensure that the vine is able to continue to photosynthesize throughout the summer. Even in the professedly 'dry-farming' vineyards of Germany, the watering of steep slopes is allowed; it is carried out in the finest vineyards – Brauneberger Juffer, the Rüdesheimer Berg sites and Maximin-Grünhauser Abtsberg – in hot years. These vineyards have little natural moisture, and therefore in dry years the development of their sugar content is retarded as there is not enough water to feed the ripening grapes. But it is a small step from adding enough water to enable vines to continue to grow to adding water in order to increase the eventual crop.

Adding water to a cask of wine before selling it is among the oldest and easiest of adulterations. After all, about 85 per cent of wine is water. The producers of the excellent Chiantis which were shipped to England in the seventeenth century eventually lost their market here because dishonest merchants added water to them. In France early this century, retailers and bar owners used habitually to 'baptize' wine by adding about 20–25 per cent of water. This was perfectly legal, as long as the alcohol content of the wine did not fall below 10 per cent. [17] Since then the law has changed; practices, it seems, have not. In the autumn of 1987 the satirical magazine *Le Canard enchaîné* published a report sent by the Fraud Squad to the Minister of Agriculture concerning its tests on the produce of the 1986 vintage. These revealed widespread overchaptalization, and illegal chaptalization in those *appellations* where it was not permitted. Among the illegally chaptalized wines were a Côtes du

Roussillon *rosé* and a sweet white Bergerac: having by this means attained an excessive alcoholic degree, they were then diluted with 15 per cent and 20 per cent of water respectively.[18]

[1] P. Morton Shand, *A Book of French Wines*, Penguin edn., 1964, pp. 54–5.
[2] J. L. W. Thudichum and August Dupré, *A Treatise on the Origin, Nature and Varieties of Vine*, 1872, p. 548.
[3] Emile Peynaud, *Knowing and Making Wine*, Wiley, 2nd ed., 1984, pp. 109–10.
[4] M. J. Lavalle, *Histoire et statistique de la vigne et des grands vins de la Côte d'Or*, 1855, p. 30.
[5] Hanson, p. 245.
[6] 'Il est plein de feu, de montant, et de légereté; il est presque tout esprit; il est enfin le plus excellent de toute la Bourgogne.' Claude Arnoux, *Dissertation sur la situation de Bourgogne*, 1728.
[7] Noël Cossart, *Madeira*, Christie's Wine Publications, 1984, pp. 102–3.
[8] Peynaud, p. 252; Jean Ribéreau-Gayon et al., *Sciences et techniques du vin*, vol. 3, Dunod, 1976, p. 705.
[9] Quoted in *Decanter*, December 1984, p. 36.
[10] Pascal Ribéreau-Gayon, 'Wine Flavour', in G. Charalambous (ed.), *The Flavour of Foods and Beverages*, Academic Press, 1978, pp. 355–79.
[11] Burton Anderson, *Vino*, Macmillan, 1982, pp. 168, 375.
[12] Cossart, p. 115.
[13] Peynaud, p. 191.
[14] *Wine Advocate*, no. 48, December 1986, p. 13.
[15] Cossart, p. 109.
[16] René Pijassou, *Le Médoc*, Tallandier, 1980, pp. 783–4.
[17] Theodore Zeldin, *France 1848–1945*, vol. 2, Oxford University Press, 1973, p. 760.
[18] *Le Canard enchaîné*, 14 October 1987, p. 4.

KEEPING UP WITH THE JAYERS

If many of us prefer the taste of young wines, how come old vintage dates are so sought after that they have frequently been faked? Rioja shippers, for example, could not, in the past, always be trusted as to the date of the vintage they quoted on their labels. During his researches in the 1950s into the wines of Jerez, the wine writer Julian Jeffs was assured that one of the Rioja shippers had registered 'Vintage 1929' as his trade mark; but then, according to local bar-room gossip, sherry producers who sold dated *soleras* used their telephone numbers.[1]

When, at the end of the last war, the American government lifted restrictions on bottled wine from Portugal, the market was flooded with madeira bearing fictitious dates. One Chicago merchant sold over 400 cases of 1874 madeira in 1949 and 1950 – probably more vintage wine than was ever made in that year, when production was reduced by phylloxera. Spurious vintage dates may not pose a problem today, but dated *soleras* do. These boast the vintage when wine was first put in the cask, since when, at regular intervals, between 10 and 25 per cent of the wine has been drawn off and replaced with younger wine. Laws have recently been introduced which limit to ten years the period during which it is permitted to 'refresh' a dated *solera* with younger wine. *Soleras* began after phylloxera when the shippers simply did not have enough wine to lay down as single-vintage madeiras. In his book on madeira, Noël Cossart seeks to justify them on the grounds that otherwise all the pre-phylloxera vintages would by now have been drunk.[2] But are not some consumers misled into thinking that *solera* madeiras are genuine vintage wines?

So-called 'vintage' cognac used to be made by such a *solera* system. How else could Bisquit Dubouché have fulfilled the claim in their advertisements in the 1930s that they were able to supply apparently unlimited quantities of the 1865, 1834 and 1811 vintages?[3] Unless there exists documentary evidence to prove the age of a cask of cognac, which there almost never does, the use of a vintage date is today illegal.[4] This prohibition applies, however, only to cognac producers and merchants within France. There is nothing to prevent a British wine merchant from bottling and selling a cognac with a vintage date, providing it was imported into Britain in cask before it was six years old, bearing a certificate of age from the Bureau National Interprofessionnel de Cognac, and providing that he states on the label the year in which the cognac was imported, in which case its veracity can be verified by checking customs documents. Vintage armagnacs are allowed, but only a few of the cellars contain enough casks of different sizes of any one vintage to allow for genuine topping-up of old vintages. The wine writer Nicholas Faith believes that the Armagnaçais illegally practise the sort of *solera* system the Cognaçais used to use.[5]

Once a wine has been provided with a fictitious date, it is quite easy, by heating it, to make it appear as though it has achieved that age of its own accord. The Romans manufactured 'smoked wines' by storing their amphorae full of wine above a smoke-room from which smoke rose up and heated them. In 1830 the Italian Ulisse Novellucci started experimenting with heating sealed bottles in water, bringing them up to near the temperature level at which alcohol vaporizes for a few minutes and then cooling them down. He said that this procedure gave the wine the same 'taste it would have in 8 to 10 years time, except for a very tiny difference which the connoisseurs can detect and describe as being "cooked" '.[6] Ageing wine by heating reproduces some of the process of cask-ageing; the slower it is, the better. Anyone with a cellar at room temperature, rather than the recommended 10°C, will see his wines develop relatively fast. That is why the same wines taste much older in Texas than they do in Scotland. Restaurants which serve fine wines far too young are therefore right to store them at room temperature, not least because this reduces the period of 'bottle-sickness' (during which the wine is recovering from the shock of being bottled).

Various other methods of ageing wine artificially have been tried. In 1890 Cesari Bernardi tried subjecting red wines to electrolysis, and found that, after four to five days, they 'acquired a delicate perfume and became fuller-flavoured and more velvety'.[7] In fact, though electrolysis certainly changes the character of a wine, causing simultaneous oxidation at the cathode and reduction at the anode, the result does not at all resemble the ageing process. More recently irradiation has been tried, and found to be even less successful, since it causes chemical decomposition and changes the odour of the treated substance. After all, one of the main uses of ultra-violet light, apart from irradiation, is to deodorize buildings. Experiments carried out in 1986 involving the irradiation of Pilsener beer with gamma radiation not only reduced the colour but produced a totally unacceptable smell of bad eggs (hydrogen sulphide). Some years ago the radiologist William Levett tried irradiating a bottle of Château Latour from a recent vintage. It tasted disgusting – but that may have been because, in his calculations beforehand, he had put a decimal point in the wrong place, and thus subjected the wine to ten times as much radiation as he had intended.

But why should we believe so fervently that old wine is better that we seek to produce it artificially? In the Middle Ages and the Renaissance no one actually chose to drink old wines. But some wines did survive longer than others in the casks in which they were stored. Wines which survived to old age without going off were demonstrably better than wines which had to be drunk young, before they went off. This was the origin of the belief that old wine is good wine. There was never any suggestion that it improved in the ageing process.

Had medieval man believed that wine was ameliorated by ageing, he could perfectly well have put this belief into practice. His lack of lead crystal bottles would not have stopped him. Wine can perfectly well be aged in cask. It does not oxidize, providing that the cask is kept filled to the brim and regularly topped up to replace the liquid lost through evaporation. Indeed, a cask is a far better medium for ageing than the wide-mouthed earthenware amphorae used by the Romans, which were ineffectually sealed with wax, and whose contents frequently had to be preserved with pitch and resin; yet this did not prevent the produce of the first great vintage of Roman times, that of 121 BC, from surviving for 200 years. When today we accuse a poor, oxidized wine of having been kept too long in cask, we may be confusing statistical with causal correlation: oxidation is caused by poor wine-making and careless storage.

The development of wines intended for ageing was, it has been suggested, the consequence of the closure to Bordeaux of its traditional markets when English and Dutch merchant ships were chased away in the second half of the seventeenth century by protectionist French trading policies. At war with France, England developed the vineyards of the Douro in Portugal as an alternative source of wine to that which she had enjoyed for 500 years. When the English market was again opened to them after the signing of peace in 1713, the Bordelais found that they could not compete on price with port, because they had to pay higher customs duties. Furthermore, the *haut bourgeois* proprietors of the Bordeaux city suburbs were being undercut in their local markets by the produce of the recently drained, newly planted and more fertile marshland. Their only way out was to convert to quality-wine production, to produce wines which were intended not for immediate consumption, but for laying down.[8]

The clarets of the late seventeenth and early eighteenth century were the first fine wines, in the modern sense, to be produced. But they were not available to everyone, not even for ready money. Social climbing was not easy in the eighteenth century, since many objects of prestige could only be obtained through personal contacts. Wine was one of these. By the nineteenth century it had become easier for the *nouveaux riches* to get their hands on the wines hitherto enjoyed only by the aristocracy. At the same time the Industrial Revolution saw the creation of a new, large, acquisitive middle class, who aspired to upper-class tastes even though they could rarely afford to indulge in them. This class placed a premium on one-upmanship and petty snobbery, and its members were quite happy to pay money for artificially aged wines, if the genuine article was beyond their means.

It is the values of this class which dominate today. We pay money principally for exclusivity rather than for taste. Young wines are in plentiful supply, because they have not yet been drunk; therefore they are not, on the whole, exclusive. For some people even the latest vintage of Château Pétrus or Romanée-Conti is neither expensive nor exclusive enough. They are the sort of people who pay £105,000 for a bottle of Château Lafite 1787 at auction. This particular bottle was purchased by the New York publisher Christopher Forbes in December 1985. He placed it in his museum, under spotlights. These caused the cork to dry out and fall into the wine. Clearly he had not bought this wine for the taste. Indeed, it had only fetched as high a price as it did because the bottle bore what were supposed to be Thomas Jefferson's initials.

In seeking out exclusive products, we are paying money for what marketers call 'added value'. This means conferring an image on a product that makes it seem worth more than it is. The 'added value' is the extra money a consumer can be persuaded to pay above the intrinsic worth of a product in order to make a statement about himself, that he is fashionable, has good taste, has lots of money, or is otherwise desirable. In the chapter on wine-tastings, I mentioned the comparative tasting of malt and blended whiskies carried out at St Mary's Hospital, Paddington, in 1983, in which the tasters were not significantly more successful in distinguishing malt from blended whiskies than a group of monkeys would have been. Yet malt whisky is fast becoming the fashionable alternative to cognac. The reason is that people buy malt whisky in order to make personal statements about their status as discriminating, successful, well-travelled people, rather than because of the intrinsic taste of the whisky. Those are not my words. They are those of the marketing manager of a leading brand of malt whisky, Glenfarclas.[9]

The most obvious example of a drinks product whose high price can be accounted for only in terms of the added value it offers is champagne. In terms of taste champagne offers very poor value for money, but in terms of added value it is positively cheap. A bottle of champagne costs much less than the other elements of a 'champagne lifestyle'; it even costs less, and lasts a little longer, than an ounce of caviare. Thus, in terms of the added value it confers, champagne is underpriced. That is why, given the tendency towards conspicuous consumption in Thatcherite Britain, sales of the cheapest element of conspicuous consumption doubled between 1982 and 1985.

If people will pay more for champagne than for equally good sparkling wines from elsewhere, it is because these other wines lack the added value of the association with a 'champagne lifestyle', a feature which is assiduously and expensively promoted by the major producers of champagne. That is why the big champagne houses were so terrified when, in their advertisement for their own-label sparkling Saumur, Sainsbury's suggested that it might be mistaken for champagne. Actually, today Sainsbury's own-label Blanquette de Limoux is a much better wine than their sparkling Saumur.

Price itself creates added value because it makes a product exclusive – or least creates an image of exclusivity. By asking, and obtaining, a high price, it is possible to persuade consumers that a product is high-quality. Pommery have greatly increased the sales of their champagne in France since 1985, not by improving the product, but by the simple expedient of putting up their price. It is not surprising that people think that, if a wine costs more, it is better. If no objective criteria exist to distinguish between different wines, if you do not know anything about the product you are buying, then it is not ludicrous to take price as a guide to quality. After all, price is a guide to reputation.

A wine's reputation, however, is created as much by its price as by its quality. It is only by charging a high price that the image can be achieved which will bring consumers to accept that the price is justified by the quality. Certainly it would be hard on any other grounds to justify the ludicrous prices which are asked for *cuvée de prestige* champagnes. These have been introduced by many champagne houses in the last ten years or so, largely because ordinary champagne has become too cheap. When, in the autumn of 1983, following two enormous harvests, the price of a bottle of champagne in a supermarket fell to £5.95, it could be said that for many people even champagne had become an affordable, everyday product. *Cuvées de prestige* are simply champagnes with a fancy image sold in fancy bottles at a fancy price. They exist to fulfil the needs of those who consider that ordinary, non-vintage champagne is no longer expensive or exclusive enough.

The image of *cuvées de prestige* as exclusive products has to be cultivated assiduously – and at the expense of the truth. The medallion man's *cuvée de prestige*, Dom Pérignon, from the people who gave you Moët et Chandon, is everywhere sold 'on allocation'. Yet it is not exactly in short supply. According to my estimates, based on figures provided by Moët et Chandon's London office, roughly one million bottles are produced each year – more than the entire production of white wines in the village of Puligny-Montrachet in Burgundy. (Admittedly the châteaux of Bordeaux play a similar game, restricting supply in order to inflate demand by releasing only 50 per cent of their crop when they first place their wine upon the market.)

The situation is quite ridiculous. Champagnes which are considerably better than swanky *cuvées de prestige* sell for one-third the price. In the village of Le Mesnil, one of the three best white grape villages in Champagne, the cooperative is contracted to sell three-quarters of its production to the big houses for use in their *cuvées de prestige*. I would not be surprised if it were the best quarter of its production that the cooperative keeps for sale under its own label. André Jacquart, a grower in the village, sells wine to Taittinger which they include in their Comtes de Champagne. I can only say that I prefer the wine he sells under his own label, at £12 compared with £35 for the Taittinger.

Indeed the bourgeois proprietors of Bordeaux are perfectly open about the fact that the image of higher quality is achieved by charging a higher price. The success of this policy can be seen in the rise to prominence of Château Pétrus in the 1950s, which Edmund Penning-Rowsell ascribes in no small degree to the fact that its proprietress, the late Mme Edmond Loubat, who believed that her wine was the equal of the first growths of the Médoc, refused to sell her wine for a price any lower than theirs.[10] But the châtelains of Bordeaux vie with each other to see who can charge, and obtain, the highest prices, not because they are greedy for money – if they can afford to run a classed-growth château they don't need that – but because they are greedy for prestige. Jean Sanders, the Belgian proprietor of Château Haut-Bailly, describes the pricing policy of 'many Bordeaux châteaux' as 'stupid and very dangerous. It's a *marché de voisinage* [a matter of keeping up with the Joneses] where everyone is far too busy worrying about what his neighbour is getting. Whose are the most fairly priced wines? The ones from châteaux which belong to businessmen.'[11]

In the 1960s the prices of classed-growth clarets were forced up by the rivalry between Elie de Rothschild, the owner of Château Lafite, and his cousin Philippe de Rothschild, the owner of Château Mouton-Rothschild, who vied with each other to see who could charge the higher price, in the belief that whichever wine fetched the more money was the better one. This competition contributed to the collapse of the market in 1974. The fear is sometimes expressed that a similar rivalry today between the 'super seconds', Châteaux

Léoville-Lascases, Ducru-Beaucaillou and Pichon-Lalande, will lead to a similar collapse.

This is a game the Bordelais have always played. M. de Rauzan, the proprietor in the eighteenth century of the then-united estates of Châteaux Rausan-Ségla and Rauzan-Gassies, became dissatisfied with the price offered for his wine in Bordeaux. Therefore he chartered a ship which he loaded with casks from two good vintages and sailed for London. Using his ship in the Thames as an office, his initiative won him both publicity and orders. But he still did not consider the price high enough. He announced that, unless he obtained what he considered a fair price, he would throw the casks into the river, one by one. After he had thrown away four of the casks, the onlookers could stand it no longer and gave way.[12]

Clearly the new fine wines which were developed in the late seventeenth and early eighteenth centuries could not be sold, even to wealthy Londoners rejoicing in the proceeds of a first stock-market boom, unless some effort were put behind their promotion and added value were created in order to justify their price. The first claret to make a name for itself was Château Haut-Brion, thanks to the marketing skills of the owner, Arnaud de Pontac, who sent his son François-Auguste to London in 1666 to open a tavern, called The Sign of Pontac's Head, off Newgate Street, in order to promote his wines. This tavern became the most fashionable meeting-place in London. The superior status of Haut-Brion was established by selling it for 7s a bottle when other perfectly good wines could be purchased for a quarter as much, and, within a decade, the cost of the wine if purchased direct from the château had doubled because rich Englishmen ordered it to be bought at any price. In his book on the wine trade in the eighteenth century, Alan Francis argues that, after 1715, there was no profit in importing anything but expensive Bordeaux wines into England.[13]

As, in the 300 years since fine wines were invented, it is from France that we have traditionally bought them, we find difficulty in shaking off the belief that the only fine wines worth paying money for come from France. If countries other than France want to sell fine wines, they have to compromise their identity by planting Cabernet Sauvignon or Chardonnay. We also have trouble believing that certain of the most celebrated French wines, with the noblest history, are no longer worth the sums that are asked. Château Lafite has a great reputation, which reached its zenith in the nineteenth century, when it was so much the snob name that in 1836 the St James's Club purchased 100 barriques of Ch. Latour 1831 under the name 'Lafite'.[14] From the late 1960s until the late 1970s, Lafite was living on that reputation. The 1971 – from a good, though not great, vintage – was never much better than plonk, and went over the hill some years ago. Yet it sells for about £40–50 a bottle retail. Clearly it has not achieved this price on grounds of quality.

But tradition is not all. If it were, German wines would still attain their historic status. The exception to the rule that wines were drunk young until 200 years ago can be found in the wines of the Rhineland, which, from the sixteenth century on, were matured in enormous vats on a *solera* system, and kept to a great age. In the last century the best German wines attained prices higher than first-growth Bordeaux. A Harveys of Bristol list of 1867 quotes Steinberger Auslese 1862 (which might well have been dry) at £9 a case, compared with £4 14s for Château Lafite 1864, a great vintage. Today you can buy wines from the best estates in Germany, such as Langwerth von Simmern in the Rheingau, the State Wine Domain in the Nahe, and Bassermann-Jordan in the Rheinpfalz, for £5–10 a bottle. German wines suffer partly because, as I have already mentioned, their system of nomenclature is often confusing, sometimes misleading and always open to abuse, and partly because they are not branded.

Burgundies, too, suffer for not being branded. They may seem expensive, but that is because of their scarcity value. Though the price of white burgundies has been forced by world demand to soar out of all relation to its quality, red burgundies are still cheaper than clarets of comparable quality. In their opening offer of 1985 red burgundies, Justerini and Brooks asked £343 for Henri Jayer's Echézeaux. When they had offered the 1985 clarets the previous year, Château Mouton-Rothschild cost £507 a case. Yet the total production of Henri Jayer's Echézeaux is only about 1 per cent that of Château Mouton-Rothschild. Its scarcity should have made it much more expensive.

In Burgundy, the Rhine and Mosel, most vineyards enjoy multiple ownership. In Burgundy the noble and monastic estates were expropriated during the Revolution and divided between a number of smallholders. If the Domaine de la Romanée-Conti can command much higher prices than its rivals – upwards of £100 a bottle – it is because its holdings were not split up when they were sold after the Revolution, and it enjoys sole ownership of two of the best *grand cru* sites in the region. On the other hand, Clos de Vougeot, whose reputation predates that of the Domaine de la Romanée-Conti by several centuries, was divided between six purchasers in 1889 and now, thanks to the French practice of multigeniture, is owned by more than eighty.

Because the vineyards are divided into a large number of very small holdings, most top-class burgundy and German wine is sold under the names of sites rather than those of estates. In Burgundy only the Domaine de la Romanée-Conti has been given exemption from the rule that no company may use as part of its name the name of any of the *appellation contrôlée* vineyards in which it owns land; in this case, the *grand cru* Romanée-Conti. The vineyards are brand names in themselves, from Clos de Vougeot and Bernkasteler Doktor downwards. But this has led to abuse. Whereas in Bordeaux the reputation of the brand – the château – depends on one single wine, in Burgundy and Germany, with a few exceptions, the reputation of the brand – the site – depends on many growers, who make wines of varying qualities. In general, the reputation of the sites has been established by dedicated growers, and then abused by unscrupulous growers who share ownership. I cannot imagine that the grower in Piesporter Goldtröpfchen who was reported to have produced an average crop of 500 hectolitres per hectare over the four vintages from 1979 to 1982 can have been solicitious of the reputation of the vineyard.

Vineyard sites in Burgundy are classified according to their potential quality. But frequently one man's straight Vosne-Romanée is superior to another's Vosne-Romanée les Beaumonts – a *premier cru*, and therefore theoretically superior; so too is one man's Vosne-Romanée les Beaumonts superior to another's Echézeaux – a *grand cru*, and thus in theory at the top of the tree. The classification is only really of use in choosing between wines made by the same wine-maker from the produce of different sites. It is certainly possible to see the ascent in quality from plain Vosne-Romanée through Vosne-Romanée les Beaumonts to Echézeaux in the wines made by Etienne Grivot for the estates of his father Jean Grivot and his aunt Jacqueline Jayer (cousin to the great Henri).

The abuse of the reputation of site names, and their misrepresentation of a wine's quality, could be circumvented by producing a classification of growers, if it were not that the reputations of winemakers are too volatile to provide a reliable basis for classification. Certainly the leading producers in Bordeaux are classified, but they enjoy a flexibility with their raw material which is not open to vine growers in Germany and Burgundy; and their classification is still wholly unreliable. Officially the disappointing Château Cantenac-Brown precedes its celebrated neighbour Château Palmer in the list of third growths. Even if it had not been produced more than 130 years ago (as was that of the Médoc), even if it is updated every now and then (as is that of Saint-Emilion), such a classification will always be out of date by the vintage after its publication, as new stars emerge and old ones fall.

The famous 1855 classification of the Médoc has served to reinforce the reputation of the leading estates. It was only following this classification that most of the châteaux began to sell their wine under their own names rather than those of the merchants who sold them. Although it has been suggested that the classification was made by the trade in order to stop price competition between growers,[15] its consequence was both to widen the price between the first and other growths, and artificially to elevate the price of lesser growths. A classification of growers will never be introduced officially in Burgundy or in Germany because the less conscientious growers in good sites would recognize its likely consequences and never agree to it.

The survival of the 1855 Bordeaux classification is often justified on the grounds that it rates châteaux according to the potential of their soil. Thus, even if a château is producing bad wine at the moment, when it does pull its socks up, it will be making wine up to the level of its classification. There is some truth in this. From the middle of the nineteenth century until the Depression of the 1930s, Léoville-Poyferré was considered to produce possibly the best wine in Bordeaux after the first growths. The estate then fell into a decline. Though classified as a second growth, it was doubtful whether it was producing wine even of fifth-growth quality. In 1982, after the old cellarmaster was knocked over and killed by a car while crossing the main road that separates the vineyards from the cellars, the owner's son, Didier Cuvelier, took charge and persuaded his family to make an overdue investment in improving the wine-making equipment. Since the 1982 vintage the wine has returned to second-growth quality.

A revindication of the 1855 classification? No. The 1855 classification had nothing to do with the potential of the soil in the vineyards. In the first case it was based on the prices – not the quality – of the wines in the early 1850s. As A. d'Armailhacq, the proprietor of what is now Château Mouton-Baronne-Philippe, wrote at the time of the classification, 'The brokers and merchants never pay for a wine according to its real quality, but according to its reputation.'[16] Secondly, it classified the brand names of the châteaux, not their vineyards. Thus châteaux are able to keep their classification even if they have moved or enlarged their vineyards – as most of them have. The quantity produced under the names of the second growths has increased from an average of 2,000 cases in 1855 to 20,000 or more today, though yields have only doubled or at most trebled in that period. Château Siran, an unclassified château in Margaux, has about 40 per cent of its vines on land which had been part of classified châteaux in 1855, including two-thirds of the vineyards which had belonged to the third-growth Giscours and fifth-growth Dauzac.

The manner in which châteaux migrate can be seen in the reconstruction by the Russian-born American Alexis Lichine of Château Cantenac-Prieuré, a fourth-growth Margaux which he bought in 1951 and renamed Prieuré-Lichine. He has enlarged it from 11 to 58 hectares. There are thirty different plots in five communes within the Margaux *appellation*, some as far as 3 or 4 kilometres away from the château. (In Burgundy a journey of 4 kilometres would also take you across five different communes: from Gevrey-Chambertin to Vosne-Romanée.) The vineyards include parcels which previously belonged to the second growths Dufort-Vivens and Brane-Cantenac, and to the third growths Palmer, Ferrière, Kirwan, Giscours, Issan and Boyd-Cantenac. I would not be surprised if they also include land which did not belong to classified châteaux in 1855, but we are not told about that. Alexis Lichine is still trying to extend his domaine. He says that 'we glean from the best of the *appellation* of Margaux'[17] – no suggestion of trying to express the character of an individual site. Château Prieuré-Lichine is basically a (very) up-market blended Margaux.

In his *Really Useful Wine Guide*, Robin Young suggests that châteaux are even allowed to buy in grapes from other producers, and sell the wine under the château name.[18] They certainly do so, but they are not allowed to, since French *appellation contrôlée* laws do not permit a château name to be used on a label unless the wine is produced exclusively from grapes grown on the estate. But it is undoubtedly true that the only restriction on the brand identity of the classed-growth châteaux of the Médoc is the law of *appellation*, which requires that all the wine sold under the label of a château in a particular village must come from that village – and this law too is ignored. Châteaux have plots of land all over the place. Three-fifths of the vineyards of Pichon-Lalande are in Pauillac, two-fifths in Saint-Julien. The château used to be obliged under *appellation contrôlée* regulations to sell three-fifths of the crop as Pichon-Lalande from the village of Pauillac and two-fifths as Pichon-Lalande from the village of Saint-Julien. This was patently ridiculous, since the wine was all the same. In the 1960s the château was given permission to use the *appellation* – Pauillac – in which the majority of the vines lay. Brand names are clearly considered to be more important than *appellation contrôlée* regulations.

It has been suggested that this process of enlarging vineyards beyond all recognition could be prevented if each Bordelais vineyard were given its own *appellation*, as in Burgundy. This would also prevent the abuse of the names of classed-growth châteaux, as is currently enjoyed by such blended Bordeaux as Mouton-Cadet and Chevalier de Lascombes. After all, no one is allowed to sell blended burgundy as Chambertin Cadet, or blended Côtes du Rhône as Chevalier d'Hermitage.[19] But the Burgundians *do* abuse famous names by hyphenating them on to names of villages. Moreover, it is tempting for a vine grower who owns small patches of vines in a number of different vineyards and villages to sell as much wine as he possibly can under the name of his most famous vineyard. If some of the grapes in his holding in a *grand cru* vineyard happen to be destroyed by hail, when that year's wine is finally produced the damage will mysteriously have been transferred to one of his holdings in a less prestigious vineyard. This does not matter, since the smallness of his holdings may have led him to vinify the produce of several of them in the same vat, giving the result various different names – one reason why 'different' wines from the same producer often taste the same. This blending can work to the benefit of the wise consumer rather than to his disadvantage. After all, if an Echézeaux and a plain Vosne-Romanée are fermented together in the same vat, the Echézeaux may not be as good as might have been expected, but the Vosne-Romanée will be better. It is sometimes suggested that this is what Jacques Reynaud does at his Châteauneuf-du-Pape estate of Château Rayas with his Côtès du Rhône from Château de Fonsalette, in theory a separate estate. He has a guaranteed sale of Château Rayas to Michelin three-star restaurants all over France; Château de Fonsalette is sold to (relatively) impoverished wine-lovers. Might both wines not emerge from the same vats? Certainly what is sold as Château de Fonsalette is a remarkable wine; certainly Jacques Reynaud is a mysterious man.

In 1984 the classification of Saint-Emilion was revised and the imposition introduced that for ten years no classed growth was to increase the declared vineyard area covered by the classification. In 1985 it was decided to declassify Château Beauséjour-Bécot from the top group of twelve Premier Grands Crus Classés to the second group of ninety Grands Crus, on the grounds that the proprietor had in 1979 included, without permission, two Grand Cru (Classé) vineyards in his property, thereby increasing its size from 20 to 35 hectares. Effectively, a new law was being imposed retrospectively, as, up till 1984, Michel Bécot had been perfectly entitled to do what he did. But this may have been only the excuse chosen to punish him. It was rumoured in Bordeaux that the real reason was that a powerful merchant had lent Bécot money on the understanding that he was to be given the exclusive right to distribute his 1982 vintage, and that Bécot failed to keep his end of the deal. At the time of writing, the declassification of Château Beauséjour-Bécot is expected to be reversed.

Producers of champagne find themselves in an even more fortunate position than those of Bordeaux. Not only can they charge higher prices because of the security afforded the consumer by well-known brand names, but they can also increase the production of the wine under those brand names to meet demand. I have already discussed earlier in the book (see Chapter 10) how champagne is blended for marketing purposes and not for any qualitative reasons; that producers have nevertheless succeeded in persuading consumers to part with extra money for the added value of their skill in blending inferior wines to produce a marvellous one; and that production can be increased at the last minute by buying ready-made champagne and slapping your own label on it.

Since the 1960s, the area under vine in Champagne has doubled and the amount of wine produced has trebled. This is important. Few producers of fine wines can hope to acquire an international reputation without being able to produce enough to enable people to get their hands on it. Most consumers of fine wines want to be seen drinking a wine which their peer group will know. Until the end of the first century BC, Greek wines enjoyed the same sort of reputation in Italy as French wines do in Britain today. They were the most sought-after, and the most expensive. But from then on Greek wines fell out of fashion. The reason, Edward Hyams believes, is that the Greeks were unable to change the pattern of their industry, to turn from small-scale to large-quantity production. The Romans wanted a wine which was good and expensive but which was also plentiful.[20] Today, burgundies are expensive partly because they are scarce; but the produce of the best growers might command more of a premium if it were not quite so hard to obtain. The entire vineyard area of the commune of Morey-Saint-Denis is the same size as the single branded wine, Château Lafite; and I know of sixty-four growers in the village, each of whom makes several different wines.

Champagne prices have not, however, increased as those of claret have. In 1968 a bottle of Château Figeac 1962 would have cost you little more than one of non-vintage champagne, about £1 10s or £1 15s. Today a bottle of Château Figeac 1982 would cost you about £25, three times as much as one of non-vintage champagne. Retail prices have increased eightfold in the period, which means that, while the relative cost of champagne has actually fallen by about 50 per cent, that of the top clarets has doubled. Why?

The answer is simply that claret has become an object of investment. It is possible to invest in wines only if they are branded, that is to say, well-known, easily recognizable, and available in commercial quantities. By this criterion both claret and champagne qualify. But investment in wines is a long- rather than a short-term commitment. Therefore it is essential that the wines invested in should be perceived not only to be long-lived, but also to improve on keeping. This criterion excludes champagne but includes claret.

According to Hugh Johnson, 'Today, the principal virtue of a *vin de garde* is that it remains a tradeable commodity for longer.'[21]

It was investment in claret as a commodity which caused the collapse of the market in 1974. People were encouraged to invest in claret because the prices paid for mature wines in the London auction rooms rose steeply in the 1960s. Wine appeared to be a good investment because of the sharp increase in the rate of inflation, which made the return offered by traditional investments much less satisfactory than that obtained by investing in apparently 'inflation-proof' luxuries – paintings, postage stamps, wine. Unsatisfactory vintages in 1968 and 1969 concentrated investors' attention on the much better 1970 and 1971 vintages. Demand exceeded supply; what had been a buyer's market became a seller's one. The growers were encouraged, after a generation of largely poor returns from poor vintages, to increase their prices substantially even for their generally very bad 1972s. Prices peaked in 1973, and then, given a push by the Cruse scandal, collapsed in 1974.

Can such a crash occur again? Michael Broadbent, then as now a director of Christie's, said just before it happened that 'there is a hell of a lot of wine in Bordeaux'.[22] Well, there is a hell of a lot of wine sitting in Bordeaux unsold today. Not just from the mediocre vintage of 1984, but from good vintages – 1982s, 1983s, 1985s, 1986s. Many wine merchants do not even taste the wine they buy *en primeur*, in the spring after the vintage, more than a year before the wine is bottled. Certainly the majority of the 1985s which were put on the market in the spring of 1986 had been bought, untasted, by brokers who were interested in making a quick profit, not in supplying wine merchants with wines of a quality that they wanted. Consumers are continuing to buy each new vintage *en primeur*, presumably in the hope that what happened to the 1982s will happen again. But then the commercial position was uniquely propitious. Awakening American interest in fine wines coincided with a dollar which bought twice as many francs as it had when the 1978s had been offered. The opening prices were condemned in England as excessive: 50–80 per cent up on those charged for the last outstanding vintage, 1978. Yet if you had bought almost any of the leading châteaux at opening prices in the spring of 1983 you could have made a 100 per cent profit if you sold the wine when it had actually been shipped, in the autumn of 1985.

The longer-term performance of the wine investment market has, however, proved much less exciting. If you had bought 1975 clarets in 1976 and sold them at auction in 1986, you would have realized just enough money to replace them with an equivalent quantity of wine of equivalent quality from the 1985 vintage. Having sold your 1975s, it would have proved difficult to justify replacing them with 1985s, when the equally good 1981s were available for 25 per cent less and four years closer to maturity. It would indeed have proved very difficult to justify selling your 1975s at all. I can see no reason for buying clarets *en primeur* at current prices, whether for future selling or future drinking, except for the wines of a few estates in Pomerol which are impossible to get hold of when they are older.

The investment and auction markets for claret have driven the amount that is paid for leading clarets out of all relation to their intrinsic quality. One Bordeaux merchant justified the spiralling prices of classed-growth clarets in the early 1980s on the grounds that 'if you are dying of thirst in a desert and somebody offers you a glass of water at 10 million francs, the price is a fair one'.[23] Had he not read the story of Abe's sardines, which Simon Loftus took as the sub-title of his brilliant book about the inner workings of the wine trade? 'Abe bought a shipment of sardines that had already been traded many times and each time profitably. Unlike previous buyers, Abe took the trouble of procuring a box of his purchase. The sardines were terrible. He telephoned Joe from whom he had bought them only to be told, "But Abe, those sardines are for trading, not eating." '[24] Who will ever be able to afford to drink today's classed-growth clarets, traded at ever-increasing prices?

[1] Julian Jeffs, *The Wines of Europe*, Faber & Faber, 1971, p. 418; *Sherry*, 3rd ed., Faber & Faber, 1982, p. 226.
[2] Noël Cossart, *Madeira*, Christie's Wine Publications, 1984, p. 124.
[3] Maurice Healey, *Stay Me With Flagons*, Michael Joseph, 1940, p. 246.
[4] Production of vintage cognacs, this time under close supervision, has resumed with the 1987 vintage, which we can expect to see on the market some time next century.
[5] *Wine and Spirit*, December 1986, p. 63.
[6] Cosimo Ridolfi, *Orali lezioni*, 1862, vol. 2, p. 299, quoted in Lamberto Paronetto, *Chianti*, Estampa, 1970, pp. 190–92.
[7] *Brewers' Guardian*, 1890, p. 340.
[8] Henri Enjalbert, 'Comment naissent les grands crus: Bordeaux, Porto, Cognac', *Annales*, 1953, pp. 457–63.

9 Mark Elliott, brand manager for Glenfarclas, quoted in *Wine and Spirit*, November 1985, p. 37.

10 Penning-Rowsell, pp. 363–4.

11 Quoted in *Wine and Spirit*, June 1987, p. 55.

12 Penning-Rowsell, p. 270.

13 A. D. Francis, *The Wine Trade*, A. & C. Black, 1972, p. 235.

14 Penning-Rowsell, p. 167.

15 This view was expressed by Bruno Prats, the dynamic proprietor of Château Cos d'Estournel, in *Decanter*, August 1983, p. 24. I have been unable to substantiate it.

16 A. d'Armailhacq, *De la culture des vignes, la vinification et les vins dans le Médoc*, 1855, quoted in Penning-Rowsell, pp. 232–3.

17 *Decanter*, December 1984, p. 32.

18 Robin Young, *The Really Useful Wine Guide*, Sidgwick & Jackson, 1987, p. 44.

19 Christopher Fielden in *Decanter*, October 1984, p. 19.

20 Hyams, p. 90.

21 *Decanter*, September 1985, p. 4.

22 Quoted in a letter to *Decanter*, December 1983, p. 9.

23 *Wine and Spirit*, October 1986, p. 50.

24 Loftus, p. 77, quoting from Peter Sichel's 1971–2 Bordeaux vintage report.

THE FALERNIAN SYNDROME

The price of wines bears no direct relation to their quality but derives from their image. The 'added value' afforded by this image is, however, necessary for quality-wine production, since without first creating a high price for his wines a producer cannot afford to lavish the expense necessary to produce top-class wine. What would seem to be the natural relationship between quality and price is in fact inverted. A wine-maker has to create added value in order to be able to afford intrinsic value.

I have already mentioned that, although it is overpriced in relation to its intrinsic worth, given the amount of added value it offers, champagne is cheap. Indeed, it is too cheap. The costs of actually making it and of marketing and advertising are so high that the very important aspect of ageing has to be skimped. This ageing cannot be carried out by the consumer after he has bought the wine; it has to be carried out in the cellars of the producer while the yeasts are still in the bottle. During the champagne's long period of conditioning in contact with its yeast cells, the yeasts give back to the wine substances, notably amino acids, which they have previously taken from it. The value of this long yeast contact is evident from Bollinger RD, the one *cuvée de prestige* which possibly is worth the price. This ages for ten years in contact with its yeasts before the yeasts are expelled and the champagne recorked for shipment.

The higher the price a merchant charges for his champagne, the more money he has to give the vine grower from whom he has bought the grapes. This prevents merchants from ripping off growers. But it also prevents them from increasing their price to finance a longer period of ageing, since the extra money goes to the grower rather than into investment in stockholding. It has been said that it is a poor vine grower in Champagne who has to drive his Mercedes himself. Yet if champagne is to justify its high price, a longer period of ageing is necessary. Currently most champagne is young, green and over-sugared. When champagne cost more, greater care could be taken in its production. On his travels in France just before the Revolution, Arthur Young visited Champagne and ascribed much of the fine flavour of the wine to the care taken by pickers in selecting only healthy bunches of grapes.[1] Today rotten grapes are usually picked and pressed along with healthy ones; the must is then filtered to take away the taste.

The most famous example of a wine which became so uneconomic to produce as – in the case of some estates – to disappear altogether is that of Sauternes, which can only be produced by selectively picking grapes affected by noble rot. Since noble rot does not strike all the grapes in a vineyard at once, the bunches have to be picked individually, by hand, sometimes in several passages through the vines over a period of months. On top of the labour costs, the size of the eventual crop is small. This is the consequence partly of the concentrating of the grapes by noble rot, partly of the fact that not all the grapes are affected, and partly of the need to reject a lot of the grapes which have been picked because they have been spoilt by grey rot or diluted by rain. It is sometimes mentioned as though it were something extraordinary that Château d'Yquem, which produces the most celebrated and expensive wine in Sauternes, yields on average only 9 hectolitres per hectare, going up to 12 or 13 in good years. In fact all the leading Sauternes châteaux achieve similarly low yields, ranging from 9 to 18 hectolitres per hectare. The leading red wine châteaux of Bordeaux regularly achieve yields of between 50 and 60 hectolitres per hectare.

Sauternes is not cost-effective to produce unless a high price is charged for it. Though the selective picking of Sauternes was known in the eighteenth century, it was not adopted – at least not for commercial purposes – until someone could be found who was prepared to pay the price. The first vintage of Château d'Yquem as we know it today was produced because the Russian Grand Duke Constance/Constantine, brother of the Tsar, paid £800 – five times the odds – for a *tonneau* (100 cases' worth) of the 1847. Château d'Yquem has established a reputation – added value – which today enables it to charge a price two to three times as high as that of its rivals. Therefore it can afford to spend as long as is necessary to pick the grapes: sometimes the pickers make nine or ten passages over three months. The château can afford to pick fast when necessary, as in 1984, in the week of 15 October, when it employed 130 pickers at an approximate cost of £15,000 for the week. Its rivals cannot always afford such care. The first-growth Château Suduiraut notoriously produced a 1985 Sauternes lacking in concentration, because they finished picking too early. They ended on 20 November, a month before Yquem.

In the 1960s consumers were not prepared to pay for Sauternes. Many of the top châteaux, unable to afford the indulgence of several selective pickings of nobly rotten grapes, started making dry white wines instead. Even Château d'Yquem did so, beginning in 1959. Some châteaux pulled up their white-grape vines and planted black. Max de Pontac, heir to the family which invented fine red Bordeaux at Château Haut-Brion in the late seventeenth century, ploughed up the vineyard at the second growth, Château Myrat, in 1976. Sauternes might have gone the way of Monbazillac, 50 miles away, which earlier this century used to produce wines equal to those of Sauternes. Today most producers can no longer afford selective picking. Yields, at 40 hectolitres per hectare, are far too high to make good sweet wine. *Appellation* regulations in Monbazillac forbid mechanical harvesting, since the wine is supposed to be made by a selection of nobly rotten or at least overripe grapes. In fact a number of growers harvest by machine, and they say that officials turn a blind eye to the practice.

In Sauternes it is, by and large, the good vintages which are cheap, and the bad vintages which are expensive. In 1983 the grapes all become nobly rotten at once: Château Raymond-Lafon (owned by the manager of Yquem) made only four or five passages and were able to bottle 90 per cent of the crop under their own label. In bad vintages the pickers have to make more passages through the vines. In 1974 Raymond-Lafon made ten passages but still had to sell off the entire crop to merchants as generic Sauternes.

The same is true of the red wines of the region: bad vintages are more expensive to produce. How is this expense to be financed? By what is commonly referred to in the wine trade as 'blackmail'. If a merchant, importer, retailer or consumer wants to buy a sought-after wine in a good vintage, he has to buy it also in bad vintages: for example, 1984, which was not *that* bad a vintage, but was given a bad press. Opening prices, both in Bordeaux and in Burgundy, were about 10–15 per cent higher than for the far superior 1983s. In order to justify asking more for their 1984s than they had for their 1983s, the Bordelais piled on the excuses: the need for a lot of expensive spraying, the loss of Merlot grapes through floral abortion, etc. But the only way they persuaded merchants to buy their 1984s was by 'blackmail'.

Up until the 1974 crash, stocks of clarets were held by merchants in Bordeaux. Since then everything has changed. The merchants no longer have the capital (nor can afford the interest involved in borrowing the money) required to finance every vintage. Instead of being stockholders, as formerly, they have become dependent on selling recent vintages on a commission basis; they have been transformed from merchants into brokers. They are interested in quick sales, however they are achieved. They want to pass on the tins of sardines as fast as possible.

The 'blackmail' travels down a chain until it reaches the eventual consumer. It stops here. Of course, if a wine merchant wants to employ this ruse on his customers, he has to be subtle about it. I have not seen it more beautifully put than in Corney and Barrow's opening offer of the 1984 clarets, in which they told their customers that they felt that this was a vintage which customers would like to have represented in their cellars. In their autumn 1986 list they admitted their failure and reduced prices. Their stocks of the wines nevertheless remain largely unsold. At £5.64, Château Labégorce-Zédé could probably be said to offer reasonably good value for money.

In Burgundy and now in the Northern Rhône, 'blackmail' is the essential consequence of the domaine-bottling movement, for peasant vine growers cannot afford to finance the poor vintages. We consumers cannot have it both ways. If we believe that we should buy our burgundies and Northern Rhônes direct from the growers rather than indirectly through the blends made up by merchants, then we have to finance them. If we won't do so willingly, then their alternative is either to 'blackmail' us – or to go back to selling to merchants who will mix up their wine with the produce of other growers in a blending vat. Certainly anyone who wanted to buy the 1985s from Gérard Chave in Hermitage, Robert Jasmin in Côte-Rôtie or Auguste Clape in Cornas in the Northern Rhône from Yapp, the sole importers, would have been disappointed had he not bought, or been prepared to buy, their 1984s as well.

It is very tempting, however, for growers who employ this system out of necessity to become greedy when the market turns in their favour, and, like many estate agents in London, start gazumping their customers. This practice has become common among white wine producers in Burgundy's Côte d'Or, the prices of whose wines doubled between the 1982 and 1985 vintages. Corney and Barrow enjoy a good relationship with a number of estates in the region, but no longer with any in Chassagne-Montrachet. In one of their wine-lists, their buyer, John Armit, described how they used to buy wine from Ramonet-Prudhon, but stopped doing so after it had taken two years, and the dispatch of solicitors' letters, to deliver the 1976s they had ordered. In 1979 they started to buy wine from Bachelet-Ramonet instead, but in 1984, when prices were rising by the day, they discovered that 250 cases they had ordered had already been sold *twice* to other purchasers.

Bordelais proprietors justify the system by looking at it the other way round. In certain good vintages, demand exceeds supply, so it is necessary to make an allocation. How to choose to whom to allocate the wines? 'Blackmail', the proprietors argue, is preferable to selling to the highest bidder, or operating on a basis of 'First come, first served'. But should not they, rather than their customers, bear the loss in bad vintages? It is they, after all, who make the profit in good ones. Even if Bordelais châteaux had cut their prices in 1984, they would not exactly have suffered a loss. It has been estimated that the maximum possible cost of making a bottle of classed-growth claret is 30 francs, so châteaux who were selling their product for 100 francs or more were hardly in danger of suffering economic damage.

This said, the lesser quality and higher prices of the top wines in bad vintages is offset to a certain degree by the fact that the gap between wines from the best estates and those from lesser producers is much greater in bad than in good vintages. It may be worth buying wines from less celebrated properties in Bordeaux and Burgundy in good vintages like 1982 in Bordeaux and 1985 in Burgundy, when even careless wine-makers would have had to make an effort if they wanted to produce bad wines, but, if you feel the need to buy in lesser years, it really is worth sticking with the big names. Whereas, in Bordeaux, the leading châteaux reject the majority of their vats as not up to scratch, in Burgundy, the *premier* and *grand cru* sites lie on the better-drained hillsides and are therefore not as vulnerable to the effects of too much rain as those vineyards at the bottom of the slope which are entitled only to the plain communal *appellations* (straight Nuits-Saint-Georges, etc.).

In Bordeaux, even in a good vintage, it is necessary to eliminate less good vats, in order to ensure that the quality is up to scratch. It is often pointed out that this is enormously expensive. In 1985 the second-growth Château Ducru-Beaucaillou sold for 100 francs and its second wine La Croix – the repository of its less good vats – for 40 francs a bottle. By rejecting 40 per cent of the harvest from the first wine, the owners lost a potential 6 million francs. But then the wine would not sell for the price it does if these steps were not taken to ensure quality. Moreover, one might wonder why a Bordelais châtelain should need to eliminate 40 per cent of the harvest in a good vintage.

The Bordelais use vat elimination as their standard method for reducing excess yields. They effectively operate the cascade system (this has already been explained[2]) which permitted a wine-maker to sell the same wine under various different *appellations*, up to the maximum production permitted for each, and was outlawed in 1974. Today the excess production over the limit permitted for each *appellation* has to be sold off for distillation. A disincentive for producing a big crop, one might have thought, but in fact the redrafting of the laws and the introduction of *rendements annuels* and *plafonds limites de classement* have ensured that a producer with a big crop does not suffer, and that a châtelain can produce 80 hectolitres per hectare and still be allowed to sell the whole lot as Pauillac. Of course, the resultant wine won't be worthy of a classed-growth château: no matter, the châtelain eliminates his thinner vats. 'Elimination' should not be taken too literally: in many instances, the producer does not throw the wine away or even sell it off to merchants as part of a Pauillac, Médoc or Bordeaux blend; like Jean-Eugène Borie at Château Ducru-Beaucaillou, he releases it under a 'second label' and at a price which would seem healthy to all but the greediest producers of classed-growth clarets. Still, vat elimination does at least ensure that the wine will be good, despite the excess production.

Vat elimination is a procedure which is only possible for big properties with a large production which is all sold under a single label. Therefore it is not an option open to the smallholders of Burgundy, most of whom own vines in various different vineyards from which they make wine which they commercialize under several different labels. If they think a crop is likely to be too large a one to be commensurate with good quality, they cut off some of the bunches of grapes in mid-summer.[3] This allows the remaining grapes to achieve better ripeness and concentration of flavour. The only problem with this method is that the vine growers don't really know as early as mid-summer whether the harvest is likely to be a large one or not. They sometimes guess wrong. For example in mid-summer 1982 they considered eliminating some grapes but did not do so because they remembered that the 1981 harvest had been small. The resulting wines were so dilute that they had to resort to the desperate means of running off between 10 and 20 per cent of the juice before fermentation in order to produce red wines with any degree of colour or concentration. In July 1983 they remembered the problems of 1982 and therefore did eliminate some grapes. As a result, the grapes were too concentrated, their sugar levels too high, and some of the wines had excessive levels of acetic acid. Others had to be diluted with water.

Quite apart from the smaller size of their holdings, the Burgundians have to resort to these risky and often desperate means because their black grape, Pinot Noir, is denatured by high yields. Thus they could not overcrop and then eliminate vats in the manner of the Bordelais. It is usually held that Pinot Noir cannot produce good wine if allowed to produce more than 45 or 50 hectolitres per hectare. There are, it must be admitted, those who disagree. Rainer Lingenfelder, who used to make Blue Nun Liebfraumilch for Sichel, now runs his family vineyard in the Rheinpfalz. He planted Pinot Noir vines in 1981, and in 1985 produced a superb, concentrated wine, comparable in style to a good red burgundy from the Côte de Beaune, from a crop of 80 hectolitres per hectare. He says that the Burgundians could perfectly well increase their black grape yields by 50 per cent if they had better vineyard management.

Like Pinot Noir, Merlot, the grape cultivated on Bordeaux's right bank, in Pomerol and Saint-Emilion, can be denatured by high yields. This can be demonstrated by tasting a cheap Italian Merlot which is unlikely to bear any resemblance to the versions produced in Bordeaux. In Saint-Emilion and Pomerol, bunches of grapes are sometimes cut off in mid-summer, as in Burgundy. It was particularly important in 1986, when some estates in Saint-Emilion achieved 120 hectolitres per hectare – far more than the permitted maximum yield. In Pomerol, Vieux Château Certan cut off 50 per cent of their bunches of grapes. In 1982, considered at the time an enormous vintage, at Château Pétrus one bunch in four was removed once the size of the potential harvest was apparent. As the full-time vineyard workers would have considered this to be sacrilege, the task was carried out by a few student *stagiers*.

Cabernet Sauvignon, which predominates on Bordeaux's left bank, is not denatured by high yields to anything like the same degree. Its quality may be much diminished, but it still tastes like Cabernet Sauvignon. This is partly, I suspect, a consequence of its thick skins and high tannin content. That is why overcropping followed by the elimination of thinner vats is possible in the Médoc. Thus, whereas the top Burgundian estates yield 30 hectolitres per hectare or less for their black grapes, top Bordeaux châteaux yield twice as much and then sell off up to half. For example, at Château Latour the average yield in the 1970s was 52 hectolitres per hectare, but on average only 57 per cent of total production was sold under the principal Château Latour label – which, by a stroke of casuistry, produces, in Bordelais eyes, a yield of 30 hectolitres per hectare.

But do the Bordelais, by their peculiar method of overproduction, cause quality to suffer? Certainly it is facile to believe that there exists a simple equation: the smaller the yield, the better the wine. If lowness of yield in itself indicated superior quality we would have to assume that no wines are as good as they used to be. We would have to agree that Château Latour 1970 cannot possibly be as good as the 1870 because the yield was twice as large. On this criterion, how fantastic must Nuits-Saint-Georges les Saint-Georges have been in the first half of last century when its yield averaged 1.5 hectolitres per hectare.[4]

It all depends on what causes the yield to be low. In Dão in Portugal, the low average yield of 28 hectolitres per hectare is largely the consequence of the vineyard's infestation with the fan-leaf virus. In Spain, the national average yield is only 20 hectolitres per hectare, the same level as that achieved in France 150 years ago, because not only are many of the vines unhealthy but in some years they stop growing in summer for lack of water. Irrigation is illegal in Spain for wines which claim a *denominación de origen* – the Spanish equivalent of French *appellation contrôlée*. Whereas, in Catalonia, the average yield for the *denominación* of Priorato is a ludicrously uneconomic 4 hectolitres per hectare, the vast Raimat estate, which does not enjoy a *denominación* and therefore may be irrigated, achieves yields of up to 100 hectolitres per hectare, as high as almost anywhere else in Europe; yet the wines are superb, not least a very 'Californian' Cabernet Sauvignon.

Excessive yields do, however, produce poor wines. All over Europe, grape varieties are reviled because they are normally set to work producing as much juice as they can manage. In Germany, the grape responsible for the mass of Liebfraumilch drunk in Britain is Müller-Thurgau; but it only produces poor wine, the emptiness of which needs to be concealed by the addition of substantial amounts of unfermented sweet grape-juice, because it is made to crop at 200 to 250 hectolitres per hectare. In his holding in the Bernkasteler Schlossberg vineyard in the middle Mosel, which he cultivates by 'organic' methods, Ernst Loosen yields about 40 hectolitres per hectare from his Müller-Thurgau vines (less than from the Riesling he cultivates elsewhere) and produces a remarkable wine as a result.

The relationship between yield and quality can best be explained if one understands a given area of vineyard as having a certain amount of goodness. A vine grower has the option of dividing this goodness between a small quantity of wine, producing a concentrated flavour, or between a lot of wine, and thus diluting it.[5] When vines are overcropped, the leaves simply cannot produce enough sugar by photosynthesis to enable the grapes to ripen properly and develop normal flavour. Moreover, as the yield per vine increases, the nitrogen content decreases. It is nitrogen which during fermentation helps the formation of esters and higher alcohols, producing more intense flavours and aromas; and it is possibly these which react during bottle-ageing, producing a fine wine.

The best wines are produced from the lowest yields. Strictly speaking, this does not prove a causal connection – it may simply be that producers who take the care to produce good wines are also those who crop the least. Nevertheless, it is strong circumstantial evidence. The most expensive and, I believe, best Châteauneuf-du-Pape, Château Rayas, yields about 15 hectolitres per hectare. The second most expensive and, I believe, second best estate in the region, Château de Beaucastel, crops on average 18 hectolitres per hectare. The average yield in Châteauneuf-du-Pape is about twice as large.

It is possibly the excessive yields which explain why so many German dry wines taste thin, when historically they were rated so highly. The Association of Charta Estates makes much of the fact that in 1896 Berry Bros sold top dry Rheingau wines for more than first-growth clarets. But in those days the yield of German wines was lower than that of French ones, which were busily being over-manured in order to overcome the effects of phylloxera. In Germany today, high yields are seen as a sign of a healthy vineyard. This is not unique: the same is true for white grapes in Burgundy. In Meursault, the late Guy Roulot taught his sons (who now make the wine for Domaine Guy Roulot) that, whereas too many black grapes made a bad wine, for white grapes quantity and quality go hand-in-hand. The quality of the Domaine's white wines suggests that M. Roulot may not have been entirely wrong. I do not know what the yields are on this domaine, but there are a number of white burgundy producers who now regularly crop 100 hectolitres per hectare. In Germany, the average yield had reached 100 hectolitres per hectare by the 1970s, and culminated in an average 171 hectolitres per hectare in 1982. The most quality-conscious estates, however, achieve yields only one-third to one-half this size.

Why are yields today so much higher than they used to be? Many vine growers would say that yields were lower in the past because the vine-stock was less healthy, and because their predecessors lacked the modern chemical sprays that exist to deal with disease and rot. Rot was certainly a problem in the past – that was why grapes were picked earlier – but it was *less* of a problem, because lower yields meant that the bunches of grapes were less tightly packed and therefore more easily able to dry out after rain, and so less susceptible to the spread of rot. Moreover, excessive use of nitrogenous fertilizers has produced an excess of vegetation, which causes increased humidity around the vine and makes rot more likely. Until recently, vine growers relied on Bordeaux mixture as a prophylactic against fungal diseases; a copper sulphate solution, this burned the hands of those who used it, and hardened the skins of the grapes, rendering them less liable to rot than they are today. Modern anti-rot sprays are, at best, a short-term solution, and have in some instances made the problem worse. There was substantial rot among Pinot Noir grapes in Burgundy in 1983 because the rot fungi had developed resistance to the anti-rot sprays. The produce of certain great estates, notably Domaine Armand Rousseau, was tainted with rot. If the sorting out of rotten grapes by hand has only fairly recently become common practice in Bordeaux, then it can only be because it has only recently become necessary. According to the wine merchant and wine writer David Peppercorn, it was adopted because of the disastrous results of 1963, and enabled much more successful wines to be made in 1968, despite similar weather conditions.[6] Now there are machines for eliminating grapes which have a healthy skin but are rotten on the inside. Using one such machine in 1983, Patrice Rion of the Burgundy Domaine Daniel Rion eliminated 30 per cent of the grapes, three times as many as usual.

Disease is an undying problem. Five hundred years ago, many of the vines in the Côte de Beaune were destroyed by a plague of beetles. As human efforts were of no avail, the Burgundians concluded that the plague was the work of the Devil, and sought God's assistance. A public religious procession was organized; each man was instructed to go to general confession and to abstain from swearing. When similar measures proved ineffective against another type of beetle which attacked the vines in the 1540s, the insects were excommunicated.[7] The dangers facing vines have, however, become more serious since the appearance of the oidium fungus in the middle of the nineteenth century and of the phylloxera louse and mildew fungus twenty years later. These diseases have not been conquered; their march has merely been halted. Grapes are sprayed with sulphur to prevent the onset of oidium and with Bordeaux mixture against mildew. The ravages of phylloxera were stemmed at the turn of the century by the grafting of European vines on to the roots of American species of vine, which are resistant to phylloxera because they are too tough for the louse to penetrate. In the last decade, mutant strains of phylloxera have appeared, attacking the hitherto phylloxera-resistant roots of American vines. Perhaps a new root-stock will be developed, resistant to the new Type B phylloxera. If not, George Ordish, the author of the standard work on the subject, fears that 'the world's vineyards could soon be in the position they were in just over a century ago – threatened with extinction by this tiny insect'.[8]

At present the major problem in the principal vine-growing regions of France is fan-leaf (*court-noué*), a virus which lives in the soil and causes vines to degenerate. It cannot be treated except by grubbing up and disinfecting the infected vineyard. It affects Chardonnay more than other varieties: according to Hanson, it was already causing the loss of 20 per cent of the production of Le Montrachet at the beginning of the 1970s,[9] and it has got worse since. In Burgundy, Pinot Noir too has started to degenerate; and at fifteen to twenty years of age, just when the vines ought to be producing their best and most concentrated fruit. This may help explain why yields are so low. It is hoped that the problem will be solved by the selection of healthy clones – yet no one knows what has caused it. Moreover, Pinot Noir mutates as willingly as insects under radiation. Will red burgundy as we know it survive beyond the twenty-first century? After all, Herefordshire cider, made from traditional bitter-sweet apple varieties, which is currently being revived, will never be as good as it was in the seventeenth century, when it was more esteemed by many than French wines, because the great Redstreak variety from which it was made degenerated and disappeared last century.

If yields have doubled on average in France since last century, it is because of the selection of more healthy and productive clones and the introduction of fertilizing. Both these changes have to a certain degree proved detrimental to quality.

In Burgundy in the middle of the last century the question of fertilizers was much discussed. A committee of growers and merchants, convened in order to decide upon the means of restoring the trade in Burgundy wines to its former prosperity, and re-establishing the quality and reputation of its great wines, concluded that it was necessary to stop applying nitrogenous fertilizers. Burgundy was losing its reputation because some vine growers were adding excessive amounts of manure to their fine-wine vines. Nobody objected to the manuring of vines which produced wines of ordinary quality. A questionnaire sent out round the wine-producing villages of the Côte d'Or, asking whether manuring was desirable, received the reply that 'It is helpful to manure the common varieties [Gamay, etc.], for with them the object is to produce quantity. On the other hand, it would be a mistake to manure the noble varieties [Pinots] because the increase in quantity would not compensate for the loss in quality.'[10] Whereas Pinot Noir yielded on average 15 hectolitres per hectare, a vineyard planted with Gamay and manured was capable of achieving eight times as much.

Attitudes to the manuring of fine wines changed when the vineyards were devastated by mildew and phylloxera in the second half of the last century. At Château Latour, these caused the average crop to fall by 50 per cent. So, from the 1880s on, the vineyard was fertilized heavily. Following a very large crop in 1899, 516 tons of manure and 12,750 tons of the new, untested, chemical fertilizers, were added. As a result, in 1900 the yield of the wine sold under the Château Latour label was 40 hectolitres per hectare, more than twice the average achieved in the thirty years from mid-century. I have no idea how much extra wine was produced but 'de-classified'. In Bordeaux, 1899 and 1900 are reputed as great vintage years. The wine writer Nicholas Faith has argued that the clarets produced in these vintages demonstrate that 'contrary to received opinion (and to the regulations surrounding the production of fine wines in France) the lavish use of fertilizer does not necessarily dilute the quality of the wine produced'.[11] But is this really so? In his *Great Vintage Wine Book*, Michael Broadbent says that on tasting he found the Latour 1900 to be not as full-bodied as he had expected.[12] Monsieur de Braquessac, proprietor of the restaurant Voisin in Paris, was, in 1905, more explicit. He said that there were no longer any *grands vins* in France; that Château Latour, which used to be delicious, was no better than the stuff the peasants drank; and that matters were getting worse, not better. This was in response to the investigations which the Comte de Beaumont, the château's director, was carrying out in order to discover why the price and reputation of his wine had fallen. In the first decade of this century, prices for the leading clarets fell, on average, by over 25 per cent. How far this was the result of overproduction – supply exceeding demand – and how far the consequence of a fall in quality, actual or perceived, is a moot point. Nevertheless, in 1907 several châteaux found it necessary to grant the exclusive distribution of their wines to brokers on a long-term basis; the contract which brokers made with Château Latour stipulated that chemical fertilizers were not to be used, and that manuring was not to be carried out to excess.[13]

The effects of clonal selection are equally contentious. One of the reasons for the very high yields in Germany today is that they were developing more productive clones of the Riesling grape long before similar work was begun in France. Work on clonal selection began at the vine-breeding institute at Geisenheim in the Rheingau at the end of the nineteenth century, and yields took off from the 1930s as a result. By the outbreak of war the average yield in Germany had reached 40 hectolitres per hectare, at a time when the average yields of the top wines in Bordeaux and Burgundy had fallen back to their historic figure of about 20 hectolitres per hectare. There was a very good reason to increase the yields in Germany: people were complaining about the price. It is ironic in these days, when fine German wines do not fetch a fair return, to read the book written by Hugh Rudd in the 1930s on German wines in which he seeks to justify their high prices by pointing to the need for expensive manuring every year, and to the need to prune the vines hard in the spring to achieve quality.[14]

The average yield in Bordeaux in the 1950s was 30 hectolitres per hectare, no higher than it had been in the first decade of the century and only 50 per cent up on the amount produced in the early nineteenth century. Yields in Bordeaux only took off in the 1960s because, it has been said, of the introduction of massal cloning in the 1950s: choosing the healthiest vines in the vineyard and using these for all new cuttings.[15] But I would be surprised if such an obvious procedure had not been adopted earlier. If average yields increased by one-third between the 1950s and 1960s, it was partly because many old and unproductive vines were pulled out after the frosts of 1956, and partly because mineral fertilizers were added less discriminately. The increase of yields from 1962 on brought prosperity back to the Médoc.

According to Julian Jeffs, the purpose of clonal selection has been to propagate disease-free vines, and increased yield is incidental.[16] If that is the case, how come that every instance of clonal selection has led not only to a reasonable increase in yield due to a greater proportion of healthy grapes, but to a vast increase in yield due to vines producing more and larger grapes and therefore less concentrated wine? Jeffs himself admits that in Jerez the yield of Palomino grapes on the best albariza soils has trebled, producing wines with a lower natural alcoholic strength – 11–11.5 per cent compared with 12–12.5 per cent previously – which increases to about 15 per cent following fortification and evaporation during ageing.

In *The Wines of the Rhône*, John Livingstone-Learmonth says that the nature of the Syrah grape was altered in the 1970s by clonal selection: the new strain of Syrah better resists floral abortion, but a number of growers are concerned that the new vine produces larger and more numerous grapes, which dilute the plant's fruit.[17] Similar reservations have been expressed about the Pinot Droit clone of Pinot Noir which was widely planted between the 1930s and the 1970s. It produces larger grapes and therefore more wine than traditional Pinot Noir clones. Pinots Droits may well bear some responsibility for the long-term decline in the reputation of red burgundy. But then we are demanding less concentrated wine which matures sooner, and should not shy away from admitting that, as a result of altering viticulture to suit this public demand, wines are no longer as good as they used to be.

There is another reason why yields have increased in recent years. Harry Waugh, who joined the wine trade in 1934 and bought wine for Harveys of Bristol in the 1950s, says that before the last war red burgundy was every bit as popular as claret, and the good vintages were laid down for the future as eagerly as were the claret vintages; but that since the war, perhaps on account of the small production and increasing world demand, the quality of red burgundy has been allowed to deteriorate with – inevitably – a depressing effect on its reputation.[18] In the 1970s red burgundies became lighter and thinner, culminating in the rosés of 1982, a vintage which led consumers to yearn for the Algerian blends of yesteryear.

Burgundy is not alone in this. The reputations of all the most famous wine regions of the world are being damaged by overcropping. The average yield per hectare in Champagne has increased from 50 hectolitres in the 1960s to 92 hectolitres in 1982. Of course excess yields don't really matter in Champagne. The wine is usually drunk on its own and therefore doesn't need to have the depth or body to stand up to food. In any case, how many people buy champagne for the taste?

On the whole, consumers pay for added value and not for intrinsic quality. Once a wine has established a reputation for quality, quite possibly without making a profit, then is the time to cash in. Winemakers are farmers, not wine-lovers. The wines they produce will not necessarily remain fashionable for very long. I cannot imagine, for example, that such ordinary wines as Sancerre and Pouilly-Fumé can go on obtaining the prices they do for ever. In a natural progression, high quality is followed by a good reputation, which leads to abuse and consequently to downfall. Rioja has progressed rapidly from the second to the third stage. It is not as good as it used to be, not least because the best black grape, Graciano, and the best white grape, Malvasia, yield very little and so are disappearing fast. Yet, in 1986, some estates doubled their prices. Looking back in 1775 at the claret boom of 100 years earlier, Sir Edward Barry pointed out that the popularity of the wine caused it to be overproduced and adulterated. Spanish and other wines were added to claret, causing the wine to referment. 'By these arts we have been almost entirely deprived of any genuine claret wines . . . it is therefore no wonder that the port wines are now universally preferred to French claret.'[19]

Where possible, famous wines have always been overproduced throughout history. As Pliny said of the most celebrated of Roman wines, Falernian, 'The reputation of this district is passing out of vogue through the fault of paying more attention to quantity than to quality.'[20] Château Haut-Brion lost its reputation in the early nineteenth century, and was overtaken by Lafite, because, according to a contemporary authority, 'too much manure is used'.[21] Like Falernian before it, Haut-Brion was cashing in on its reputation.

It could be argued that the only economic incentive for the production of good-quality wine is the hope of establishing for the future the sort of reputation that will enable you to rip consumers off. In many regions vine cultivation is uneconomic: in the Mosel, for instance. For the last ten years the income from wine of the average grower in the Mosel-Saar-Ruwer region has been only one-third of that of his counterpart in other regions.[22] As one leading grower has pointed out, he has to sell his Riesling wines for 5 DM a bottle – the equivalent of nearly £2, before tax – simply to break even. This situation is being partially relieved by a reorganization of vineyard holdings (*Flurbereinigung*). These used to be so diverse that growers could spend longer getting to their plots than working on them. As a result of *Flurbereinigung*, growers have exchanged plots of land with each other to make access easier, and production costs have halved. But still the production of ordinary QbAs (*Qualitätsweine bestimmter Anbaugebiete*) is uneconomic. Many wine merchants are listing 1984 QbAs from leading growers at ridiculously low prices. In their 1985 list, Russell and McIver were offering a 1984 Wehlener Sonnenhur Riesling from a good grower (in arguably the best vineyard in the Mosel) for £3.16, only 17p more than a blended Piesporter Michelsberg, which was probably made predominantly from Müller-Thurgau grapes.

The Mosel vineyards require four times as many man-hours of labour per hectare as those of Bordeaux. The base costs are so high that cheap wine can *never* be made profitably, and therefore, although it is currently uneconomic, the only hope for a long-term improvement in the economic condition of vine growers in the Mosel lies in selling top-quality wines for a high price. Such wines in the Mosel can only be made from Riesling; but Riesling wines cannot always be sold for a profit. To make a profit, a grower needs sufficiently ripe grapes to sell his wine as Spätlesen. Growers have therefore converted from the noble Riesling to the fairly ignoble Müller-Thurgau grape, because Spätlesen can be made more easily from this. In 1950 over 90 per cent of vineyards in the Mosel-Saar-Ruwer were planted in Riesling; the proportion today is less than 60 per cent. The vine growers have signed their own death-warrant.

Producers in the Northern Rhône have faced similar problems. In the Northern Rhône one man can work two hectares, in the Southern Rhône, ten. In 1983 John Livingstone-Learmonth quoted Max Chapoutier – with Gérard Jaboulet and Etienne Guigal, the best-known merchant in the region – as saying that he had lost money in Côte-Rôtie every year since 1973. In the 1890s Côte-Rôtie enjoyed as high a reputation as Hermitage, but it fell in the middle of this century because no one was prepared to work the slopes. Today only half the land permitted to bear the *appellation* has been planted in vines. The vineyard area has, however, been extended since the 1960s by planting on the plateau above the hillsides. John Livingstone-Learmonth has estimated that one-third of the *appellation's* vineyards are planted in this way.[23] Yet wine made from vines grown on the plateau can never achieve the quality of that produced from vines on the hillside. And, with the much-hyped 1985 vintage, the produce of the best hillside vineyards has begun to fetch high sums. Yapp sold Robert Jasmin's 1985 for more than twice as much as his 1982. So it can be done.

On the whole, however, the production of the world's best-value fine wines can better be explained by the fanaticism of a few hobbyists than by the prospect of economic advantage. The drop-out lawyer Edoardo Valentini makes a remarkable red

Montepulciano and an even more remarkable white Trebbiano in the Abruzzi in central Italy. This 'Trebbiano' is not in fact the much-derided Trebbiano of Tuscany but quite another grape which few people can afford to cultivate any more, because of its susceptibility to rot. Valentini declared his philosophy to Burton Anderson: 'I could have a profitable operation if I chose to mass-produce wine from my grapes. But no thanks. You've got to love it to get through what I do to make my kind of wine, but I just wouldn't have it any other way. It's hard work, and it doesn't pay, but wine is my way of committing myself.'[24]

[1] Arthur Young, *Travels in France 1787–9*, 1792, p. 383.
[2] Chapter 11, pp. 156–7.
[3] *Éclaircissage*.
[4] M. J. Lavalle, *Histoire et statistique de la vigne et des grands vins de la Côte d'Or*, 1855, p. 65.
[5] George Ordish, *Vineyards in England and Wales*, Faber & Faber, 1977, p. 64, quoting Edward Hyams.
[6] David Peppercorn, *Bordeaux*, Faber & Faber, 1982, p. 41.
[7] Camille Rodier, *Le Vin de Bourgogne*, Louis Damidot, 1921, pp. 15–17.
[8] George Ordish, *The Great Wine Blight*, Sidgwick & Jackson, 2nd ed., 1987, p. 196.
[9] Hanson, p. 95.
[10] Quoted in C. Ladrey, *La Bourgogne: revue oenologique et viticole*, 1861, p. 97.
[11] Nicholas Faith, 'Phylloxera – What Really Happened in the Médoc', in Patrick Matthews (ed.), *Christie's Wine Companion*, 1981, p. 114.
[12] Michael Broadbent, *The Great Vintage Wine Book*, Mitchell Beazley, 1980, p. 43.
[13] René Pijassou, *Le Médoc*, Tallandier, 1980, pp. 777–8, 782, 829–30.
[14] Hugh R. Rudd, *Hocks and Moselles*, Constable, 1935, pp. 10–11.
[15] *L'Appellation d'Origine Contrôlée*, 1985, pp. 78–9. The difference between massal cloning and clonal selection is that, in the former method, the new vines are a mixture of clones, whereas in the latter they are descended from a *single* mother.
[16] Julian Jeffs, *Sherry*, Faber & Faber, 3rd ed., 1982, pp. 154, 165.
[17] John Livingstone-Learmonth, *The Wines of the Rhône*, Faber & Faber, 2nd ed., 1983, p. 21.
[18] *Decanter*, October 1984, p. 60.
[19] Sir Edward Barry, *Observations on the Wines of the Ancients, etc.*, 1775, pp. 437–9.
[20] Pliny the Elder, *Natural History*, AD 77, Book 14, Chapter 8.
[21] Wilhelm Franck, *Traité sur les vins du Médoc*, 1824, p. 121.
[22] Ian Jamieson in *Decanter*, December 1983, p. 18.
[23] Livingstone-Learmonth, pp. 33–4, 81–2.
[24] Burton Anderson, *Vino*, Macmillan, 1982, p. 374.

WHAT'S YOUR POISON?

Some vine growers deliberately make things harder and more expensive for themselves by adopting so-called 'organic' methods of cultivation and vinification.

Why? Is it a con, designed to make us pay higher prices? Certainly, levels of misinformation about organic wines are considerable. Lavinia Gibbs-Smith, who sells a range of organic wines, claims in her facts sheet that 'wine produced organically has more taste than wine produced in other ways . . . chemical additives reduce taste considerably, as anyone who has eaten monosodium glutamate in food must know.' Does she really imagine that chemicals are used in wine-making as a 'taste-enhancer', as monosodium glutamate is in food production? It is sometimes hard to tell which is the more pernicious additives industry – that of adding extraneous substances to food products, or that of spreading incorrect 'scare' stories about their effects.

Moreover, organic wine-making does not exist. The rules of the group of organic wine producers called Terre et Vie permit fining with casein and bentonite, neither of which is entirely safe. In theory, both are supposed to precipitate out of the wine, taking with them substances which cause cloudiness and discoloration. But what if they do not? A quarter of a million Americans are allergic to casein, the principal protein occurring in milk. Bentonite is a clay, a compound of aluminium, the ingestion of which may well be a cause of senile dementia. It is added in very large quantities: 1 part per 1,000. If tests on beers conducted by CAMRA are anything to go by, aluminium from bentonite-fining probably does sometimes remain in the wine. CAMRA found very high concentrations of aluminium in a number of the beers they tested. One beer contained six times the recommended EEC limit for the aluminium content of drinking water. The presence of aluminium is just as likely the consequence of fining of the water with aluminium sulphate (alum) before the beer was made as of bentonite-fining of the finished beer, but this does not affect the issue: some residue remained in the beer.[1] The use of bentonite in wine-making could be avoided by heating the must or adding gum arabic instead. Apart from clarifying the wine, however, bentonite removes histamine and tyramine, the products of malolactic fermentation by undesirable strains of lactic acid bacteria, which may possibly be the cause of headaches in people who consume red wine.[2]

The term 'organic' is applied to wines which are made from organically produced grapes. The interests of organic producers lie in vine growing rather than in wine-making: the rules of Terre et Vie devote eleven pages to viticulture and one-and-a-half to vinification. Even so, no grapes are organically produced in the strict meaning of the term. All professedly organic wine-makers use sulphur sprays against the oidium fungus and a copper sulphate solution (Bordeaux mixture) against mildew. Bordeaux mixture is certainly necessary, even in a dry climate. Some Riojanos thought they were safe in their dry climate, so they used not to spray – until their 1971 and 1972 crops were destroyed by mildew. But confidence in its wholesomeness is not engendered by looking at how this was discovered. Last century, at harvest-time in Bordeaux, it was necessary to protect vines near the road from the depredations of grape thieves. At Château Latour two workmen stood on guard, armed with shotguns. Less wealthy châtelains sprayed the vines nearest the road with well-known poisons. First, they employed verdigris (copper acetate) but this became expensive when it started to be used to make the insecticide Paris Green (acetoarsenite of copper). So some of them took up spraying the vines with blue vitriol, a copper sulphate solution which looked like verdigris. This was the method employed at Château Saint Pierre-Sevaistre. In 1882 Pierre Millardet, Professor of Botany at Bordeaux University, noticed that the vines along the edge of the road – those which had been sprayed – had not suffered from mildew, whereas unsprayed vines had. So copper sulphate began to be used as a specific against mildew. Not everyone approved of its administration. It was widely believed that the copper got into the vine and affected the quality of the grapes. At the beginning of this century Dr Robin, an eminent Parisian stomach specialist, forbade his patients wine because, he said, copper sulphate produced potassium sulphate crystals which are corrosive.[3]

One might have expected organic producers to subscribe to the views of the Roman Columella, who said, after discussing the use of pitch and resin to preserve wines, that 'we regard as the best wine any kind which can keep without any preservative . . . for that wine is most excellent which has given pleasure by its own natural quality.'⁴ But in fact all professedly organic wine-makers add sulphur dioxide to their wines. In the present state of technology it is virtually impossible to produce wines which are stable without adding sulphur dioxide at some point during their manufacture, usually a little at the beginning of vinification, to prevent the wine's being spoilt by bacteria, and rather more at bottling, to guard against oxidation. A new German method which employs excimer lasers might in time serve as an alternative to sulphur dioxide for cheap wines, but the lasers affect the chemical constituents of the product and therefore could not be used on fine wines intended to age. The exception which proves (or perhaps disproves) the rule is the Greco di Bianco made from semi-dried grapes by Umberto Ceratti in Calabria in southern Italy. He kills the vineyard micro-organisms by immersing the grapes in boiling water before crushing;⁵ the wine's stability is improved by its naturally high alcohol content of about 17 per cent, but how it remains fresh and, by all accounts, delicious without any sulphur being added at bottling is beyond my ken. It would not, however, be true to say that the Greco di Bianco *contains* no sulphur dioxide; it is merely that none is added. Sulphur dioxide is produced as a by-product of yeast metabolism during fermentation. I have tasted organic wines which stink of naturally produced sulphur.

It is often difficult to know precisely how much sulphur dioxide organic wine-makers add to their wines, as they sometimes reveal only the quantity added at bottling, not the amount they add at the beginning of fermentation. Because they do not use chemical sprays against vineyard micro-organisms, they may in fact need to add more sulphur dioxide at the beginning of fermentation than more conventional vine growers, in order to prevent the action of unwanted yeasts and bacteria. To be a member of Terre et Vie, a wine-maker is permitted to include in his wine up to 100 milligrams per litre of sulphur dioxide, of which no more than 30 milligrams per litre may be free sulphur (the only form in which it can be smelt). Few of the leading organic producers add much less than this. It is hard to do without the addition of 50 milligrams per litre of sulphur dioxide to the best-made white wines at the time of bottling.

Is consumption of these quantities of sulphites[6] harmful? The EEC has laid down maximum sulphur levels at 175 milligrams per litre for red wines and 225 for white. The 1981 EEC Scientific Committee for Food reported that the average European takes in 15 milligrams of sulphites daily from food and non-alcoholic drinks; and 90 milligrams of sulphites if he drinks a bottle of wine a day. In 1973 the World Health Organization set the acceptable maximum daily intake at 0.7 milligrams per kilogram of body weight, equivalent to 49 milligrams for an 11 stone adult. So, even drinking organic wines, a bottle-a-day man exceeds that limit.

Many regular wine-drinkers certainly take in more sulphites than is recommended. If they are doing themselves any harm, however, it is because of the alcohol, not because of the sulphites. Experiments on animals have shown that large doses of sulphites are acutely toxic but that low, long-term doses have no adverse effects. We all form endogenously an average of 1,680 milligrams of sulphites every day, all of which is excreted in urine. There are, however, always some people who are allergic to a particular naturally occurring substance, and sulphites are no exception. Half a million Americans are sensitive to sulphites, and in the last five years thirteen deaths have been linked to ingestion of the chemical. The Food and Drug Administration has reacted by banning sulphite preservatives in fresh food and vegetables. (The use of sulphites to keep salads fresh in salad bars was already illegal in Britain.) In 1987 the drinks industry agreed with the Bureau of Alcohol, Tobacco and Firearms to introduce sulphite labelling before it was imposed upon them. By taking the first step, drinks producers only bear the slight imposition of having to state that a product 'contains sulphites' – there is no need to give the quantity – and this can be stated on the back label.

The question of sulphite labelling has been treated separately from that of general ingredient labelling of drinks products, which is not compulsory, as it is for packaged foods. In the USA in the late 1970s, the Carter administration introduced the regulation that beer, wine and spirits bottles must carry labels listing all the ingredients. This was cancelled by the Reagan administration; then restored by a Federal judge in Washington in 1985; the drinks industry has appealed to the Supreme Court, where it will take several years to hear the case. And so it goes on. Will ingredient labelling of drinks products ever be introduced, either in the USA or in Europe? Already the Australian government has ordered that wine labels must show the World Health Organization's anti-oxidant and preservative numbers. It is possible that the Germans will introduce it unilaterally, because of the abolition of their 400-year-old pure beer law, the Reinheitsgebot, in March 1987. In response to a case brought by the Alsatian brewers Fischer-Pêcheur, the European Court ruled that for Germany to require that beer be brewed only from malt, hops, water and yeast was an action 'in restraint of trade', since it prevented beers made with recourse to brewing adjuncts and additives from being sold in Germany. If compulsory ingredient labelling were to be introduced in Germany, then imported beers would have to declare all the embarrassing additives they have used. Certainly the list would be a long one: a chemist at one of London's best breweries told me that they used nineteen additives; others use more. But not all German breweries are squeaky-clean. In 1986 it was revealed that forty of them had made a practice of adding mono-bromacetic acid and other chemicals to their beer.

Would the compulsory ingredient labelling of wines actually work? Firstly, producers who are adding illegal substances to their wine are unlikely to advertise the fact on their labels: for example, burgundy producers who illegally add tartaric acid (E 334) to their wines; or anyone who adds water (which, in the case of foods, has to be listed if it accounts for more than 5 per cent of the total weight). The authorities in wine-producing countries have enough trouble in administering the law as it is.

Secondly, wine-makers employ a great number of processing aids, such as casein, bentonite and potassium ferrocyanide, which are not additives and therefore do not have to be declared on the label. Potassium ferrocyanide is used in Germany to resolve discoloration of the wine by a combination of iron and tannin. When it was introduced in the 1920s, it was hailed as a great advance, because it produced wine that was crystal-clear, so hock glasses no longer had to be coloured. The process is called 'blue fining' because it forms a blue precipitate – the dye Prussian blue – which is usually removed by filtration. If the filtration is not carried out properly, some of the blue precipitate may get into the bottle; and, in time, this decomposes to form hydrogen cyanide – cyanide gas – which gives the wine a bitter almond odour. To check that this has not happened, the wine-maker needs a laboratory equipped with an atomic adsorption spectrometer; this is not an item frequently to be found in the establishments of German vine growers. It was reported in the trade publication *Harpers Wine and Spirit Gazette* that in 1986 the Wine Standards Board had investigated two instances of wine to which the process of clarification with potassium ferro-cyanide had been incorrectly applied.[7] Thankfully, hydrogen cyanide in wines has never been found to be above the toxic level: nevertheless, its use is prohibited in America. Other treatments exist, such as the addition of citric acid or calcium phytate. Unlike potassium ferrocyanide, these do not diminish a wine's ability to improve in bottle. If German wine-makers could afford to invest in modern equipment, the problem would not occur in the first case.

Thirdly, labelling of the sulphur content, as opposed to merely stating that the wine in question, like all others, contained sulphites, would not be practicable. The free sulphur dioxide content varies from one week to another; the proportion of bound sulphur dioxide is more stable. But it is the free sulphur which is offensive, and it does not always form the same proportion of the total sulphur content. Existing regulations are based on the total sulphur content. If the free sulphur dioxide content were labelled at time of bottling, it would undoubtedly have changed by the time the consumer came to drink the product.

It is certainly common sense not to add an excessive quantity of sulphur dioxide to a wine. It smells unpleasant. It also destroys vitamins, particularly thiamine (B_1), of which the average concentration in wine is 8.7 milligrams per litre. This means that a glass of wine contains more thiamine than a bowl of All-Bran. We do not, however, drink wine for its vitamin content.

Sulphur has not only a negative, protective function – which might well be replaced by other methods – but a positive role as well. Many organic wines, produced with a minimum of sulphur dioxide, are kept clean by vinifying away from air, under a blanket of nitrogen. But a wine destined for bottle-ageing needs to have contact with air during vinification. Sulphur dioxide allows this to occur without the wine oxidizing. To this, a sophisticated organic wine-maker might reply that the must should certainly be oxygenated, but in the *absence* of sulphur dioxide. This way, the tannins oxidize and bind together into long chains, which are too heavy to remain in solution, and so precipitate out. They are not liable to oxidize in the bottled wine, because they are not there. Moreover, because wines which are oxygenated during fermentation do not oxidize so easily after bottling, less sulphur dioxide has to be added at bottling. If, on the other hand, sulphur dioxide is added to the must, it combines with those tannins most liable to oxidize; these tannins remain in small units rather than forming heavy chains and therefore are not precipitated out during fermentation or fining; they stay in the wine where they later evolve, turning it brown.

More harmful than sulphur dioxide is the danger that the current obsession with sulphur dioxide levels will have a deleterious effect on the quality of wines produced. A consumer survey in Bavaria in 1987 found that 44 per cent of respondents would prefer sulphur-free wines, even if they were more expensive than sulphured wines. The quantity of sulphur dioxide that needs to be added at the start of vinification can be reduced if the microbial population of the grapes is kept as low as possible by spraying regularly against rot and other infections. But if modern chemical sprays are used, this may introduce a harmful substance into the wine, and possibly cause long-term ecological damage. They may also harm the people who are using them. Jacques Beaufort, who makes an excellent champagne in the *grand cru* village of Ambonnay, went organic when his son inhaled a chemical spray he was using, one of his lungs ceased functioning, and he was temporarily paralysed.

We are always being assured by wine-makers who depend on the use of pesticides and insecticides that there is no danger of their getting into the wine we drink. If so, how come Xavier Gardinier, the new owner of Château Phélan-Ségur, had in 1987 to buy back the 1983, 1984 and 1985 vintages from merchants, because the wine (made by his predecessors) had a disagreeable odour caused by the use of the systemic insecticide acephate? (This substance is unpleasant rather than poisonous.) It has long been known that systemic insecticides, which are not sprayed on the grapes but work from the inside, through the sap of the vine, do leave a residue in the eventual product. (It is ironic in the circumstances that Xavier Gardinier made his fortune in the field of chemical fertilizers.)

Chemical sprays, whether systemic or otherwise, are liable to get into the wine if used close to the harvest. If no rain falls in between the administration of the spray and the harvest, then there will most probably be some pesticide residues in the eventual wine. Yet the very time when modern anti-rot treatments are most necessary is fairly soon before the harvest – for example, after a fall of rain, which has swollen the grapes, reduced their sugar content and therefore caused an imminent harvest to be delayed.

In the long term, we simply have no idea what ecological damage we may be causing by the administration of pesticides and insecticides. There are many examples all over Europe of fruit trees having to be uprooted because excessive treatments have at last selected resistant insects. What sort of super-bugs are we creating? A fear for the future of the eco-system justifies organic methods of growing grapes or, indeed, any other form of fruit or vegetable.

It is not usually difficult for a conscientious vine grower to rid himself of vineyard pests without recourse to chemical insecticides. He merely introduces other insects which feed on the pests in question. Another method, adopted by the Ott family at Château de Selle in Provence, is to use substances which red spiders and other insects find unpleasant to smell. There are sometimes problems with natural insecticides, however. Some German wines when young have a 'goaty' (böckser) smell. It used to be thought that this had something to do with the type of manure used, but it is now believed by some people to be the result of the attempt to use as an insecticide hydrogen sulphide produced by rotting eggs in the fridge.

Organic manure is quite a different matter. It is not necessary. How can organic wine-makers, without hypocrisy, spray a copper sulphate solution on to their grapes yet declare their opposition to chemical fertilizers which are simply natural materials obtained in a pure form as the result of a chemical process? If a soil is deficient in nitrogen, phosphorus or magnesium, why not add it in a pure form, rather than going out of your way to find a shepherd with time on his hands who is prepared to drive his sheep your way? There is no difference between the nitrogen contained in manure and nitrogen administered neat. Certainly, mineral fertilizers act more rapidly when added in pure form than when administered as manure, but the prudent vine grower will add small amounts at various times, not all at once. The harmful effects of the addition of chemical fertilizers on both the environment and the wine derive from their excessive use, not from their employment in preference to sheep's droppings, horse-manure or dead cats.

Ironically, it has been suggested that chemical weed-killing is less destructive to the soil than turning it over mechanically, which destroys the surface roots of the vine so that it cannot feed on the surface soil. The nutriments in the topsoil are very important to the vines, because this is where 80 per cent of their root-system is to be found. Also, if vineyards are not tilled, worms are not killed, and these ventilate the soil. [8]

This said, the following estates all make excellent wine by organic methods. I have listed them in approximately ascending order of price:

Guy Bossard, Muscadet.
Laurens-Teulier, Marcillac.
Castello di Luzzano, Lombardy.
Terres Blanches, Coteaux des Beaux-en-Provence.
Freiherr Heyl zu Herrnsheim, Nierstein, Rheinhessen.
Castellare, Chianti Classico.
Castello di Volpaia, Chianti Classico.
Veuve Achard, Clairette de Die (*tradition*).
Château Musar, Lebanon.
Gaston Huet, Vouvray.
Elisabetta Fagiuoli, Vernaccia di San Gimignano.
Domaine de Trévallon, Coteaux des Beaux-en-Provence.
Pierre André, Châteauneuf-du-Pape (red).
Château de Beaucastel, Châteauneuf-du-Pape [their nearby Côtes-du-Rhône estate, Cru de Coudoulet, is also organic, and considerably cheaper].
Château Vignelaure, Coteaux d'Aix-en-Provence.
Château de Selle, Côtes de Provence.
Mas de Daumas Gassac, Vin de Pays de l'Hérault.

Much of the confusion surrounding organic production arises from the tendency of organic vine growers and particularly the importers and retailers of their products to claim as their own techniques that are in common use throughout Europe. The planting between rows of vines of leguminous plants, to act as fertilizer, is not peculiar to organic viticulture: it was re-introduced by the Austrian Dr Lenz Moser in the 1920s.

Modern chemical anti-rot treatments have been abandoned by a number of vine growers, not just organic ones. The Moueix estate, owners of a number of leading Saint-Emilion and Pomerol properties from Château Pétrus downwards, experimented with modern chemical anti-rot treatments, but gave them up in 1978 on the grounds that they delayed fermentation.

Nor is a preference for natural over cultured yeasts peculiar to organic wine production. Organic wine-makers argue that the character of the wine depends on the yeasts which occur naturally on the skins of the grapes in the vineyard and that cultured yeasts produce identikit wines, smelling of pineapple and tasting of fruit salad. Certainly this is the predominant character of Californian and Australian Chardonnays, which are generally fermented with cultured yeasts. It is not, however, clear that the most important yeasts are those which live in the upper layer of the soil and are carried by insects on to the skins of the grapes. It may be that the most important yeasts are those which are to be found in the cellar. If so, questions of organic cultivation and avoidance of chemical sprays are completely irrelevant.

The importance of yeast strains in the cellar can be understood by looking at their effect on the flavour of beer. The raw material – the malted barley – is of a standard quality; it does not vary from one producer to another as grapes do. John Hammond, Head of Fermentation at the Brewing Research Foundation, believes that 'the compounds responsible for beer flavour are almost wholly derived from yeast metabolism',[9] which produces esters, acids and higher alcohols during fermentation. Different yeasts produce quite different beers from the same worts. Each brewery has its own yeast, which in some cases has been jealously guarded for a century or more. Likewise, according to Peter Vinding-Dyers, the innovative Danish wine-maker at Château Rahoul in the Graves in Bordeaux, every wine cellar has its own group of yeasts. That is why, he says, Léoville Lascases tastes different from Léoville Poyferré, which is made only a few metres away; and why grapes produced in the vineyards of one and vinified in the cellars of the other will have the character of the estate in whose cellars the wine is made.

If Vinding-Dyers is right, then this would help explain why wines made by the same wine-maker from the produce of different, often very disparate, vineyards in Burgundy, the Rhine and Mosel so closely resemble each other. They are all made with the same yeasts. (But it does not explain why merchants' burgundies, blended from wine they have bought in, taste so similar. In some instances, this similarity can have been achieved only by the illegal inclusion of wine from elsewhere.)

If most Australian wine-makers prefer to use selected yeast strains rather than rely on those which occur naturally in their cellars, it is, according to Dr Terry Lee, director of the Australian Wine Research Institute, because this 'eliminates much of the element of chance in winemaking'. It is hardly surprising that Peter Vinding-Dyers should have said, in a lecture to candidates for the Master of Wine examination, that 'the day we arrive [at this sort of uniformity in Bordeaux], Bordeaux is finished'.

The contrast between wine made using cultured yeasts and wine made using natural ones is as great as that between pasteurized and unpasteurized cheese. Pasteurization of milk kills fault-producing micro-organisms but also destroys most of the enzymes, some of which are responsible for the development of flavour as the cheese ripens. Commercial cheese-makers who pasteurize have to add starter cultures, so all their cheeses taste the same. Unpasteurized cheeses, where the naturally occurring enzymes and bacteria are allowed to work, are different every time. Certainly, pasteurized cheeses are more reliable than unpasteurized, and sometimes they are just as good, though no one would claim that the pasteurized versions of soft cheeses such as Camembert or Brie bore any relation to the unpasteurized versions. But pasteurized cheeses are never as interesting as unpasteurized. Do we want wines that all taste the same, or that taste different from every wine-maker and every vintage?

The advantage of cultured yeasts is that they start fermenting faster than natural ones. That is why some wine-makers, who would not dream of sterilizing or pasteurizing the must and then adding a cultured yeast strain, nevertheless add a starter yeast to get fermentation going. The locally adapted, naturally occurring yeasts then take over during fermentation. In his book on German wines, Fritz Hallgarten says that he has not found the use of a starter yeast to affect the flavour of the eventual wine, with one exception: a

Steinberger Trockenbeerenauslese which was so difficult to bring to fermentation that as a last resort sherry yeast was used. Nobody was told about this, but at the first public tasting experts considered that the Steinberger Trockenbeerenauslese had a special, unusual character.[10]

A further aspect of wine-making which organic vine-growers claim as unique to them is an opposition to filtration. Certainly, few organic vine growers filter their wines. But the rules of Terre et Vie permit it. An opposition to filtration has nothing at all to do with organic viticulture and everything to do with the making of top-quality wine.

In the early days of filtration after the last war, it was a dangerous procedure, because asbestos filters were used. These have not altogether disappeared. Jim Roberts, a wine-maker in New South Wales, who died in 1986 of mesothelioma, a lung disease caused by exposure to asbestos, won soon before his death substantial damages against the manufacturers of the asbestos filter pads he had been using for the previous twenty years. His family say that the same pads are still used by other wine-makers.

Any dispute over the effect of filtration today concerns the taste of the wine. In his book on wine-making, Emile Peynaud argues that the purely mechanical (as opposed to chemical) action of filtration cannot possibly have a negative effect on the quality of wines, because the foreign substances in suspension and the impurities that form the lees do not have a favourable taste function.[11] How can Peynaud say what he does, when the character of champagne depends on what is in the lees? The base wine for champagne is usually neutral-tasting, and the final product only has any flavour at all because of the break down of yeast cells during the second fermentation. Muscadet, too, is a neutral-tasting wine – unless it has spent some months in contact with its lees, without being racked from one cask to another. The unfiltered Muscadets *sur lie* made by the Chereau and Carré families from their five estates actually improve in bottle: Château de Chasseloir, Grand Fief de la Commeraie, Moulin de la Gravelle, Château du Coing à Saint-Fiacre and Château de l'Oiselinière de la Ramée. Nor is it any coincidence that the top producers of Meursault – François Jobard, Domaine des Comtes Lafon and Jean-François Coche(-Dury) – are those who keep their wines in contact with their lees for a long period. In the course of two years' ageing in cask, the Lafons do not rack their wine off its lees at all, even though this brings an increased danger of spoilage. Wine-makers who believe in lees-contact before bottling do not, however, necessarily disbelieve in filtration. In Western Australia, Moss Wood, who make a brilliant Semillon, filter the wine before bottling, after long lees-contact. Unfiltered white wines are very rare, largely because consumers who are bothered if they find sediment in a bottle of red wine are going to be totally fazed if they discover sediment in one of white. After all, white wines are rejected if they have tartaric acid crystals in the bottom of the bottle. These tend to form in cold weather unless the wine has already been chilled in the winery to encourage their precipitation before bottling. I have bought from various wine merchants at ridiculously low 'bin-end' prices a number of white wines which have formed tartaric acid crystals. One or two merchants, however, are canny enough to persuade their customers that, because the tartaric acid has precipitated out, the wine is less acidic and therefore a better, not a worse, buy.

Filtration is carried out for purely commercial reasons. Why should restaurants bother with a wine that has deposit in it, when few of their staff will have the time or ability to decant a bottle of wine off its dregs; and, if they present their customers with a bottle which has sediment in it, it will be sent back? Moreover, an unfiltered wine is more likely to go off, because it contains impurities which may cause an unfavourable chemical reaction. Unfiltered wines contain yeasts which, if the wine contains any unfermented sugar, can spring to life in warm temperatures and cause a refermentation. Robert Parker says he knows *sommeliers* in France who remove certain unfiltered wines from the list in summer because they come alive and taste 'spritzy'.[12]

How can anyone argue that filtration takes nothing out of the wine, when Beaujolais Nouveau lacks aroma and flavour because it has been heavily filtered so that it can be drunk in a stable condition within two months of the harvest? Filtered 'vintage character' port never achieves the same quality as unfiltered crusting port. The former is sold for drinking young; the latter is intended to mature for a few years in the bottle. Churchill's Crusting Port, made, they say, from the same quality of grapes as their Vintage Character, is, even two years after bottling, in another class. Unfiltered wines will develop greater complexity with age than filtered ones because a greater number of different chemical reactions are likely to occur during bottle-ageing, since essential constituents have not been removed from the wine – even if no one knows what these are.

There is a patent difference in taste between filtered and unfiltered versions of the same wine. Robert Parker tasted two *cuvées* of the 1983 and 1984 vintages of the Châteauneuf-du-Pape Domaine du Vieux Télégraphe, and in each case preferred that *cuvée* which had not been given a second filtration before bottling. Daniel Brunier, who makes the wine with his father, accused Parker of wanting to cause controversy, and said that the difference between the two *cuvées* only lasted for one month while the filtered wine recovered from the shock of the filtering process. Parker, however, tasted these wines in 1986. Daniel Brunier also said that the only reason why one of his American importers brought in an unfiltered *cuvée* was that Parker had created a demand for unfiltered wines. Parker says that, among leading producers of Côte-Rôtie in the Northern Rhône, both Etienne Guigal and Gilles Barge experimented with filtration several years ago and found that it stripped the wine of character and flavour.[13]

In Burgundy, perhaps the finest wines made in the villages of Nuits-Saint-Georges and Vosne-Romanée are those of Henri Jayer. Some of the vineyards he works are owned by Domaine Méo, and Jayer cultivates these on a share-cropping basis: Domaine Méo owns the vines; Jayer makes the wine, and gives Domaine Méo half the wine he has made in 'rent'. Perhaps the half that Jayer gives Méo is not as good as the half he keeps for himself. Certainly Jayer does not filter the wine he sells under his own name, whereas Méo filter theirs heavily. There is no doubt that Jayer's unfiltered version is superior.[14]

The burgundy merchant Louis Latour, in defence of his company's use of pasteurization, argues that to use sterile filtration instead would be to adopt a 'more brutal process', which removes colour and flavour from the wine at the same time as rendering it stable. I would not push my criticism of filtration quite so far. Pasteurization was invented as a desperate remedy for diseases of wine which are, thanks to an improved understanding of the process of vinification, no longer much of a problem. In 1863 Emperor Napoleon III asked Louis Pasteur to try to find a solution to wine diseases. Pasteur discovered that the principal disorders which afflicted wines were the result of the activity of micro-organisms, and that they could be killed by heating. He argued that it would be easier to destroy microbes after fermentation than to prevent their entrance. Unusually for a wine producer, the present Louis Latour's grandfather took a scientific degree at the end of the nineteenth century, at which time Pasteur's discoveries were all the rage. That is why Maison Louis Latour pasteurize their wines today. But Pasteur did not understand how wine matured. He thought that it matured only through the action of air, and that therefore bottle-maturation involved nothing more than slow oxidation through the cork. As I have already pointed out, bottle-ageing, though it involves a number of chemical and physical changes, the full extent of which is not yet understood, owes little, if anything, to the effect of oxygen. Louis Latour heat their red burgundies to 70°C for one minute, which causes both chemical and physical change. How can it be argued that this does not affect the taste of a wine when even the purely physical changes caused by filtration, or by chilling a wine to below 0°C in order that tartaric acid salts should precipitate out of solution before rather than after the wine is bottled, emasculate the end-product? Admittedly the difference in taste may become evident only after chemical reactions have occurred during bottle-maturation. Because it causes similar chemical changes in different products, pasteurization makes these products more alike than they might otherwise have been.

Pasteurization is suitable for cheap, everyday wines which are not intended to mature. Indeed, it is essential for the stability of sweet, low-alcohol, low-acid, virtually tannin-free wines such as Lambrusco and Asti Spumante. According to Nicolas Belfrage, it was the introduction of hot-bottling in the 1960s that was largely responsible for Italian success in selling reliable, high-volume lines. This method involves heating the wine to between 48 and 54°C and bottling it at this temperature, either chilling the bottles afterwards or allowing them to cool down of their own accord. Hot-bottling became unfashionable in the 1970s, and is no longer much used outside Sicily.[15]

When, in his book on Burgundy, published in 1982, Anthony Hanson revealed the fact that Maison Louis Latour pasteurized their red wines, and said that this was 'known in Burgundy, but no more talked about than if the King were walking about with no clothes on',[16] Louis Latour defended himself in print. Pasteurization, he said, was necessary to protect red burgundies against acetification, particularly in hot years with low acidity. He made the rather extraordinary statement, 'Scientific and technical progress has always been beneficial to wine.'[17] Yet the scientific progress achieved by Louis Pasteur occurred at the same time as less quality-conscious producers were discovering the benefits of the new azo dye magenta to give pale wines a bright red colour. This may have helped the wine, but it certainly did not help the people who drank it.

On the other hand, we should not follow organic wine-makers in dismissing scientific and technical progress. What is old is not necessarily good. Before the French Revolution, at the then monastic vineyard of Clos de Vougeot, the monks used to jump naked into the vats three times during the vinification, in order to ensure that the skins mixed properly with the juice. This exertion, called *pigeage*, was the only occasion in the year when the monks had a bath, and it was said that a real burgundy expert could declare by the taste whether a wine was pre- or post-*pigeage*.[18] Wine-drinkers, like many other classes of society, have a tendency to invent a fantastic past for themselves. They live in a world increasingly full of industrial heritage museums, which create an image of a healthy working society, to counteract today's high levels of unemployment; which present poverty as something wholesome, warm and welcoming, and create a nostalgic longing for non-existent better days.[19]

Organic wine-makers suffer badly from *la nostalgie de la boue*. Some organic producers are actually living in that lost past: they have not made a conscious decision to 'go organic'; they have simply not yet got round to using modern chemical sprays and additives. Paul Bouron at Château de Chavrignac in Bordeaux lives a life straight out of *Madame Bovary*, going around in wooden clogs, without socks, even in the depths of winter. Other organic wine-makers have re-adopted the cosmic view of our medieval ancestors. In the cultivation of Coulée de Serrant in Savennières in the middle Loire, Nicolas Joly follows the biodynamic methods created by Rudolf Steiner in Germany at the beginning of the century, which take us back into a world dominated by lunar cycles. Joly only works the earth when the moon is in Leo, Aries or Sagittarius. Remarkably, he produces the best wine in the *appellation*.

1 *What's Brewing*, November 1987, p. 9.
2 See Chapter 2, p. 15.
3 René Pijassou, *Le Médoc*, Tallendier, 1980, p. 830.
4 Columella, *De Agricultura*, c. AD 60, Book 12, paragraphs 16, 19.
5 A similar method is employed by Château de Beaucastel in Châteauneuf-du-Pape, who flash-heat the skins of uncrushed grapes to 80°C for two minutes. This is not pasteurization, as is sometimes alleged, because only the skins of the grapes are heated, not the pulp inside. Nevertheless, the process of heating cannot but affect the taste of the end-product. Sulphur is added to this wine before bottling.
6 Sulphites are the salts of sulphurous acid, which is formed by the dissolution of sulphur dioxide in wine.
7 *Harpers Wine and Spirit Gazette*, 14 August 1987.
8 J. F. Roques in *Outlook on Agriculture*, 1976, pp. 30–4, quoted in George Ordish, *Vineyards in England and Wales*, Faber & Faber, 1977, pp. 117–9.
9 John Hammond, 'The Contribution of Yeast to Beer Flavour', *Brewers' Guardian*, September 1986, pp. 27–33.
10 Fritz Hallgarten, *German Wines*, Publivin, 1976, p. 98.
11 Emile Peynaud, *Knowing and Making Wine*, Wiley, 2nd ed. 1984, p. 307.
12 *Wine Advocate*, no. 46, August 1986, p. 26.
13 *Wine Advocate*, no. 46, August 1986, pp. 3, 6; no. 48, December 1986, p. 18.
14 The position will change after the 1987 vintage, which will probably be Jayer's last. Some of Jayer's vines will go to his nephew, Emanuel Rouget; others will revert to Domaine Méo. Jayer himself will be employed by Domaine Méo as their adviser: so it is possible that Méo will become one of the great names in Burgundy.
15 Nicolas Belfrage, *Life Beyond Lambrusco*, Sidgwick & Jackson, 1985, pp. 35–6.
16 Hanson, p. 117.
17 *Decanter*, October 1982, p. 44.
18 Edward Ott, *A Tread of Grapes*, n.d., pp. 38–9.
19 See Robert Hewison, *The Heritage Industry*, Methuen, 1987.

CHATEAU LAFITE ON TAP?

One respect in which organic wine-makers are living in the past is that they are producing wine which is unnecessarily expensive. For most of its history wine has been an up-market product, within the financial grasp only of the upper classes. Rarely before modern times has the ordinary man been able to afford to drink wine. In medieval France, the peasant smallholders who produced wine could not afford to drink it; their livelihood depended on selling it. The only people who could afford to drink wine were aristocrats and the wealthy citizens of the towns. Inns were forbidden to sell wine to locals; they provided it only to travellers. Peasants drank *piquette*, made by adding water to the pulp of skins, stalks and pips left over after pressing the wine. This produced a coloured water very low in alcohol. Whenever the poor showed an increasing interest in drinking wine, wine laws were imposed in order to prevent growers from producing any sort of wine other than that which the upper classes wanted to drink: for example, Duke Philip the Bold's ordinance requiring the uprooting of all the ignoble Gamay vines in Burgundy.

The Middle Ages of wine production ended in the early eighteenth century, when the French government, in response to a 'fury of planting', issued an edict forbidding new plantings of vines anywhere in France. This was largely ignored. Standards of living in the countryside had grown sufficiently for peasants to be able to afford to drink wine.[1] At the same time, the beginnings of the Industrial Revolution produced an enormous growth in towns all over Europe. Demand outstripped supply, and the largest cities – London, Paris, Lyons, Milan and Rome – were all inundated with adulterated wine. A description of London written in 1790 claims that half the port and five-sixths of the white wines drunk in the city are in fact raisin wines, and gives an account of a factory in Lambeth Marsh which 'admirably mimicked almost every species of white wine'. The reason for the factory, the author explains, is that 'such is the prodigality and luxury of the age that the demand for many sorts exceeds in great degree the produce of the native vineyards'.[2]

Wine production was revolutionized. Noble vine varieties in northern and central France were pulled out. Pinots Noir, Blanc and Gris were replaced by the productive Gamay. After the Revolution, ecclesiastic and aristocratic vineyards, which had held out against the swing from Pinot to Gamay, were turned over to peasants. If the pre-eminence of the wines of Bordeaux was established at this period, it was because proprietors here were bourgeois as compared with the ecclesiastics of Burgundy and aristocrats of Champagne, and therefore held on to their properties. But in Bordeaux, too, the standard of the ordinary wines was going downhill fast. Vines came down from hillside vineyards and were planted in the fertile plains, where their crop was further boosted by over-manuring. Yields were thereby increased from 20-odd to 200 hectolitres per hectare. It was said that 'people don't care about quality any longer, but only about quantity'.[3] In the Midi the notorious Aramon, capable of producing 300 hectolitres per hectare or more, began to appear in the 1780s.

The wine the poor could afford to drink for the first time would have seemed revolting to our palates. John Locke, on a visit to France in the 1760s, described how wine was made at Montpellier in the Languedoc; how the grapes went into the vat rotten, and full of spiders; that 'they often put salt, dung, and other filthiness in their wines to help, as they think, its purging'; and that 'the very sight of their treading and making their wine (walking without any scruple out of the grapes into the dirt, and out of the dirt into the grapes they are treading) were enough to set one's stomach ever against this sort of liquor'.[4]

The poor did not want wine to be improved because that made it more expensive. In his guide-book to Spain, published in 1845, Richard Ford said that 'even at Valdepeñas, with Madrid for its customer, the wine continues to be made in an unscientific, careless manner'. Forty years earlier 'a Dutchman named Muller had begun to improve the system, and better prices were obtained; whereupon the lower classes, in 1808, broke open his cellars, pillaged them, and nearly killed him because he made wine dearer.'[5]

If this was not bad enough, it has been argued that, following the devastation of the French vineyards by the phylloxera louse in the latter part of the nineteenth century, the vine grower's attitude to his product changed and became a more cynical one. The replanting of the vineyards after phylloxera had involved the growers in heavy expenses, which obviously they wanted to recoup as quickly as possible. Formerly an artisan, the vine grower in the Midi now became a manufacturer, turning out increasing quantities of increasingly poor wine that for some time achieved prices out of all relation to its worth.[6] Chaptalization, necessary during the phylloxera period to give some alcoholic strength to *piquettes*, was now used to fortify weak wines from over-cropped vines.

In the Midi vine growers completed the changeover to Aramon; virtually nothing else was cultivated. This made them wealthy at first. It was said at Béziers in the 1890s that 'each vineyard owner on market days would come to buy his piano and jewels for his wife and daughters'.[7] In famous wine-producing regions, too, the need to finance replanting caused a shift from fine wines which needed to be aged in cask and did not bring a quick capital return to ordinary wines which did. Certain vine varieties disappeared, being too troublesome to cultivate; one of these was Muscat from Beaumes de Venise, where it reappeared only at the end of the 1950s.

In virtually all the most famous vineyard areas there was a major change in the varieties of vine planted. Quality seemed to be a thing of the past. In the 1930s in the Médoc wines made from Alicante Bouschet – which produces a wine with a great deal of colour but not much else – sold better and at higher prices than those made from Cabernet Sauvignon. The change in the vine varieties which were planted after phylloxera was made easier by the fact that replanting was necessary: the only effective means of stemming the progress of phylloxera was by grafting European vines on to American ones, which themselves made poor wine but were resistant to the phylloxera louse. Until this period change in the vineyards had been very slow, because vines survived for several generations. They were propagated not by creating new plants from the shoots of old ones but by burying them in the ground. This is not possible today, as the shoots would not be resistant to phylloxera. Replanting is necessary; there are few vineyards with vines older than fifty years old.

Ever since the recovery from phylloxera at the turn of the century,

Europe has been flooded with more wine than it can drink. Governments have tried to resolve this problem by a distillation programme, to rid the market of its excess of cheap wine, thereby shoring up prices and saving the peasantry from starvation. At the beginning of the century, before the distillation programme had been introduced, overproduction in the Midi caused prices to fall so low that vine growers put on masks and went begging. Today governments pay producers to dispose of their wines. The wine distillation programme has made it more cost-effective to produce bad cheap wine for distillation than good cheap wine for drinking. The European Parliament estimates that the EEC has been robbed of tens of millions of pounds each year since 1976 through wine fraud; others consider this to be a conservative estimate.[8] The methanol scandal in Italy in 1986 may have been one such fraud. Possibly the wine was bulked up with water and fortified with methanol, not with the intention of its being consumed, but in order to increase the amount of wine which qualified for subsidies for distillation. It was only decided to get rid of the contaminated wine by selling it for human consumption when this particular conspiracy was denounced by an Apulian wine merchant to a group of local distillers. Certainly many other such conspiracies exist. In 1987 sixty-four people in northern Italy were charged with trying to defraud the EEC by concocting 80 million litres of artificial wine out of water, sugar and chemicals between 1984 and 1986.

In his book about the Common Agricultural Policy, *The Sacred Cow*, Richard Cottrell argues that the EEC should phase out subsidies and let the market find its own level.[9] Why should we continue to support a class of peasant vine growers in France and Italy if there is no market for their products? In 1982 there were 429,000 people making wine in France, of whom 236,000 regularly sell commercially. If they lose a guaranteed market, they will have to face a choice between changing career or looking for the market – which they can do by growing better-quality grapes. In fact many of the younger generation have moved away from rural areas, and the total area of land under vines in France fell by 56 per cent between 1962 and 1981. The decrease in area under vines has mainly occurred in regions producing poor-quality wines for mass consumption.

As the demands of consumers change, the attitude of vine growers to their product is changing once again, this time for the better. Historically, much of Italian viticulture was 'promiscuous': that is to say, vines were cultivated, not just together with, but in the same soil as other plants. Vines were trained on trees and had to compete for sustenance with them and with other crops. According to Nicolas Belfrage, up to the 1960s half the vineyards in Tuscany were still cultivated in this fashion.[10] Early last century, in a book of agricultural advice, Ignazio Malenotti argued that 'it is wrong to restrict a vine to produce only one bunch of grapes when it is able to supply a hundred or more, as it does when it is trained on trees or trellises. Why condemn the vine to such sterility? Would not anyone who obliged an olive-, fig-, pear- or peach-tree to produce only one fruit be considered extravagant, or idiotic?'[11]

These attitudes still apply to food, but not to wine, production. If organic wines are unnecessary, and organic foods necessary, it is because there is no quality market for the best varieties of tomatoes or potatoes, cropped to the sort of low yields that will produce the best flavour. The only way that better-tasting vegetables can be marketed at a price which makes them economic is by adopting the 'organic' tag. Wine production, on the other hand, is geared to quality. You don't have to call a wine 'organic' in order to charge, and obtain, a fancy price. Therefore, from the point of view of quality, there is no need for wine to be produced by organic methods. After all, organic production is for most people an agent in the search for quality, not an end in itself.

Many fruits and vegetables are nowadays available in only a very few varieties, all of them bland in taste; the direst example is perhaps the Moneymaker variety of tomato. In a book on the chemistry of food tastes, James Boudreau of the University of Texas at Houston has argued that 'taste is no longer a factor in food production. Fruits and vegetables are grown for yield and ease in transportation and are ripened by artificial means.' He says that the reliance on a few fertilizers with a high nitrogen content produces foods with a different chemical composition; and that the use of other chemicals has not merely destroyed good tastes but produced bad ones. For instance, the chemicals used to loosen oranges for mechanical picking have been found to introduce new chemicals with off-tastes into the orange. 'Many of the foods selected over millennia for flavour have, in the last twenty or thirty years because of changes in chemical composition, become bland or even objectionable in flavour.'[12]

On the other hand, the demand for cheap and tasteless or frequently nasty wine among the French and Italian peasantry and proletariat has continued to fall. In 1950 an average French adult drank 120 litres of wine, of which only 4 were of *appellation contrôlée* quality. By 1982, his consumption had fallen to 85 litres, of which 15 were of *appellation contrôlée* wines. But *appellation contrôlée* does not necessarily mean expensive. Many can be bought in this country for less than £2 a bottle, be they Muscadet or Minervois. The great triumph of the second half of the twentieth century is the development of a technology which enables good wine to be supplied cheaply.

Of course this is a secular process. The great growth in the consumption of cheap wines in the nineteenth century was made possible by the development of the railways. No longer did the areas of wine production need to be close to the main areas of consumption. Vineyards became concentrated in the Midi, where the weather was best and therefore the greatest yields could be achieved. The Midi converted from polyculture to the monoculture of vines which cover much of the region today.

Likewise, methods of wine production became in many respects more sophisticated last century, having up to then changed very little since Roman times. How improved production methods affected prices is evident from the cost of champagne. Because the system of manufacture could not be relied upon, in the 1820s champagne cost twice as much as Meursault and not much less than old Chambertin. By the 1860s it was possible to judge the amount of sugar left in the bottle after the first fermentation, and breakages were much reduced. Champagne now cost the same as Meursault and less than half as much as Lafite or Chambertin. This change coincided with a growth in conspicuous consumption among the English middle classes, and exports of champagne increased by 250 per cent between 1844 and 1869.

Conventional wisdom has it that making white wine is 25 per cent grapes and 75 per cent wine-making, whereas for red wine it is 60 per cent grapes and 40 per cent wine-making. That would help explain why it has always been easier to find good cheap red than good cheap white wine – because black grapes from hot, dry countries tend to be in good condition, even if overcropped, and it is not always easy for the wine-maker to ruin them. Moreover, the tannin which red wine takes up from the grape-skins, pips and stalks in the fermenting vat helps to protect it against all but the most incompetent of wine-makers. White wines, on the other hand, are not fermented in contact with their skins, because neither tannin nor colour is desired. If vinified at a high temperature and exposed to air, the wine all too easily oxidizes; if fermented at a low temperature and protected from contact with air, the wine rapidly oxidizes once the bottle is opened and it is exposed to air for the first time. Nevertheless, the introduction in the course of the last twenty years of temperature-control mechanisms permitting low-temperature fermentation has turned many bad white wines into acceptable ones.[13] Twenty-five per cent more fatty-acid esters, which contribute to a fruity aroma, are found in a wine which has been vinified at 20°C than in one which has been fermented at 30°C.[14]

Fermenting white wines at a low temperature is a means of avoiding faults rather than of achieving quality. Admittedly, a few oustandingly aromatic white wines are made by this process, such as the single-vineyard Frascati, *vigneto* Colle Gaio, from Colli di Catone, which is fermented for six months at 12°C – this may seem absurd, but the Malvasia grape from which it is made oxidizes very easily. On the whole, however, fermenting a wine at a temperature such as this produces a clean but tasteless product, whose main characteristic is an aroma of bananas. Certain of the leading insti-gators of cold fermentation of a generation ago have realized that it is time to take a step backwards. Giacomo Tachis, the wine-maker for Antinori in Tuscany, who helped invent Galestro, one of the most tasteless of all cold-fermented white wines, as a means of getting rid of the white grapes which had previously been added to Chianti, has now been experimenting with fermentation tempera-tures up to 25°C. According to the Australian Murray Tyrrell, '10°C over six months is a load of bloody nonsense.'[15]

Cold fermentation might produce wines without any faults – but faults are necessary to produce an interesting wine. White wines which have spent long periods in cask in contact with their lees may stink, when young, of bad eggs (hydrogen sulphide), but the lees-contact produces more complex mature wines. In the eyes of some oenologists, Château Pétrus suffers from a disastrously high pH (which more or less means that it lacks acidity). Does that mean it is fit only for *lamproie à la bordelaise*? The world's most disappointing and overpriced wines are those which have sought technical perfection at the expense of character or flavour.

Like the building of tower-blocks, cold fermentation was the response of one generation to the problems of its predecessor, but has created a duller, sadder world for its successor. Conditions in the vineyards have changed since the 1960s. It is now possible to bring in to the winery untainted, ripe white grapes, whose juice does not need to be separated from the skins as quickly as possible in order to prevent the wine from being contaminated by off-tastes. The skins contain both the chemical constituents which give the wine a disagreeable flavour and the aromas and flavours which give each grape its particular character. If the juice of the white grapes is allowed to remain in contact with the skins for a period of anything between a few hours and a few days, and fermentation is prevented either by chilling the must or by having disinfected the cellars beforehand so that there are no yeasts which can get to work, the flavouring elements can be extracted from the skins of the grapes without drawing out much in the way of colour or tannin. This method of pre-fermentation maceration is becoming increasingly popular. Sometimes it occurs whether it is wanted or not, as in Australia and New Zealand, where grapes may be carried hundreds of miles in refrigerated trucks, and undergo a pre-fermentation maceration during the journey. Some Australian and New Zealand Chardonnays have a grape-skin taste which distinguishes them from the general run of Chardonnays, produced to a formula, which might come from anywhere. The Chardonnay produced by the Morton Estate in New Zealand goes perhaps a little too far, since it tastes rather like Sauvignon (the grape of Pouilly-Fumé and Sancerre). But that is common enough. I have tasted a number of dry white Bordeaux, made principally or entirely from Sémillon, which also have the grassiness of Sauvignon. The first vintage (1986) of the white wine from Mas de Daumas Gassac, made 80 per cent from Viognier grapes (which are also used to make the vogueish Condrieu of the Northern Rhône), the juice of which macerated for four days in contact with their skins, is a brilliant, if expensive, dry wine which tastes as though it were made from Muscat.

Pre-fermentation maceration may seem like a game, but the potential for white wines made using it is enormous; it enables better-tasting wine to be made from the same raw material, without restricting yields or planting Cabernet Sauvignon or Chardonnay.

Where will technology take us? Will it be possible to produce good wine without recourse to the grape at all? There is a long history of the production of fake wine, but most of it has been disgusting, such as the 'phoney wine' made in Italy in 1966 by an eight-hour process in which were mixed together tap-water, sugar, ox-blood, chemicals and the sludge from banana boats. A more promising report in 1986 suggested that scientists in California had come up with a method of reconstituting the vital 1 per cent of wine which is neither water nor alcohol. This was developed in order to fuel demand for alcohol-free wine; but of course it is perfectly possible to add alcohol as well as water to the substances which have been developed in order to replicate the taste of wine. As yet, this is at an experimental stage.

Though there are several hundred flavour components of red wines, only about fifteen of them are really important. Leo McClosky, who owns the Felton-Empire winery in California, believes the most significant of these to be a substance he calls oenin, which he says represents up to half the flavour of red wine. McClosky has developed means of accelerating the natural development of oenin, which is formed by the grouping together of tannins as a red wine matures. 'We should soon be able to deliver wines that possess this very desirable flavour more often and better, so that fine wines will be more available and cheaper.' He says, however, that it would be too expensive to synthesize oenin – though I expect someone will eventually find a way of doing so cheaply.

Until a means is effected of offering us Château Lafite on tap, we must needs rely on the produce of those vine-growing regions where technology has been revolutionized by modern methods. With pre-fermentation maceration, the revolution in white wine is only just beginning. Very few well-made inexpensive white wines as yet exist: that is why so many supermarkets and off-licence chains stock the Vin de Pays des Côtes de Gascogne sold under a number of different labels – Domaine du Tariquet, Domaine de Planterieu, Domaine d'Escoubes et al. – but all produced by the Grassa family. In the case of red wines, thanks to a reduction in yields, the introduction of temperature control and judicious use of *macération carbonique*, the revolution has already occurred. The wines we buy from the South of France today are not made from vines grown in the fertile plain, cropped at 200 hectolitres per hectare, blended with Algerian wine, and relabelled Nuits-Saint-Georges on entry into Britain. They are produced from vines on the infertile hillsides, where it is rarely possible to reach the maximum permitted yields for the Minervois and Corbières *appellations* of 50 hectolitres per hectare, and sold, under their own names, for little more than £2 a bottle. Today's wine snob is not the man who turns up his nose at Château Léoville-Poyferré 1970 because Robert Parker only marked it 65 out of 100. He is the man who only drinks Sainsbury's Corbières because he does not believe that it is worth paying more. In part, at least, he is right.

[1] This improved standard of living was one of the preconditions of the French Revolution, because it increased expectations without a commensurate increase in freedom or political power. The Revolution was precipitated when these rising expectations were dashed by an economic recession after 1778.
[2] Thomas Pennant, *Of London*, 1790, p. 31.
[3] Monsieur de la Grange, Member of Parliament for the department of the Gironde, in 1844, quoted in Germain Lafforgue, *Le Vignoble girondin*, Louis Larmat, 1947.
[4] John Locke, *Observations Upon the Growth and Culture of Vines and Olives*, 1766, pp. 21–2.
[5] Richard Ford, *Gatherings from Spain*, 1846, p. 148; *Handbook for Travellers in Spain*, 1845, p. 309.
[6] Charles K. Warner, *The Winegrowers of France and the Government*, Columbia University Press, 1960, pp. 1–16.
[7] De Romeuf, 1909, quoted in Warner.
[8] Richard Cottrell, *The Sacred Cow*, Grafton Books, 1987, p. 104.
[9] Cottrell, pp. 176–81.
[10] Nicolas Belfrage, *Life Beyond Lambrusco*, Sidgwick & Jackson, 1985, pp. 10–11.
[11] Ignazio Malenotti, *L'Agricoltore Istruito*, 1840, p. 127.
[12] J. C. Boudreau (ed.), *Food Taste Chemistry*, American Chemical Society, 1979, p. 24.
[13] The transformation of white Riojas has been discussed in Chapter 2.
[14] Pascal Ribéreau-Gayon, 'Wine Flavour', in G. Charalambous (ed.), *The Flavour of Foods and Beverages*, Academic Press, 1978, pp. 355–79.
[15] Quoted in *Wine and Spirit*, September 1985, p. 70.

CONVERSION TABLES

In this book, yields have been given in hectolitres per hectare:

> 1 hectolitre = 100 litres;
> 1 hectare = 2½ acres.

A yield of 50 hectolitres per hectare is thus roughly equivalent to the production of 2,500 bottles per acre.

I have expressed alcohol content in per cent of alcohol by volume. Various other forms of measurement are encountered. The original gravity (OG) of beer, the ° Oeschle of German wines and the ° Brix of Californian wines are measurements of the sugar content of the must, i.e. the *potential* alcohol content. The alcohol level actually achieved depends on how much of the sugar turns to alcohol. Rough equivalences are:

sugar content (grams per litre)	°Brix	°Oeschle	OG	potential alcohol (%)
70	7	30	1030	4
110	11	50	1050	6
145	14.5	65	1065	8
180	18	80	1080	10
215	21.5	95	1095	12
250	25	110	1110	14
290	29	130	1130	16

ESSENTIAL READING

BOOKS

This is a collection of some of my favourite drinks books. It does not include all the standard works which one would probably want to have in a representative collection of wine books, nor is it a homage to the published sources I have used, which have been given their due accreditation in footnotes to the text.

An asterisk indicates that the book is out of print, in which case try one of the specialist mail-order second-hand wine book sellers:
John Roberts, 130 St Leonards Rd, London SW14 (01–876 1534)
Tony Shepherdson, 2 Foresters Way, Bridlington, Humberside (0262 603 472)
Peter Willis, Newmarket House, Nailsworth, Glos. (045 383 3198)
The Wine Book Club, Woodlands, Hazel Grove, Hindhead, Surrey (042 873 5069)

Dion, Roger, *Histoire de la vigne et du vin en France* (Flammarion, 1959).* A controversial attempt to explain why the famous French wines really are famous, concentrating on the Middle Ages. Long.

Embury, David A., *The Fine Art of Mixing Drinks* (Faber & Faber, 1953). Written by an American before we had our cocktail revolution, so don't expect a Slow Comfortable Screw Up Against The Wall, but Embury does explain why cocktails are made as they are, unlike the authors of the various glossy books which appeared during the cocktail boom of the early 1980s.

Enjalbert, Henri, *Histoire de la vigne et du vin: l'avènement de la qualité* (Bordas, 1975).* Short but magisterial history of fine-wine production. Disagrees with Dion.

Forbes, Patrick, *Champagne* (Victor Gollancz, 1967). Though patently out of date, and written with an understandable bias towards the big merchants (Forbes used to work for Moët), it is the one book on the subject which can be approached as champagne should be – self-indulgently.

Foster, Terence, *Dr Foster's Book of Beer* (A. & C. Black, 1979).* A layman's guide to the science and history of English beer. Unlike the authors of the other books on the subject which appeared at about the same time, Foster does not subject his readers to a pro-CAMRA, anti-big-brewery tirade.

Hallgarten, Fritz, *Wine Scandal* (Weidenfeld & Nicolson, 1986). A bit disjointed but has some good stories, which I have tried, as far as possible, to avoid duplicating.

Hanson, Anthony, *Burgundy* (Faber & Faber, 1982). Brilliant, complex, controversial – like a good bottle of red burgundy – though not much use as a guide to the growers to follow today.

Hyams, Edward, *Dionysus: a social history of the wine vine* (Sidgwick & Jackson, 1987). A welcome reissue of a book written in 1965. It describes why and how vines came to be planted where they grow today. It shows both the advantages and the failings – Hyams sometimes gets it wrong – of applying polymathy to the problems of vinous history.

Loftus, Simon, *Anatomy of the Wine Trade*: *Abe's Sardines and other stories* (Sidgwick & Jackson, 1985). I cannot praise this too highly. It is even better than the wine-lists he writes for Adnams. It makes wine *exciting*.

Penning-Rowsell, Edmund, *The Wines of Bordeaux* (Penguin, 5th ed., 1985). More a work of history than a guide to which châteaux to follow today.

Robinson, Jancis, *Vines, Grapes and Wines* (Mitchell Beazley, 1986). A brave, if not altogether successful, attempt to produce a standard work on grape varieties which is actually readable.

Younger, William, *Gods, Men and Wine* (Michael Joseph, 1966).* A large history of wine, concentrating on Britain. Written in the grand manner.

MAGAZINES

For people who can afford to drink fine wine, the two best guides to what to buy are the *Wine Advocate*, P.O. Box 311, Monkton, Maryland 21111, USA (Robert Parker), and the *Vine*, 2 Sunderland Rd, London W5 (Clive Coates). They are complementary, since the *Wine Advocate* comprises mostly tasting notes, whereas *The Vine* also contains a lot of historical information and some details of wine-making techniques. Clive Coates can, however, be excessively uncritical at times. This is not a criticism which can be levelled at Robert Parker. I also recommend *Wine* magazine, for all its irritatingly gushing style and reliance on largely meaningless tasting notes. *Decanter* is boring, full of puffs, and worth reading only for the outstanding consumer columns of Robin Young and Christopher Fielden. If this book owes its origins to anyone, it is to them.

ESSENTIAL DRINKING

This is a list of the importers of all the wines mentioned in this book except for those whose importers are given in the text, those whose source is obvious (for example, supermarket own-labels), and well-known, widely available brands, including those of champagne, claret and port. A wine is listed under every chapter in which it is mentioned, even if it has been referred to before. An asterisk indicates that the importer does not sell direct to the public, but a telephone call to the importer will elicit the name of your nearest retailer. I have not, on the whole, mentioned retailers who are not importers because they are usually more expensive and they cannot be depended upon to continue to stock the same wines; the *Which? Wine Guide* gives some idea of the range of all the leading retailers. Importers' addresses and telephone numbers are given at the end of this section.

CHAPTER 2

Lopez de Heredia, Rioja: Laymont and Shaw, Moreno, Walter Siegel*.
Marqués de Murrieta, Rioja (white): Oddbins, Waitrose.

CHAPTER 4

Domaine Marquis d'Angerville, Volnay: O. W. Loeb.
Bouchard Père et Fils: Peter Dominic.
Domaine du Conroy, Brouilly: H. Allen Smith.
René and Vincent Dauvissat, Chablis: Domaine Direct.
Georges Duboeuf: Berkmann, Davisons.
Domaine Henri Gouges, Nuits-Saint-Georges: O. W. Loeb.
Louis Jadot: Victoria Wine, Hatch Mansfield*.
Louis Latour: Parrot*, Arthur Rackham.

Vincent Leflaive, Puligny-Montrachet: Adnams, Corney and
Barrow.

Mastroberardino: Belloni, Millevini.

Moillard: Lawlers*.

Domaine Armand Rousseau, Gevrey-Chambertin: Domaine
Direct, O. W. Loeb.

CHAPTER 5

Robert and Michel Ampeau, Meursault: Peppercorn and Sutcliffe*.

Gaston Barthod-Noëllat, Chambolle-Musigny: Bibendum.

von Bühl, Rheinpfalz: H. Allen Smith.

B. and J.-M. Delaunay, Gevrey-Chambertin: Peppercorn and
Sutcliffe*.

André Delorme, Rully: Peppercorn and Sutcliffe*.

Bernard Faurie, Hermitage: Nigel Baring.

Forstmeister Geltz/Geltz-Zilliken: Lay and Wheeler.

Marius Gentaz-Dervieux, Côte-Rôtie: Bibendum, Lockes.

Haut-Poitou Cooperative: Peppercorn and Sutcliffe*.

Jean-Marie Lombard, Brézème: Yapp.

André Ostertag, Alsace: Morris and Verdin.

Pothier-Rieusset, Pommard: Ballantynes.

Schloss Rheinhartshausen: Henry Townsend.

Rolly-Gassman, Alsace: Bibendum, Richard Harvey Wines,
Lockes, Henry Townsend.

Domaine des Varoilles, Gevrey-Chambertin: Peppercorn and
Sutcliffe*.

CHAPTER 6

Budweiser (Czechoslovakia): Waitrose.

CHAPTER 7

Guy de Barjac, Cornas: Adnams, Bibendum, Corney and Barrow,
Justerini and Brooks.

Bassermann-Jordan, Rheinpfalz: Bibendum, Richard Harvey.

Château de Beaucastel, Châteauneuf-du-Pape: Adnams, Bibendum, S. H. Jones, Justerini and Brooks.

Gérard Chave, Hermitage: Yapp.

Jean-François Coche(-Dury), Meursault: Domaine Direct, Lay and Wheeler.

Badia a Coltibuono, Extra Virgin Olive Oil: Charles Carey*.

Sélection Jean Germain: Davisons.

Grange Hermitage: Majestic, Oddbins, Sainsbury.

von Hövel, Saar: Windrush Wines.

Alain Hudelot-Noëllat, Chambolle-Musigny: Berkmann, Corney and Barrow.

Robert Jasmin, Côte-Rôtie: Yapp.

François Jobard, Meursault: Bibendum, Haynes Hanson and Clark.

Domaine des Comtes Lafon, Meursault: Domaine Direct, Morris and Verdin.

Nahe State Domain: Lay and Wheeler, O. W. Loeb, Henry Townsend.

Petaluma, South Australia: Les Amis du Vin, Geoffrey Roberts*.

Jean-Marie Ponsot, Morey-Saint-Denis: Ballantynes, Morris and Verdin.

Sassicaia: Belloni, Corney and Barrow, Winecellars.

Wolf Blass, South Australia: Averys, Alex Findlater, Hedges and Butler.

CHAPTER 8

Fratelli Adanti, Umbria: Istituto Enologico Italiano*.

Beringer, California: Hatch Mansfield*, Victoria Wine.

Domaine des Bernardins, Beaumes-de-Venise: Oddbins.

Weingut Gert Breuer, Alex Findlater.

Deinhard: Deinhard*.

Forstmeister Geltz, Saar: Lay and Wheeler.

Fritz Haag, Mosel: La Vigneronne.

Domenico Ivaldi, Piedmont (Moscato Passito): Winecellars.

Cru Lamouroux, Jurançon: Richard Harvey Wines.

J. J. Prüm, Mosel: O. W. Loeb.

Weingut St Johannishof Dr Loosen: Alex Findlater, Walter Siegel*, Windrush Wines.

Tokay: Adnams, Berry Bros.

Schloss Vollrads, Rheingau: Peter Dominic, Eldridge Pope.

CHAPTER 9

Domaine Simon Bize, Savigny-lès-Beaune: Domaine Direct, Haynes Hanson and Clark.

Gérard Chave, Hermitage; Yapp.

Château de Haute Serre, Cahors: Michael Druitt*, The Wine Society.

Frédéric Lafarge, Volnay: Haynes Hanson and Clark.

Alois Lageder, South Tyrol: Oddbins, Trestini*.

Lupé-Cholet (Côte de Nuits-Villages): Berry Bros, Jackson Nugent*.

Domaine de Montille, Volnay: Domaine Direct, O. W. Loeb.

Domaine de la Pousse d'Or, Volnay: Ballantynes, Domaine Direct

Domaine de la Romanée-Conti: Percy Fox*, Hungerford Wine Co., T. and W. Wines.

Marcel Vincent, Pouilly-Fuissé: Domaine Direct, Lay and Wheeler.

CHAPTER 10

Champagne Michel Arnould: T. and W. Wines.

Champagne Pierre Arnould: Champagne de Villages.

Badia a Coltibuono, Chianti: Parrot*, Winecellars.

Bigi, Umbria ('Marrano'): Enotria*.

Arnaldo Caprai, Umbria: Marske Mill House.

Paço do Cardido, Vinho Verde: Tanners, Wineforce*, Wines from Paris.

Quinta do Cotto, Douro: Bibendum, Alex Findlater, Lockes, Wineforce*.

Etienne and Marcel Guigal, Côte-Rôtie: Justerini and Brooks, Henry Townsend.

Henri Jayer, Vosne-Romanée (Passe-Tout-Grains): Bibendum, Peatling and Cawdron.

Monsanto, Chianti: Bibendum, Raeburn Fine Wines.

René Rostaing, Côte-Rôtie: Nigel Baring, Justerini and Brooks.

Herbert Tiefenbrunner, South Tyrol: H. Allen Smith.

Antonio Vallana, Piedmont: Hedges and Butler.

CHAPTER 11

Caves Aliança: J. W. Wines.
Avignonesi, Tuscany (Vin Santo): Winecellars.
Blandy's 10-year-old Malmsey: Oddbins, Tesco.
Fürstlich Castell'sches Domänenamt, Franconia: Carl Koener*.
Pierre Coursodon, Saint Joseph: Justerini & Brooks.
José de Sousa Rosado Fernandes, Reguengos de Monsaraz: H. Allen Smith.
Emile Florentin, Saint Joseph: Bibendum.
Luis Pato, Bairrada: Bibendum, Alex Findlater, Wineforce*.
Pojer e Sandri, Trento: Winecellars.
Rautenstrauch'sche Weingutsverwaltung Karthäuserhof (Christoph Tyrell), Saar: O. W. Loeb.
Château Rayas, Châteauneuf-du-Pape: O. W. Loeb.
Rutherford & Miles' 10-year-old Malmsey: Pavilion Wine Co.; Rutherford, Osborne and Perkin*.
Sassicaia: Belloni, Corney and Barrow, Winecellars.
Sella e Mosca, Sardinia: Italian Wine Agencies*.
Roberto Voerzio, Piedmont: Millevini.

CHAPTER 12

Antinori, Tuscany (Solaia), Umbria (Cervaro della Sala): Belloni, Corney and Barrow, Winecellars.
Avignonesi, Tuscany: Eurowines*, Winecellars.
La Bastide Blanche/Les Restanques, Bandol: The Wine Society.
Mas de Daumas Gassac: Adnams, Bow Wine Vaults, Justerini and Brooks, Pavilion Wine Co.
Angelo Gaja, Barbaresco: Trestini*, Winecellars.
Michel Guigon, Thouarsais: Yapp.
Iron Horse: Les Amis de Vin, Geoffrey Roberts*.
Jekel Vineyards, California: Sunday Times Wine Club.
Lequin-Roussot, Santenay: Bibendum, Henry Townsend.
Marqués de Murrieta, Rioja: Percy Fox*, Moreno.
Nahe State Domain: Lay and Wheeler, O. W. Loeb, Henry Townsend.
Castello di Neive, Barbaresco: Istituto Enologico Italiano*, Millevini, Winecellars.
Château Rayas, Châteauneuf-du-Pape: O. W. Loeb.

Ridge Vineyards, California: Adnams, Geoffrey Roberts*.
La Roque Cooperative, Bandol: Peter Dominic.
Domaine Tempier, Bandol: Ballantynes, Windrush Wines.
Torres, Penedès (Gran Coronas): Thresher, Waitrose.
Murray Tyrrell, New South Wales: Averys, Alex Findlater.
Vasse Felix, Western Australia: Alex Findlater.
Vega Sicilia, Ribera del Duero: Laymont and Shaw.
ZD Wines, California: Great American Food and Wine Co.

CHAPTER 13

Cosecheros Alavesas, Rioja: Arriba Kettle.
Gérard Brisson, Morgon: Pugsons.
Gérard Chave, Hermitage: Yapp.
Cossart-Gordon, Madeira: Berry Bros (under own label), Hedges and Butler.
Georges Duboeuf (Côtes du Rhône): Berkmann.
Château Fortia, Châteauneuf-du-Pape: Windrush Wines.
Angelo Gaja, Barbaresco: Trestini*, Winecellars.
Grassa, Gascony (Cuvée Bois): Tesco, Waitrose.
Maximin Grünhaus, Ruwer: S. H. Jones, Lay and Wheeler, Henry Townsend.
Lopez de Heredia, Rioja: Laymont and Shaw, Moreno, Walter Siegel*.
Masi, Valpolicella (Fresco): Hedges and Butler, Winecellars.
Domaine de Nalys, Châteauneuf-du-Pape: Peter Green, F. and E. May*.
Luis Pato, Bairrada: Bibendum, Alex Findlater, Wineforce*.
Sella e Mosca, Sardinia: Italian Wine Agencies*.
Domaine du Vieux Télégraphe, Châteauneuf-du-Pape: S. H. Jones.

CHAPTER 14

Bassermann-Jordan, Rheinpfalz: Bibendum, Richard Harvey.
Château de Fonsalette, Côtes du Rhône: O. W. Loeb.
Jean Grivot/Jacqueline Jayer, Nuits-Saint-Georges: Haynes Hanson and Clark.
Champagne André Jacquart: Morris and Verdin.
Henri Jayer, Vosne-Romanée: Bibendum, Justerini and Brooks, Henry Townsend.

Champagne Le Mesnil: Bibendum, Richard Harvey, Lockes.

Nahe State Domain: Lay and Wheeler, O. W. Loeb, Henry Townsend.

Langwerth von Simmern, Rheingau: Adnams, Alex Findlater, S. H. Jones, Lay and Wheeler, O. W. Loeb.

CHAPTER 15

Château de Beaucastel, Châteauneuf-du-Pape: Adnams, Bibendum, S. H. Jones, Justerini and Brooks.

Chapoutier: Berry Bros (under own label), Parrot*.

Colli di Catone, Frascati: Oddbins, H. Allen Smith.

Weingut Lingenfelder, Rheinpfalz: Adnams, Carl Koenen*.

Ramonet-Prudhon, Chassagne-Montrachet: O. W. Loeb.

Château Rayas, Châteauneuf-du-Pape: O. W. Loeb.

Château Raymond-Lafon: Alex Findlater, La Vigneronne.

Domaine Daniel Rion, Nuits-Saint-Georges: Morris and Verdin.

Domaine Guy Roulot, Meursault: Berkmann, Domaine Direct.

Weingut St Johannishof Dr Loosen (Müller-Thurgau): Walter Siegel*, West Heath Wines.

Edoardo Valentini, Montepulciano d'Abruzzo: Millevini.

CHAPTER 16

Veuve Achard, Clairette de Die (tradition): West Heath Wines.

Pierre André, Châteauneuf-du-Pape (red): West Heath Wines.

Château de Beaucastel, Châteauneuf-du-Pape, and Cru de Coudoulet, Côtes du Rhône: Adnams, Bibendum, S. H. Jones, Justerini and Brooks.

Champagne Jacques Beaufort: West Heath Wines.

Guy Bossard, Muscadet: Bibendum, Richard Harvey.

Castellare, Chianti: Trestini*, Winecellars.

Château de Chasseloir, Muscadet: Michael Druitt*, Lorne House Vintners, Majestic Wine Warehouses, Market Vintners.

Churchill Port: David Baillie, Morris and Verdin, H. Allen Smith (under own label), Henry Townsend, Windrush Wines.

Jean-François Coche (-Dury), Meursault: Lay and Wheeler, Domaine Direct.

Coulée de Serrant, Savennières: Old Street Wine Co., Reid Wines.

Mas de Daumas Gassac, Vin de Pays de l'Hérault: Adnams, Bow Wine Vaults, Justerini and Brooks, Pavilion Wine Co.

Elisabetta Fagiuoli, Tuscany (Vernaccia di San Gimignano): Adnams, Bibendum.

Freiherr Heylzu Herrnsheim: West Heath Wines.

Gaston Huet, Vouvray: Bibendum, Ilkley Wine Cellars, Old Street Wine Co., The Wine Society.

Henri Jayer, Vosne-Romanée: Bibendum.

François Jobard, Meursault: Bibendum, Haynes Hanson and Clark.

Domaine des Comtes Lafon, Meursault: Morris and Verdin, Domaine Direct.

Louis Latour: Parrot*, Arthur Rackham.

Laurens-Teulier, Marcillac: Sookias and Bertaut.

Castello di Luzzano, Lombardy (Bonarda): Peter Green, Oddbins, Winecellars.

Moss Wood, Western Australia: Peter Diplock*, Alex Findlater.

Château Musar, Lebanon: Sainsbury, Waitrose.

Château de l'Oiselinière de la Ramée, Muscadet: Market Vintners.

Château de Selle, Côtes de Provence: Mentzendorff*, André Simon.

Terres Blanches, Coteaux des Beaux-en-Provence: La Vigneronne.

Domaine de Trévallon, Coteaux des Beaux-en-Provence: Yapp.

Domaine du Vieux Télégraphe, Châteauneuf-du-Pape: S. H. Jones.

Château Vignelaure, Coteaux d'Aix-en-Provence: D. Byrne and Co., Michael Druitt*, La Vigneronne.

Peter Vinding-Dyers, Château Rahoul, Graves: Bordeaux Direct; Domaine Benoit: Hungerford Wine Company.

Castello di Volpaia, Chianti Classico: Adnams, Alex Findlater, Peter Green, Christopher Tatham*.

CHAPTER 17

Colli di Catone, Frascati (*vigneto* Colle Gaio): Winecellars.

Mas de Daumas Gassac (white): Adnams, Pavilion Wine Co.

Morton Estate Chardonnay, New Zealand: Berkmann, Alex Findlater, Margaret Harvey*.

ADDRESSES

Adnams, The Crown, High St, Southwold, Suffolk (0502 724222).

Les Amis du Vin, 51 Chiltern St, London W1 (01–487 3419).

Arriba Kettle, Buckle St, Honeybourne, near Evesham, Worcs. (0386 833024).

Averys, 7 Park St, Bristol (0272 214141).

David Baillie, Sign of the Lucky Horseshoe, Longbrook St, Exeter (0392 221345)

Ballantynes, Stallcourt House, Llanblethian, Cowbridge, South Glamorgan (04463 3044).

Nigel Baring, 11 Stanhope Place, London W2 (01–724 0836).

Belloni, 12–32 Albert St, London NW1 (01–267 1121).

Berkmann Wine Cellars, 12 Brewery Rd, London N7 (01–609 4711).

Berry Bros, 3 St James's St, London SW1 (01–839 9033).

Bibendum, 113 Regent's Park Rd, London NW1 (01–586 9761).

Bordeaux Direct, New Aquitaine House, Paddock Rd, Reading (0734 481718).

Bow Wine Vaults, 10 Bow Churchyard, London EC4 (01–248 1121).

Bowlish House Restaurant, Wells Rd, Shepton Mallet, Somerset (0749 2022).

Brooklands Restaurant, Barnsley Rd, Dodsworth, Barnsley (0226 299571).

D. Byrne and Co., 12 King St, Clitheroe, Lancs. (0200 23152).

Charles Carey (01–602 7040).

Champagne de Villages, Park House, Fonnereau Road, Ipswich (0473 56922).

Corney and Barrow, 12 Helmet Row, London EC1 (01–251 4051). Wine bars: 118 Moorgate, London EC2 (01–628 2898); 44 Cannon St, London EC2 (01–248 1700); 109 Broad St, London EC2 (01–638 9308); (Coates Café) 45 London Wall, London EC2 (01–256 5148).

Croque-en-Bouche Restaurant, 221 Wells Road, Malvern Wells (06845 65612).

Davisons (head office 01–681 3222).

Deinhard (01–261 1111).

Peter Diplock (01–734 2099).

Domaine Direct, 29 Wilmington Square, London WC1 (01–837 3521).

Michael Druitt (01–493 5412).

Eldridge Pope, Weymouth Avenue, Dorchester (0305 64801).

Enotria (01–961 4411).

Eurowines (01–994 7658).

Alex Findlater, 77 Abbey Rd, London NW8 (01–624 7311).

Percy Fox (0279 635771).

Great American Food and Wine Co., J. O. Sims Building, Winchester Walk, London SE1 (01–407 0502).

Peter Green, 37A/B Warrender Park Rd, Edinburgh (031–229 5925).

Margaret Harvey (01–482 0093).

Richard Harvey Wines, The Old Court House, 37 West Borough, Wimborne Minster, Dorset (0202 881111).

Hatch Mansfield (01–930 6056).

Haynes Hanson and Clark, 17 Lettice St, London SW6 (01–736 7878).

Hedges and Butler, 153 Regent St, London W1 (01–734 4444).

Hope End Country House Hotel, near Ledbury (0531 3613).

Hungerford Wine Co., 128 High St, Hungerford, Berks. (0488 83238).

Ilkley Wine Cellars, 52 The Grove, Ilkley, Yorks. (0943 607313).

Istituto Enologico Italiano (01–251 8732).

Italian Wine Agencies (01–459 1515).

J. W. Wines (John Withers), Broadlands Garden Centre, 220 London Rd, Waterlooville, Hants (0705 251489).

Jackson Nugent (01–947 9722).

S. H. Jones, 27 High Street, Banbury, Oxon (0295 51177).

Just Around The Corner (restaurant), 446 Finchley Road, London NW2 (01–431 3300).

Justerini and Brooks, 61 St James's Street, London SW1 (01–493 8721).

Kenwards Restaurant, Pipe Passage, 151a High Street, Lewes (0273 472343).

Carl Koenen (01–636 7274)

The Lantern (restaurant), 23 Malvern Road, London NW6 (01–624 1796).

Lawlers (0306 884412).

Lay and Wheeler, 6 Culver Street West, Colchester, Essex (0206 67261).

Laymont and Shaw, The Old Chapel, Millpool, Truro, Cornwall (0872 70545).

Lockes, 5 Jewry Street, Winchester (0962 60006).

O. W. Loeb, 6 Southwark Bridge Road, London SE1 (01–928 7750).

Lorne House Vintners, Unit 5, Hewitts Industrial Estate, Elmbridge Road, Cranleigh, Surrey (0483 271445).

Majestic Wine Warehouses (head office, 01–731 3131).

Market Vintners, 11–12 West Smithfield, London EC1 (01–248 8382).

Marske Mill House (Harry Faulkner), London Rd, Sunninghill, Ascot, Berks. (0990 22790).

F. and E. May (01–405 6249).

Mentzendorff (01–222 2522).

Millevini, 3 Middlewood Rd, High Lane, Stockport, Cheshire (06632 4366).

Moreno, 2 Norfolk Place, London W2 (01–723 6897).

Morris and Verdin, 28 Churton St, London SW1 (01–630 8888).

Old Street Wine Co., 309 Old St, London EC1 (01–729 1768).

H. Parrot and Co. (01–480 6312).

Pavilion Wine Co. and Bar, Finsbury Circus Gardens, London EC2 (01–628 8224).

Peat Inn, near St Andrews (033484 206).

Peatling and Cawdron (head office, 0284 5948).

Peppercorn and Sutcliffe (01–262 9398).

La Potinière, Main St, Gullane, Lothian (0620 843214).

Pugsons Food and Wine, 82 Wandsworth Bridge Rd, London SW6 (01–736 6145), (now Caves de la Madeleine).

Arthur Rackham (head office, 09323 51585).

Raeburn Fine Wines, 23 Comely Bank Rd, Edinburgh (031–332 5166).

Reid Wines, The Mill, Marsh Lane, Hallatrow, Bristol (0761 52645).

Geoffrey Roberts (01–636 4020).

Rutherford, Osborne and Perkin (0703 35252).

Sainsbury Bros, 3 Edgar Buildings, George St, Bath (0225 60481).

Walter Siegel (01–627 2720).

André Simon, 14 Davies St, London W1 (01–499 9144).

H. Allen Smith, 24–5 Scala St, London W1 (01–637 4767).

Sookias and Bertaut, The Cottage, Cambalt Road, London SW15 (01–788 4193).

Sunday Times Wine Club, New Aquitaine House, Paddock Rd, Reading (0734 481718).

T. and W. Wines, 51 King St, Thetford, Norfolk (0842 63855).

Tanners, 26 Wyle Cop, Shrewsbury (0743 52421).

Christopher Tatham (0794 515500).

Henry Townsend, York House, Oxford Road, Beaconsfield, Bucks (04946 78291).

Trestini (01–377 6464).

The Ubiquitous Chip, 12 Ashton Lane, Glasgow (041–334 5007).

La Vigneronne, 105 Old Brompton Rd, London SW7 (01–589 6113).

West Heath Wine (Andrew Williams), West Heath, Pirbright, Surrey (04867 6464).

White Horse Hotel, Williton, Somerset (0984 32306).

Winecellars, 153–5 Wandsworth High St, London SW18 (01–871 2668).

Wineforce (01–405 7172).

The Wine Society, Gunnels Wood Rd, Stevenage, Herts. (0438 314161) (members only).

Wines from Paris, The Vaults, 4 Giles St, Leith, Edinburgh (031–554 2652).

Yapp, The Old Brewery, Mere, Wilts. (0747 860423).

INDEX